ANGELS OF POWER
and other reproductive creations

Susan Hawthorne's fiction, poetry and critical writings have been published widely in magazines and anthologies in Australia, New Zealand, USA and Europe. Her books include: *Difference* (1985); *Moments of Desire* (1989, with Jenny Pausacker); *The Exploding Frangipani* (1990, with Cathie Dunsford); and she is co-author of *Silver-Tongued Sapphistry* (1990). In 1989 she won the Pandora Florence James Award for Outstanding Contribution to Women's Publishing.

Renate Klein is a biologist and researcher in Women's Studies. She is widely published in the area of reproductive technology and genetic engineering. Amongst her books are *Test-Tube Women* (1984, with Rita Arditti and Shelley Minden); *The Exploitation of a Desire* (1989); *Infertility* (1989) and *Broadening the Debate: A Non-Aligned Critique of RU 486* (1991, with Janice Raymond and Lynette Dumble). She was a founding member of FINRRAGE (Feminist International Network of Resistance to Reproductive and Genetic Engineering) and is currently active in its Australian chapter.

Spinifex Press is an independent feminist press publishing innovative and controversial fiction and non-fiction by Australian and international authors. Direct mail-order enquiries are welcome. Also available from selected, good bookshops.

The publishers would particularly like to thank Claire Warren and Sylvana Scannapiego for their patience, hard work and commitment in the production of this book.

ANGELS OF POWER
and other reproductive creations

Edited by
Susan Hawthorne
and Renate Klein

Spinifex Press

Spinifex Press Pty Ltd
4/49–59 Stanley Street, West Melbourne 3003

First published by Spinifex Press, 1991

Production by Sylvana Scannapiego, Island Graphics
Typeset in 11pt Garamond by Claire Warren
Printed and bound in Australia by The Book Printer, Victoria
The contents of this book have been printed on 100% recycled paper

CIP

Angels of Power and other reproductive creations.

   Bibliography.
   ISBN 1 875559 00 0.

   1. Human reproductive technology – Literary collections. 2. Genetic
   engineering – Literary collections. 3. Australian literature – 20th
   century. I. Hawthorne, Susan, 1951–   . II. Klein, Renate.

A820.80355

Contents

Renate Klein and Susan Hawthorne

INTRODUCTION

Reproductive technology and genetic engineering have been in the news constantly during the last decade. Reports have oscillated from 'miracle cures' for infertility to 'designer children': healthy, happy and 'better from glass'. The community at large has been confused by the complexity of the issues arising out of this new technological wizardry.

At the same time, radical feminists internationally have issued warnings as to who it is that benefits from these technologies and who pays the price. International networks such as FINRRAGE (Feminist International Network of Resistance to Reproductive and Genetic Engineering) have exposed 'benevolent' *in vitro* fertilization for its dangers in its use of fertility drugs and the dramatic emotional and economic exploitation of women. Feminists have pointed out the high failure rates (90–95 women out of 100 leave the programs without a child), and have challenged the hegemony of technodocs and pharmaceutical companies.

Importantly, the feminist critique highlights the sociopolitical dangers inherent in these developments: potentially a society composed of 'children made to order'; the eradication of genetic diversity; and the imposition of a 'norm' that is uncomfortably eurocentric, white and male. Scientists and doctors have fiercely rebuked feminist prophecies, attempting to discount their logic by calling them hysterical, and 'over the top'. But every prediction, from freezing embryos to flushing them out of women's bodies as well as the attempt at using an artificially constructed womb as an incubator, has proven true. With the advent of 'technologically assisted' surrogacy, that is egg donation from one woman to another, the definition of 'mother' has been undermined. Post-menopausal women in their fifties can now give birth, and we are close to the day when foetuses can become 'mothers' by removing immature eggs from their developing ovaries and maturing them in the lab! Scientists continue to believe that whatever *can* be done *should* be done.

Our predictions that reproductive and genetic engineering will increasingly be pushed on to fertile women and so-called people 'at risk' have also come true. This moves the debate from one that focuses on the 'needs' of infertile people to one about the social implications for the human race in general and, in particular, women's fate. In other words, the consciousness of people is shifted so that we all begin to think that these are necessary technological interventions to guarantee a healthy child.

In the tradition of Mary Shelley's *Frankenstein* (published in 1818), the writers in this book have used the technological developments as their starting point in tracing the consequences of reproductive technologies. This is the first contemporary anthology which deals, through fiction, drama and poetry, with these powerful issues. Fictional writing provides a door for looking at issues from a number of perspectives; it also makes it possible to look into the future to see what some of the long term implications of such technological interference might be. In addition, as 'Angels of Power' demonstrates, women can unite across political persuasions to resist the power of the god-like scientists who long to create monsters and angels.

Sandra Shotlander's play mixes the mythic with the futuristic by drawing on three heroines: Biblical Mary, mother of god and in this play, mother of the god/scientist; Greek Athena, proud and virginal, and by some accounts a woman who plays the man's game better than the men; and Roman Diana, huntress, a goddess of childbirth and a figure with close links to nature. In their contemporary manifestations they take on some of their predecessors' mythic characteristics but, of course, attuned to contemporary conditions. These women in the play are all members of parliament and, although ideologically at odds with one another, are eventually brought together by the issues surrounding reproductive technology; issues that affect women's well-being, and which have long term consequences, not simply for affluent women in western cultures, but for all women everywhere, whether fertile or infertile, whether they decide to have children or not.

Amongst the issues raised in the play is that of women's control over their reproductive capacities. Do women know for what purpose their donated eggs are being used? Should any one scientist, or small group of scientists, be permitted to decide who will or will not be born into the next generation? These issues are picked up again in other contributions. In Mary O'Brien's dismal depiction of the future, one in which there is total control over 'quality testing' of people, the social structure has become extremely hierarchical, and Elly, the 'last error' with dark skin, begins to wonder whether girls have ceased to be born.

Some authors have chosen to depict women in control of certain areas of reproductive technology or genetic engineering. Melissa Chan explores the possibility of marriage to men who, through genetic diagnosis, are certain to die of heart failure in mid-life. Maurilia Meehan's Manager of the Repository for Germinal Choice pursues a different kind of control when she finds that her friend,

Jacki, has conceived naturally because of the low level of success from artificial insemination at the clinic.

IVF is a central concern for several writers. Carmel Bird takes a humorous look at the procedures in the form of a laconic fairy tale. Susan Hawthorne takes a more contemporary look at IVF, and the adverse effects of hormonal cocktails. She traces the shifting attitude of a journalist who is in favour of the 'miracle cures'. The journalist over time learns more about these dangers, and has to decide whether to expose malpractice or whether to hold to her previous public stance. Atholee Scott looks at the disappointments for those few women who do successfully conceive the 'miracle baby' on IVF programmes. Linley's life is certainly changed, but we are left wondering if it is for the better.

The poets in the collection range over a number of issues, and central to their concerns is the use to which language is put in promoting the new biotechnologies. There are *'the men without skin who want our skin/they pierce, excavate,/turn us inside out'* of whom Cait Featherstone writes; or Susan Eisenberg's *'Knights of the Laboratory/design/test tubes/that will not suffer/nausea or back pain...'*; or Susan Hawthorne's domestic imagery of *'Petri dishes, test tubes – a world/of marital glassware...'* Thalia, in the highly condensed form of concrete poetry, expresses the pain and bewilderment women experience when they enter the high-tech world of modern medicine. Using the tradition of stenography, the sequence represents the interaction between language, representation, politics and science.

The related issue of surrogacy is picked up in Lucy Sussex's story of twin sisters who engage in so-called altruistic surrogacy. She explores the dynamics of the relationship and the 'choice' of those involved in the arrangement. We are left with questions such as: what constitutes altruism? what do we mean by choice? and what is consent?

Karen Malpede's play, 'Better People', looks at the competition between scientists working on the Genome Project/genetic engineering, for the great honours of international prizes, and closer to home, of funding for research from pharmaceutical companies or Departments of Defence. The play draws parallels between the use to which Nazi scientists put their research and those of contemporary scientists working in these fields. The justification for all this competition and for the glory of experimentation is succinctly expressed by Rosaleen Love, whose Dr Neville says of his own 'little experiment' that: 'We did it because it was there.' This collection is a challenge to the scientific ethic that is simply an extension of the colonialist ethic: if it moves, shoot it, if it doesn't, chop it down. In order to survive on this planet, such ideologies must be challenged and their proponents made accountable for the consequences.

This book, with its authors from Canada, USA, New Zealand and Australia, is designed to contribute to the debate and foster international resistance to reproductive technologies. Imagination, vision and a good joke have the power to show up these technologies for what they are and to carry us into a different future: one in which diversity and human variation are not only valid, but also valued; one in which women are no longer 'test sites' for science's fantasies of a grey future; and one in which the Yenga women of BarbaraNeely's tale won't need to search for their cave.

Renate Klein and Susan Hawthorne
February, 1991

Sandra Shotlander

ANGELS OF POWER
A modern myth in two acts

Author's Note
This anthology is being published to coincide with the world premiere of 'Angels of Power' in the Beckett Theatre, Malthouse, Melbourne, Australia. As this publication goes to press the actors will begin rehearsal. There will be changes to the play in the rehearsal process, particularly to the plot in the last ten pages. This version is not the final text. Any performance or public reading of 'Angels of Power' is forbidden unless a licence has been received from the author. The purchase of this book in no way gives the purchaser the right to perform the script in public, whether by means of any kind of production or a reading. Those wishing to perform the play should contact the author through the publishers.

‖ CHARACTERS ‖

DIANA HUNT	MP Independent
PATRICIA FORBES	Radio announcer
MARY MADRES	MP Left Wing
ATHENA	MP Right Wing
MARTA	Daughter-in-law of Mary
ASSISTANT DIRECTOR OF CLINIC	IVF scientist
DAVIES	MP Right Wing
JACK FENNEL	Leader of the Opposition, Right Wing
PRIME MINISTER	Left Wing
FRED	MP Right Wing

THOMAS DIDIMUS MADRES	Son of Mary
PROF. BARON BODIE	Head of Clinic
VERNON FLANK	Radio personality
PM'S PRIVATE SECRETARY	

VARIOUS REPORTERS, A MINISTER, LOGGER AND OTHER VOICES

‖ THE SETTING ‖

The play mainly takes place in and about the corridors, the House and the offices of Federal Parliament. Other scenes are set in a squash court, MARY MADRES' living-room, a bar of a private club, a laboratory and director's office of Tartonside Fertility Clinic, and a hill overlooking Parliament. At the back of the stage is a radio studio where the announcer and VERNON FLANK broadcast.

NB. The use of music. It is intended that MARY, DIANA and THENA should each have a theme: MARY – organ; DIANA – a clear forest sound, pipe; THENA – bouzouki. Their uses are indicated in the script to heighten the effect of the archetypes.

‖ MYTHOLOGICAL FOOTNOTES PROGRAM NOTES ‖

Athena: Greek virgin goddess of wisdom, daughter of Zeus and Metis (the goddess of wisdom of the old order). Zeus, afraid Metis would bear a child to supercede him, swallowed her. She counselled him from his belly and he gave birth to Athena, who sprang to earth from his head, fully dressed in armour.

Diana: The Hunter, Roman virgin goddess, daughter of Jove, twin sister of Apollo (Greek name Artemis). Moon goddess, keeper of the wilderness, protector of young animals, a childbirth goddess.

Mary (Virgin): Was she the first surrogate mother?

‖ ACT I ‖

SCENE I

Sounds of an anti-logging protest in Pennington Forest. Chants, angry loggers, sounds of the bulldozers.

ANNOUNCER: War in the forests. Angry sounds at Pennington as tension mounts between loggers and protesters. Speculation as to whether the federal government will intervene in the dispute.

> [*The corridors of Parliament.* DIANA *enters, gauche, determined, suit and high heels, carrying piles of notes and books. Trips, scattering the books and documents.*]

DIANA [*looking at the heel of a shoe*]: Damn!

ANNOUNCER: Independent MP Diana Hunt, catapulted into Parliament last election, created uproar, when she announced she would consider joining protesters from the wilderness movement fasting on the lawns of Parliament.

DAVIES: Ms Hunt, let me help you. [*Picks up a document.*] Brushing up on the law of the jungle?

DIANA: The forest.

DAVIES: The forest, of course. [*Chants of the protestors can be heard on the lawns.*] They're ready for blood. [*Hands her the document and walks off.*]

DIANA: Thanks.

> [MARY *has entered.*]

MARY: Here let me help you.

DIANA: I shouldn't wear them. I can't get used to high heels or corridors.

MARY: It's taken some of these men years to develop a corridor walk. You should wear sneakers like me.

DIANA: I will.

MARY: You seem to have your whole office here.

DIANA: I'm always on the move.

MARY: What do you mean?

DIANA: My office has been moved again. I'm in a cupboard now. I'm being asphyxiated.

MARY: So that's why you're occupying the corridors. You should complain.

DIANA: I have. I'm not going to waste any more energy. [*The chants rise.*] I wish I was with them, out of my damn cupboard at any rate – in the forest on my horse.

MARY: I'm not familiar with horses but I've ridden donkeys.

DIANA: Have you?

MARY: Family treks. That was quite a threat you made today.

DIANA: I'll do it.

MARY: I don't doubt that.

DIANA: I think a lot of the government would support me.

MARY: Fasting is very good for you, but it won't get the numbers. It's the economy, Diana. Trees aren't part of the balance of payments unless they're turned into woodchips.

DIANA: We need a new party.

MARY: I'll keep it in mind. I'll see what I can do about your office.

DIANA: Would you?

MARY: Can't have you asphyxiating. A word in the right place you know.

DIANA: Thanks.

MARY: Can you manage or will I carry some for you?

DIANA: I'll be all right.

    [*Chants rise.* MARY *listens.*]

MARY: It should be simple for God's sake. People like trees.

DIANA: Most people don't give a flying-fuck.

MARY: That will have to change. [*Places the shoes on top of* DIANA *'s books.*]

Scene II

THENA *works at her desk.* DAVIES *enters.*

THENA: So this is the list of names of those wishing to depose Treddle. Farron, Butcher. Peters has signed it.

DAVIES: Yes, she was a little reluctant but she saw the wisdom in the end.

THENA: Did she?

DAVIES: No one is against Treddle but we all know he couldn't win an election. Now come on Thena, don't you want to be with us.

THENA: When the saints come marching in, hey?

DAVIES: We won't win with him.

THENA: I know.

DAVIES: Then what are you worried about?

THENA: Your way of doing things.

DAVIES: What's wrong?

THENA: You bastard Davies! How did you persuade all those people to sign.

DAVIES: Fennel is a leader. Anyway we have the numbers.

THENA: Then you don't need my signature.

DAVIES: Am I to understand you'll be against the new leadership?

THENA: No, but I think it should be put to the vote in the usual way.

DAVIES: And we'd have your vote?

THENA: Yes.

DAVIES: Good.

THENA: And now you'll present that list of names to Treddle I suppose?

DAVIES: You're very hard on me Thena.

THENA [*Sighs and signs*]: And it's a great day for the party.

DAVIES: Good girl. You're doing the right thing. You won't regret it.

THENA: I'm not a child.

DAVIES: What? Oh, good woman.

THENA: Thank you.

DAVIES: Not at all. Thank you. There is one more thing, this new girl – new woman – Diana Hunt. She's on the Environmental Impact Committee.

THENA: That's hardly surprising.

DAVIES: I find her most extraordinary. I just met her in the corridor, on the floor, amongst a pile of debates.

THENA: She's unusual but she's smart.

DAVIES: Not smart enough – coming late for the vote and calling out for the doors to stay open. Never seen anything like it.

THENA: But did you see the men on the doors? They almost waited.

DAVIES: She damn near caused a riot.

THENA: Exactly.

DAVIES: She could have the casting vote on that committee.

THENA: Then it could be exciting.

DAVIES: We need a recommendation in favour of the industry.

THENA: The environmental vote is getting bigger.

DAVIES: So is the national debt. I don't think the government can afford to be wedded to preserving forests.

THENA: She'll try to keep them to their election promises.

DAVIES: You seem to think this woman will have some effect.

THENA: I wouldn't underestimate her.

DAVIES: She has no idea of government, she's uncompromising. Find out something about her.

THENA: What in particular would you like to know?

DAVIES: You'll think of something. Dig up some dirt.

THENA: I could play squash with her.

DAVIES: Yes she's the athletic type, isn't she?

THENA: I used to play a mean game of squash myself.

DAVIES: Good. You'll deal with her then? I knew I could count on you. I can't promise anything yet mind you, but I think you'll find the new leadership recognizes talent.

[DAVIES *exits.*]

SCENE III

ANNOUNCER: Jack Fennel entered the political arena today in his new role as Leader of the Opposition.

[*To the background of the sounds of a party rally,* FENNEL *enters, acting as a crooner making a mouthed speech, while behind the rally 'I'm Just a Gigolo' is heard.*]

ANNOUNCER: Deposed Leader, Brian Treddle, had earlier given his allegiance to his party's new leadership. [*We see* TREDDLE *here with* FENNEL *The two shake hands and then freeze in a photograph pose.*] The Prime Minister said he wasn't surprised by the disharmony in the opposition and said Government achievements spoke for themselves.

[*Music and rally fade under sounds of Parliament.*]

SCENE IV

MARY *and* DIANA *enter down the corridor.*

MARY: I hope you don't have to fast.

DIANA: I don't see myself as a long-term politician anyway.

MARY: It's a good idea to stay alive until the next election. Gives the voters a sense of security.

DIANA: There's a lot more at stake than trees.

MARY: I Know. Come in. I'm expecting a message from my son, Thomas.

DIANA: Would you rather be alone?

MARY: No it's fine. Now sit down. I'll just clear a space. I have a new secretary, poor woman. I like everything to be immaculate. I don't understand why people want to reduce everything to woodchips any more than you do, Diana. Do sit down. [*Grabs a paper.*] Just a minute. What's this? Another begging letter, probably. Oh [*calling off*] Magda, another unsigned cheque has been returned. New, poor woman. There's so much to learn these days. Thomas never phones any more. We have a computer link. I don't know, perhaps I'm obsolete. I'm to be a grandmother.

DIANA: Congratulations.

MARY: My daughter-in-law's in an *in vitro* fertilization program.

DIANA: Oh!

MARY: I do have misgivings. Give men an instrument and they will probe with it.

DIANA: Give them high-powered saws and they'll cut down the forests. If women aren't careful, they'll be put on the assembly line.

MARY: I had my twins by artificial insemination.

DIANA: Did you?

MARY: Yes, Jesus and Thomas Didimus. We weren't intending to have children. We didn't have a cent. The idea came quite out of the blue.

DIANA: What do you mean?

MARY: It just popped into my head one night, clear as a voice. I wasn't even sure what it meant.

DIANA: But you still went ahead.

MARY: It was experimental. We were pioneering. We caused quite a stir. People came from everywhere to observe. We were the centre of attention. Don't you ever think about motherhood?

DIANA: Not in that way. I've never wanted children, but I've attended births.

MARY: Have you?

[*A note, a sound almost like a pipe calling across the forest.*]

DIANA: Oh yes. You see I trained as a midwife.

MARY: There's a lot I don't know about you. I have the strangest feeling we've met before. [*The sound of the pipe*] Funny. Could we have mutual friends? [*Notes sound again*] I'm sorry. Anyway, go on.

DIANA: I don't tell people very often. I don't tell much about that period of my life.

MARY: Is there something wrong with being a midwife?

DIANA: Oh no. It was simply an everyday part of my existence.

Mary [*confidentially*]: I've attended births too.

DIANA: You didn't mention it.

MARY: It's hardly part of government is it?

DIANA: But it is. That's where we are going wrong.

MARY: I'm there when I'm asked for, Diana. People do call on me. You and I have things in common. We should bear it in mind.

DIANA: Don't you think it's time for a new party.

MARY: What sort of party?

DIANA: One with principles, that doesn't serve the masters of commerce and technology. It has to start from a woman's point of view.

MARY: You don't have the basis of support I have in the government. I even have a woman's caucus.

DIANA: We need more than a circus – a caucus. We need a parliament of angry women. I thought you might be interested.

MARY: Oh no, no, no, no, no, I'm not the party-forming type.

DIANA: Yes you are. You have warmth and common sense and zeal when you're really worked up.

MARY: I haven't been worked up for a long time. I just sit demurely on the back bench while the dollar fluctuates and the back bench flatulates. Occasionally I'm asked to intercede. 'Mary get through to the man at the top. Mary put in a word.' I'm tired of interceding.

DIANA: You were a fighter in the old days.

MARY: Oh yes, after my son's death. It was for him. My campaign was for him, poor boy, shot on a street corner . . . I need a mission Diana, something to sacrifice myself for . . . [*Cuts off abruptly.*] I think you're wise not having children, not in this world. Frankly I'm glad I'm past all that.

DIANA: You're needed for other things. To create havoc for example.

MARY: That's not in my line.

DIANA: No, perhaps you're right, but it's in mine.

MARY: What are you thinking?

DIANA: We would be powerful together.

MARY: Tell me are you the party-joining sort?

DIANA: No, I'm not really.

MARY: Then we're just talking.

DIANA: I'm a very loyal ally, and when the right occasion occurs, I'm willing to learn some new habits.

MARY: Are you? I see. Diana, this has been a most interesting talk. Still no message from my son, but I have to go, I'm afraid. I have someone waiting to lobby me.

DIANA: Why would Thena ask me to play squash?

MARY: Did she really? Now, there's a party woman. She knows how to work the system. I don't like her politics but she's good at it.

DIANA: Maybe I should accept.

MARY: You'll have to, to find out why she asked you.

DIANA: I'm curious about her. She's very self-possessed. She has a corridor walk.

MARY: She was a champion in the martial arts. Probably very good practice for politics.

DIANA: All right, I'll give it a go.

MARY: I'll be interested to hear what happens. Now don't overdo the fasting. Be careful.

Scene V

Sounds of the squash court as Thena *and* Diana *play towards the end of the game.* Diana *is winning a point, but not easily.*

Diana: You're giving me a hard game.

Thena: I'm putting up a battle.

Diana: You're in good trim though.

Thena: Thank you. [*Goes to hit but can't reach the ball.*] I'll have to improve my speed.

Diana: You just need some practice. You have a wonderful backhand.

Thena: Yes, I've worked on that.

Diana: I hear you were a champion in the martial arts. [*They play.*]

Thena: I was before I went into politics. Now my fighting is done on the floor of the house.

Diana: It's a kindergarten.

Thena: It does seem that way.

Diana: And the decisions aren't made there.

Thena: I could do with a change, some relief.

Diana: You sound disillusioned.

Thena: Every day I face the same barriers. [*Smashes and misses.*] Your shot.

Diana: Good try.

Thena: I'm glad you could play. I thought Pennington Forest would be taking up all your time.

Diana: It is.

Thena: Since we're both on the committee, I'd like to talk about it.

Diana: Oh, yes.

Thena: Where do you get it?

Diana: What?

Thena: Your detachment.

Diana: You'll have to explain.

Thena: You let everything pass over you, all that fuss

about your wanting to join the protestors. You don't play by the rules.

DIANA: Oh, rules.

[*They play.* THENA *is kept on the run.*]

THENA: You must have lots of allies somewhere.

DIANA: This week has been hell.

THENA: It's that bad.

DIANA: It's getting worse. I can't wait to get away.

THENA: Then you're not so detached.

DIANA: I've been thinking about your persistence.

THENA: I like problems. I like it here in spite of the frustrations. [THENA *misses. She's exhausted.*] You're too good for me. [*They both bend down to reach for the ball.*] That's an interesting pendant you're wearing.

DIANA: It's ancient Greek and feminist.

THENA: I know the labrys and the double-headed axe of the Amazon. Is that how you see yourself? [DIANA *smiles.*] I had a friend who . . . Isn't it lesbian?

DIANA: It was given to me by a friend. [*As she hits the ball catching* THENA *off guard.*] It's the sign of a strong woman.

THENA: I'm glad you agreed to play. I thought you might be worried we'd be seen together?

DIANA: Why would you think that?

THENA: We're not known as political friends. This could create rumours.

DIANA: Oh, I see. I'm an independent. I can please myself, or does every action have to be calculated around here?

[*They stop play.*]

THENA: More or less.

DIANA: I was wondering why you asked me to play.

THENA: All right, I'll be honest. Since we're on the committee, I wanted to know you better.

DIANA: I like to keep fit. I used to partner my brother.

THENA: You don't have to justify to me. My father believed in some sort of ancient sporting purity. He was an idealist. Sport above politics and so on. He tried to teach me that. He taught me everything.

DIANA: Do you believe all that?

THENA: Well . . . [*smiles*]

DIANA: I play sport for pleasure. I love to move fast.

THENA: Yes, I can see. You do it very well. Come on then. After all, if you have an axe to grind, it might as well be double-headed. [*Grasping her racquet.*] I'm ready.

[*As they play the announcer is heard.*]

ANNOUNCER: Dollar plummets.

Government promises tax cuts.

Genetic testing for chain store employees.

Walt Disney thaws out in power strike.

The Prime Minister supported the Supreme Court ruling in favour of conservationists in the Pennington Forest dispute.

[*The voice of the* PRIME MINISTER *is heard under* DIANA*'s reaction as she runs to another part of the stage to find* MARY, *who is lying on the floor.*]

PRIME MINISTER: We are pleased to say the appropriate actions have been taken, between the opposing interests in this matter, and unequivocally give our support to the decision, which, had it not been made, could have caused serious repercussions – a tragedy even.

[DIANA *speaks over the* PRIME MINISTER.]

DIANA: Mary, we've won. We've won. [*Sees her on the ground.*] Mary, what's the matter?

MARY: Just relaxing. Have you ever tried to levitate?

DIANA: Mary, we've . . .

MARY: How was the squash game?

DIANA: Mary, we've done it.

MARY: Done what dear?

DIANA: There's an injunction against the logging until after the committee report.

MARY: Well done.

DIANA: Come on. Let's celebrate. Then we'll levitate.

[THENA *is performing a Japanese martial exercise. Just before* DAVIES *speaks, she stands with knees bent, body arched back and head back, holding her racquet over her head with both arms extended, on one breath chanting a long 'ah'.*]

DAVIES: Any dirt on Hunt yet Thena? [*The 'ah' continues as* DAVIES *waits.*] Thena?

THENA [*after a moment turning her head to him*]: I'm working on it.

DAVIES: You're not there just to play squash.

THENA: I'm getting fit. I have to.

DAVIES: I'm relying on you to get rid of the injunction.

THENA: Don't worry. [DAVIES *exits.* THENA *resumes the 'ah'.* DIANA *hits the ball to her, the 'ah' ends in a groan as* THENA *tries to smash and misses. She staggers on the court. The two are then seen changing shoes, etc.*] Congratulations. Quite a coup. Two wins in one day. Well, so much for ancient sporting purity.

DIANA: You never give up though.

THENA: Daddy's little warrior. Are you going?

DIANA: I'd like to stay but . . . Your father must have meant a lot to you.

THENA: I adored him and he wouldn't let me out of his sight. He was Greek, from Athens. He was very ambitious for me. That's why I studies politics and law. [*Hear the notes of the bouzouki.*] He was incredibly handsome, godlike, at least I thought so and so did a lot of other women. Is that my racquet?

DIANA [*passing the racquet*]: I didn't really know my father.

THENA: I never knew my mother.

DIANA: Oh.

[*A pause,* DIANA *watching* THENA.]

THENA: Father said she abandoned me, but when I was in therapy I dreamt he destroyed her, swallowed her up.

DIANA: How weird.

THENA: It was intriguing. [*As she speaks, we hear notes from a bouzouki.*] There was an olive grove, owls hooting, claps of thunder, a metallic sound, jarring like an axe striking a helmet.

DIANA: How symbolic. Did you find out what it meant?

THENA: No.

DIANA: And you never saw her.

THENA: I have a photo. It was buried in the back of a cupboard.

DIANA [*taking the photo which* THENA *took from her wallet.*]: There's a likeness.

THENA: Do you think so?

DIANA: Around the forehead. Dark, sad eyes.

THENA: They're my father's relatives surrounding her. It's just after she'd left her village.

DIANA: And that's your father?

THENA: Yes.

DIANA: Looks like he could consume her.

THENA [*laughs*]: He told me I didn't need a mother. I was his little warrior. I gave him my loyalty. I never questioned.

DIANA: But you went into therapy.

THENA: Something felt wrong. Days were like trudging in mud. The therapist was a wonderful woman, like a mother to me, at least she became that in my mind. I didn't tell my father I was going to her. I felt closer and closer and then I began to feel disloyal.

DIANA: What happened?

THENA: After the dream, I cried on her shoulder and then I stopped going.

DIANA: So that was the end?

THENA: I certainly haven't looked for her since then. We'd better go.

DIANA: It's all right, I'm not in a hurry any more.

THENA: Oh . . . fine.

DIANA: What would you have done if your father hadn't been around?

THENA: The same I suppose – studies, lawyer's office, politics. [*Laughs*] What about you?

DIANA: My mother was the giant figure in my life. She brought me up. I took her name not his.

THENA: But you knew him.

DIANA: He was an occasional visitor. We lived in the forest area near Pennington.

THENA: So this committee is very personal for you?

DIANA: I love the area. Have you seen the devastation after clear-felling? It's never the same again.

THENA: I'm a city person really.

DIANA: I might have known.

THENA: Don't assume I'm against you. I've argued with members of my party over this one. The environmental vote is growing.

DIANA: You only think in terms of the vote.

THENA: My father didn't teach me to care about forests.

DIANA: Nor did mine. [*Suddenly flaring*] He wasn't around long enough. He was too busy building his empire. Trees, land, women were all for his use and profit. He wouldn't know how to protect a wilderness. I think I'd better go after all. Sorry I do have to rush.

[*Exits, leaving a quizzical* THENA.]

[MARY *passes her in the corridor.*]

MARY: My son sent a message. They're on their way to visit.

DIANA: Is it good news?

MARY: He didn't say. How are the squash games?

DIANA: I think I've had enough.

MARY: Oh. Something wrong?

DIANA: Can't talk now.

[*Hurries on, leaving a puzzled* MARY.]

[*Night.* THENA *enters* DAVIES' *office.*]

THENA: It's her father.

DAVIES: Incest.

THENA: Sorry to disappoint you. However, I think Parliament could see it that she has undeclared private interests.

DAVIES: Well . . .?

THENA: Diana's father has offshore interests, in the Philippines, the meranti forests, and those interests own Jove Enterprises, whose Australian subsidiary, Apollo is the parent company for Pulp Makers Incorporated, who used to be Tasmania Paper Inc.

DAVIES: Yes . . .

THENA: Who have just won the wood-chipping contract for the Pennington area. There's a packet of shares in her name. I knew if I searched long enough, I'd find it. Tax dodge or deliberate.

DAVIES: Wonderful.

THENA: It's highly likely she's not aware of it. She says she's entirely independent.

DAVIES: Who's going to believe her? What's their relationship?

THENA: Estranged. [*Throws down a paper.*] It's all there.

DAVIES: It's worth a try.

THENA: Oh, yes.

DAVIES: Thank you Thena. Dinner tonight – again? [*They both look at each other and smile.*]

SCENE VI

A room in a club prior to dinner with a table and three chairs. MARTA *and* THOMAS *already seated opposite each other for pre-dinner drinks. Other people are in the room or about to enter, so the scene is conducted as a private argument in public.*

MARTA: I think she should know.

THOMAS: Don't go on Marta. We agreed we'd tell her at the right moment.

MARTA: Well, when is the right moment for God's sake?

THOMAS: It would only upset her now, with the forthcoming election.

MARTA: There isn't a forthcoming election.

THOMAS: There must be – there always is – people have to vote.

MARTA: Thomas we agreed your mother should know.

THOMAS: I've told you it's not the right time.

MARTA: I'm not sitting through dinner without telling her. I feel sick anyway.

THOMAS: Marta, please try to pull yourself together.

MARTA: Don't you understand? I don't want this baby.

THOMAS: I didn't force you into the *in vitro* program. We agreed we wanted a baby.

MARTA: Not this baby, you monster – not this freak.

THOMAS: It's not a freak. It's a perfectly respectable embryo.

MARTA: But it's not mine.

THOMAS: Now stop it Marta, people will hear you.

MARTA: I don't care.

THOMAS: Mary will be here in a moment. She'll see you're upset.

MARTA: Good! I want her to see.

THOMAS: But you look awful. Your eyes are all red. Here, take my handkerchief. Now don't cry. Don't cry Marta. Mother!

MARY: Marta! Thomas! How lovely. Marta, what's the matter? You look upset. Thomas, you're very pale too. You don't look at all well. Has he been eating properly Marta?

MARTA: Don't ask me, I never see him.

MARY: Thomas I must have a serious talk with you. It's a mistake to neglect your family. Marta looks terrible.

Thomas [*to* MARTA]: There you are. I knew you'd spoil this visit. [*to* MARY] How's Parliament? Any new laws in the offing? Anything of importance?

MARTA: If he won't tell you, I'm going to.

THOMAS: Can't we just wait for five minutes?

MARY: Thomas, what's happened?

THOMAS: We do have some news mother.

MARY: Are you . . .? Is it? But this is exciting.

MARTA: The baby I'm carrying isn't my baby.

THOMAS: I'm afraid there's been an unfortunate case of mistaken identity.

MARTA: Why don't you confess? You did it deliberately.

MARY: What are you talking about?

THOMAS: Mother, Marta has never shared my enthusiasms.

MARTA: What has that got to do with it?

THOMAS: If you did, you would support me now.

MARTA: I've done everything in my power for you Thomas. I've cooked for you, I've cleaned for you, I've washed your socks, I agreed to IVF but now I find out I'm not this baby's mother.

THOMAS: It depends how you look at 'mother'.

MARY: Will someone please explain?

THOMAS: We are talking about a whole new concept of motherhood.

MARTA: And a whole new concept of morality, I'd say. What about that?

THOMAS: Mother, Marta knew from the beginning, the laboratory is not a place of certainty.

MARTA: Mary, I'm pregnant.

MARY: So I understand, but it's obviously not a cause for celebration.

THOMAS: It's a scientific discovery.

MARTA: I'm not interested in scientific discovery any more. You can go and lock yourself in your precious laboratory as far as I'm concerned and cram yourself full of hormones until you have babies coming out of your – ears, and see how you like it.

MARY: Marta, whatever is the matter?

MARTA: I'm pregnant with Thomas's former mistress's baby.

THOMAS: *De facto* – she's referring to my *de facto*.

MARY: But that's impossible.

MARTA: No it's not – ask him.

MARY: Am I to understand that Marta is carrying Helen's baby?

MARTA: You've understood it exactly.

THOMAS: Mother you have to accept that times have changed.

MARY: This is very disturbing.

THOMAS: There was a confusion of embryos but it's all right.

MARTA: It's not all right.

THOMAS: I don't know what you're complaining about. She was beautiful, gifted, intelligent and she played the piano accordion. You could have a child with a musical talent.

MARTA: I don't care if she conducted an orchestra, I don't want to carry her baby.

MARY: But you can't. Helen's dead.

WAITER: Your drinks and hors d'oeuvres. [*Places two drinks and plate of caviar. To* MARY] Would you like something to drink?

MARY: No, not now, no thanks.

MARTA: I went into hospital to have our baby but Thomas has transferred Helen's baby into my womb.

MARY: Why would he do that?

MARTA: To see if he could do it. [*To* THOMAS] But you won't get away with this, let me tell you. I'll take you through every court in the land. I want compensation. I want storage fees for carrying your mistress's baby. Do you think I'm a cow? You're nothing but a vet, a baby maker, an egg snatcher, a poacher.

THOMAS [*helping himself to caviar*]: Mother, Marta is upset at the moment, but I have to tell you our marriage is not at a high point.

MARTA: High point! As far as I'm concerned, it's just moved into an all-time subterranean hell.

MARY: I feel faint. This family has a history of strange births.

MARTA: I am not going to have this baby. Do you understand?

THOMAS: Marta, everything would be perfectly all right if

you would calm down.

MARTA: How can you say everything is all right?

THOMAS: Now, don't get hysterical.

MARTA: I'm not getting hysterical, [*Standing leaning over table trying to grab* THOMAS] but I'm not going to sit here and watch you eat. You can't even respect a fish's eggs. Some poor fish was sacrificed for those eggs. [*Takes it out of his mouth and grabs him.*]

MARY: Marta please sit down. [*Sits her down*] There. Try to relax. Are you in pain? [MARTA *shakes her head. Mary takes her hand and strokes it.*] There, there. Now Thomas I want to know everything. I want the truth and I want you to explain it simply, not in complicated scientific terms.

THOMAS: Mother, Helen always supported me.

MARTA: So did I, you criminal.

MARY [*puts her arm around* MARTA]: All right Marta.

THOMAS: She was always trying to think of ways to help me. She left her body to science.

MARY: Yes, you told me that. It's not something I could do.

THOMAS: After that car accident, I recovered some of Helen's eggs and I froze them. Well, it's led to a far greater thing than Helen would ever have dreamt of.

MARY: What's that?

THOMAS: You see what I've been trying to tell Marta and what she refuses to understand is that this is a major scientific breakthrough.

MARTA: A breakthrough. [*Almost before he says it.*]

THOMAS: You see, I worked with frozen eggs, and not only that – they were immature eggs which I matured. Now this has been done with cattle but not with humans.

MARTA [*exclaims*]: Oh!

THOMAS: I'm about to publish a paper which shows how I've taken immature eggs, frozen them, thawed them, matured them, fertilized them – all in the laboratory.

It's quite a scramble, but it got Marta pregnant. I'll show you. [*Takes pen and notebook from coat pocket*] Normally the follicle that holds the egg is like this and it has to ripen, and then we go in and make a pick up, but we have to give you hormones because you don't produce enough eggs.

MARTA: You see we don't even produce enough eggs.

MARY: We've produced enough eggs in the past Thomas – enough for world over-population.

THOMAS: Not enough for the *in vitro* process Mother, so we superovulate you with hormones, but I couldn't do that with Helen because she was dead. So I took the eggs still immature.

MARTA: Immature! You think you're a god, Thomas. If you want to make something, why don't you play with plasticine?

THOMAS: This paper will make me famous. Don't you see? We have terrible problems getting eggs, what with all the regulations. Now I could use Mother's eggs, a new-born baby's eggs – technically, even a foetus's eggs. The next step is to grow an ovary and of course, the artificial womb.

MARY: I don't understand. A womb, an ovary – whatever for, when there are women?

MARTA: And what has happened to my eggs, may I ask, or am I being too bold? Flushed down the sink no doubt, or used in another game of musical babies.

THOMAS: If you must know, it's not my sperm either.

MARTA: Not your sperm! That's wonderful. Now I find not only am I mother to another woman's eggs but I'm babysitting some unknown man's sperm.

THOMAS: Men have had to put up with this since Adam.

MARTA: What do you mean?

THOMAS [*imperiously*]: How does a man know his sperm fathered the baby?

MARY and MARTA: Thomas, don't be ridiculous.

THOMAS: I'm not being ridiculous, there's always that

doubt. Science is simply equalizing the situation.

MARTA: Equalizing! Birth goes into the laboratory and nobody can be sure of anything any more. Is that what you want?

THOMAS: We are addressing a question of equality.

MARY: Equality my arse. Why don't you just try living with the doubt. It sounds like a case of womb envy to me. This is very distressing.

THOMAS: There's nothing to carry on about. It's all in the family.

MARTA: It's what?

THOMAS: Yes, you see, when I fertilized Helen's eggs, I used my brother's sperm.

MARTA: Jesus! You used Jesus's sperm?

MARY: Thomas you can't go around resurrecting eggs from the dead here and sperm from the dead there.

THOMAS: He was short of money, so he donated some sperm.

MARY: Your twin brother's sperm . . . My poor son, conscripted into war, never the same again, preaching pacifism on street corners to be shot by a fascist maniac.

THOMAS: Mother, this child might just lay that ghost. This is a child of science.

MARTA: And what have I become? Incubator to another saviour, to some crackpot scientific idea? Don't you realise this embryo has no relationship to me?

THOMAS: Yes it does. He's your nephew.

MARY: By marriage, Thomas.

THOMAS: And he's your legitimate grandchild, mother.

MARTA: And you're his half-brother, I suppose?

THOMAS: No, I'm his uncle.

MARTA: And how do you know he's a boy? Have you seen to that as well?

THOMAS: Well that's a simple procedure these days.

MARY: Thomas you're my son. I've supported you in everything you've done and I haven't always liked it, but your brother's sperm!

MARTA: Where's our embryo? That's what I want to know. What have you done with it?

THOMAS [*stands*]: I don't know.

MARTA: You what? You don't know?

THOMAS: The assistant couldn't find it. It just disappeared.

MARTA: Embryos don't just disappear. This sounds like a course of wilful destruction.

THOMAS: We wanted a baby. This baby will be a miracle, a scientific breakthrough.

MARY [*who has been in her own world of thought*]: When Jesus told me he wanted to be a conscientious objector, I said to him, 'You have to obey the law my son.' I'll never forgive myself.

MARTA: If you won't tell me the truth about our baby, I'll have an abortion.

THOMAS: You can't.

MARTA: Why not?

THOMAS: It's not your child.

MARY: I was told his birth would be a great thing, so I consented. I said do whatever you want.

THOMAS: Don't forget me, mother – you had twins.

MARTA: Aha. So now we come to the question of ownership.

THOMAS: Its closest relations are Mary and me. Anyway it's mine. I created it.

MARTA: It's what? I see. Well, if it's yours, I suppose you'll look after it, give up your job, because you'll have to. I don't want anything to do with the child. I don't want anything to do with this family. I'm leaving.

THOMAS: You won't leave me.

MARTA: Oh yes I will.

THOMAS: Mary will look after it.

MARY: No she won't.

MARTA: That's not the point. It is in my body, Thomas, and I want the truth. I don't believe you just lost that embryo.

THOMAS: It can happen.

MARY: For heaven's sake, Thomas, you don't expect us to believe that?

THOMAS: My sperm wouldn't take. You failed the procedure.

MARTA: What do you mean I failed the procedure?

THOMAS: We wanted a child. We would have had to adopt. Now let's order dinner and stop all this nonsense.

SCENE VII

Recorded sounds of a bar.

THENA [*walks to a politician having a drink*]: Hello Fred.

FRED: Theen.

THENA: Do you mind if I join you for a moment?

FRED: No, no. What are you drinking Theen?

THENA: Nothing, thanks Fred.

FRED: You're looking stunning. Sure you won't have a drink?

THENA: Not just now.

FRED: Go on, it's on me.

THENA: Fred I need to talk . . .

FRED: Gee, you're looking sexy Thena. Go on, have one with me.

THENA: Come on Fred, you're an old windbag. Now, how's your farm?

FRED: Best thing we ever did to buy a farm. Wife loves it, loves it.

THENA: Roses doing well? How are your old-fashioneds?

FRED: Never better, never better, came into bloom last week, wonderful.

THENA: Used the cow manure under the cypress trees did you?

FRED: Oh yes, never use anything else, no need, plenty

of cow manure, with the mulch from the cypress trees, never use anything else.

THENA: No, why should you when you have access to cows and cypress trees?

FRED: My wife uses droppings from the fowlyard.

THENA: Does she?

FRED: Sure you won't have a drink?

THENA: No thanks. Talking about fowl droppings Fred. Have you heard about our protectress of the forests?

FRED: Who?

THENA: Diana Hunt.

FRED: Oh, Diana Hunt, yes Diana Hunt. She's come across a bit strong lately, hasn't she? Yes, Diana Hunt.

THENA: I find it very odd.

FRED: What's that?

THENA: Her father.

FRED: Yes?

THENA: Allied to Jove Enterprises.

FRED: Jove Enterprises – never heard of them.

THENA: Offshore interests, logging and woodchipping. She doesn't use his name. I'm not surprised. Quite embarrassing for her really, a father with interests like that.

FRED: Like what?

THENA: Woodchipping. Don't you think Bill would be interested in that?

FRED: Got a moment Bill. Thena's just been telling me this Diana Hunt's mixed up in woodchipping. Her father's Jove Enterprises. Seems she's got undeclared private interests.

[*As the following recorded voices are heard,* THENA *exits into corridor and to her office. She crosses* MARY *in the corridor but is hardly aware of her.* MARY *watches her go into her office.*]

RECORDED VOICES: By Jove woodchipping.

She's got undeclared private interests.

Who has?

Diana Hunt, Diana Hunt.
Woodchipping! She's pushy.
Got an eye for the media.
Dug a hole for herself this time.
I'll tell the chairman of committees.

ANNOUNCER: Serious allegations in Parliament about conservationist, Diana Hunt. Investigations into her connections with woodchipping. She wasn't available for comment but the opposition are calling for her resignation.

DIANA [*entering* THENA*'s office*]: You started this witch-hunt. It was you.

THENA: Hardly a witch-hunt.

DIANA: Well what else are you going to tell them? I told you all about my relationship with my father and you used it. Well, I don't receive one cent from him and you know it. You've been in endless therapy and still haven't resolved your relationship with your father. They might be interested in that. I'm just going out to the press.

THENA: What?

[*She exits straight into a press conference.*]

REPORTER 1: Ms Hunt, will you be resigning from the committee?

DIANA: I see no reason to resign.

REPORTER 2: You say you were unaware of your father's links with woodchipping?

DIANA: That's correct.

REPORTER 3: Or his interests in the Philippines?

DIANA: My father has many interests. He's always wheeling and dealing.

REPORTER 1: What about the shares in your name?

DIANA: I have no intention of receiving money connected with woodchipping or logging. If my father has put shares in my name without telling me, he will have to answer for it.

REPORTER 2: Have you contacted him?

REPORTER 3: In what way will he have to answer for it?

REPORTER 1: Why would he put shares in your name without telling you?

DIANA: That is for my father to answer.

[*On another part of the stage,* THENA *speaks in Parliament.*]

THENA: And Mr Speaker, I ask the members of this House to consider, that the representative of conservationist interests in this Parliament, the self-appointed goddess of the wilderness is unaware of her own father's involvement in logging operations in the Philippines. While he destroys the remnants of the meranti forests, she profits.

DIANA: I do not follow every movement of his business dealings. How could I?

THENA: Isn't it her business to be aware? Isn't it every politician's business to be aware? [*Uproar in the House.*]

DIANA: We have nothing to do with each other. We are totally opposed.

REPORTER 2: Hasn't your father supported you in the past?

DIANA: He has never supported me.

REPORTER 3: Financially?

DIANA: Financially or in any other way.

REPORTER 3: What about your education?

THENA: Perhaps the member for conservation hasn't been as totally independent as she would like us to believe.

DIANA: It's not true. I've always been self-supporting.

REPORTER 1: Your father claims he's supported you.

DIANA: What?

REPORTER 2: What are your feelings about your father?

REPORTER 3: Could you benefit from other interests of his?

REPORTER 1: Did he support you Ms Hunt? [*All three question at once.*]

DIANA: He has never supported me, he has never supported my mother and now when it suits his purpose, he turns around and puts money in my name. He never even married her. He treated my mother like a call girl. I have no respect for him, no respect. Now he plays the benign father.

REPORTER 2: So it's a personal vendetta?

THENA: . . . A personal crusade . . .?

DIANA: No, no . . .

REPORTER 2: But your campaign would be closely linked with your feelings about your father?

REPORTER 3: Will your credibility with the wilderness movement be affected?

REPORTER 1: What about your electorate?

THENA: And therefore I call for her resignation from the Environmental Impact Committee . . .

DIANA: I care about forests, about the land, about preservation, about life. It has nothing to do with my father. I hate him.

REPORTER 1: Ms Hunt.

REPORTER 2: Ms Hunt.

REPORTER 3: Ms Hunt.

[*Blackout.*]

|| ACT II ||

SCENE I

A bar of music of the VERNON FLANK *talk-back show can be heard.* VERNON *is in the broadcasting box at the back of the stage.* THENA *sits listening in her office.*

VERNON: You are listening to the Vernon Flank show on 3GR and we are taking calls on 300771 concerning allegations against conservationist MP, Diana Hunt and her father's interests in woodchipping. I have another caller on the line. Hello.

CALLER 1: Hello Vernon, am I on?

VERNON: Yes, you are on.

CALLER 1: Am I on Vernon, am I on?

VERNON: Yes, your name?

CALLER 1: Yvonne.

VERNON: Hello Yvonne, and your comment?

CALLER 1: I'm all for her, Vernon. It's all a storm in a teacup if you ask me. I hope she's listening: good on you, Diana, and they shouldn't throw you out of Parliament even if your mother's a prostitute.

VERNON: Thank you. I think she did say call girl more as a figure of speech. I have another caller on the line.

CALLER 2 [*broad Scottish accent*]: Hello Vernon. This is George McNee from Broadmeadows. Eh. I'd like to say I'm ashamed to be an Australian. I heard those reporters last night and I think the way they hammered that lass was disgraceful and that's all about it.

VERNON: Of course if you're a politician you've got to be able to take it.

CALLER 2: I don't think anyone should have to take that. It's nobody's business who her parents are. It's a private matter. There's no respect for privacy these days.

VERNON: Thank you for your call. There's time for another caller.

CALLER 3: Hello Vernon.

VERNON: Your name?

CALLER 3: Doug Farrow, Morang Young Farmers. I just want to say, I don't agree with Diana Hunt's politics. I've got no time for conservationists, but the girl stood up for herself well and I just think you know we don't choose our parents, we don't have control over what they do, and if we had more time I could tell you a thing or two about my old man.

VERNON: Thank you, time has run out. Tune in tomorrow. We will be talking about impregnating whales with dolphin . . .

DAVIES [*enters* THENA*'s office. She turns the radio off without a word*]: You've made her into a national bloody heroine!

[*Exits.*]

SCENE II

Tartonside Clinic.

THOMAS [*In his white coat in hospital.* MARY *with him.*]: I wish you'd given me warning mother, I'd have got in some gin.

MARY: There's no need for that. I've very little time. I've spoken to Marta, Thomas.

THOMAS: I haven't seen her for a week. It feels very strange.

MARY: She wants a public investigation.

THOMAS: If there's a scandal it'll affect you.

MARY: I'm not afraid of that. I have to do it Thomas, I'm about to begin a campaign.

THOMAS: Against your own son?

MARY: No, not against you, but to restore sanity. You're

obsessed with these embryos, and I can only blame myself after the circumstances of your birth.

THOMAS: Oh Mother, with you it's always *mea culpa*.

MARY: But this isn't just an ordinary mistake Thomas, not just a matter of mistiming like some pregnancies or careless passion.

THOMAS: I feel very passionate about this child Mother.

MARY: Yes, but it's not the right sort of passion, you've gone too far.

THOMAS: But it's of the utmost benefit to mankind.

MARY: What about Marta and the child she's carrying?

THOMAS: She would learn to love it.

MARY: You've dreamt this child up. You are forcing her to have your brainchild. You've put your brainchild into Marta.

THOMAS: I could never do anything right by you Mother.

MARY: I know you've always doubted my love. Would you agree not to publish your paper? It's what Marta wants.

THOMAS: Not publish. Why?

MARY: You're making her a vehicle for your scientific glory.

THOMAS: I can't suppress information.

MARY: All this transferring of eggs and sperm, it's not healthy Thomas and to do it deceitfully as you have.

THOMAS: How could she ask me to do that?

MARY: I see. I'm to lose you both it seems, both sons.

THOMAS: What are you going to do?

MARY: I'm going to bring it up in Parliament.

[*The sound of the organ –* MARY *'s theme.*]

SCENE III

Collage of people in the corridors, sounds of the House, etc. under the announcer.

ANNOUNCER: A scandal erupted in Parliament when Labor backbencher, Mary Madres asked for an investigation into the activities of her son, an embryologist at Tartonside Hospital Fertility Clinic. [*Her voice fades under the reporters.*] It is alleged that her son illegally implanted an embryo from . . .

    [*Press in the corridor besiege* MARY *and* MARTA.]

REPORTER 1: Will you keep the baby?

MARY: My daughter-in-law cannot answer any questions.

REPORTER 2: Will you comment on your son?

MARY: No comment.

REPORTER 1: Will there be a full enquiry into reproductive technology?

MARY: That is a matter for the Minister.

REPORTER 2: Would you like to see one?

MARY: Yes.

REPORTER 1 [*to* MARTA]: Is it true your husband used the sperm of his brother? Will it be your husband's brother's child?

REPORTER 2 [*to* MARY]: What action will the government take?

MARY: There's the Minister. Ask him. Quick Marta.

    [*Pulls her around. The reporters brush past towards the* MINISTER. *In the confusion,* MARTA *is pushed against* THENA *who approaches down the corridor. Further confusion.*]

MARTA: Christ!

MARY: Marta, are you hurt?

MARTA: I'm sorry. I didn't see you.

THENA: Are you all right?

MARTA: Just a bit shaken. [*General confusion.*]

MARY: I have a rescue remedy in the office. If anything happens to the child, I'll have these reporters up for bodily assault.

    [*As* THENA *and* MARY *take* MARTA *to* MARY'*s office, the press find the* MINISTER *on another part of the stage.*]

REPORTER 1: Minister? [*Places microphone in front of him.*]

MINISTER: I have initiated proceedings, so that the hospital will institute its own appropriate proceedings in the governing of this matter. Now should decisions taken arising from these proceedings require further action, let us say a general enquiry into *in vitro* fertilization procedures for example, my department will look at that very seriously.

REPORTER 2: You will look at that?

MINISTER: Oh yes we will. We'll look at anything that has to be looked at.

SCENE IV

MARY's *office.* MARTA *is sitting,* MARY *fussing around her with a Bach-flower remedy. During this scene* THENA *stands uncertainly at the window, sipping a drink also provided by* MARY. MARTA *is greatly distressed.*

MARY: It won't harm you. It's flowers with a bit of spirits.

MARTA: It's none of their business. Doesn't anyone understand? It's none of their business.

MARY: Don't think about it Marta. Here, drink this.

MARTA: I trusted him. I always supported him. How dare he.

MARY: I know. I know.

MARTA: And you. I came to you for help. Out there in the corridor, you were only concerned for the child.

MARY: Oh no, believe me Marta, I'm concerned for you.

MARTA: Everyone goes on and on about the child. I'm going away. I have to.

MARY: Don't. Don't go on your own.

MARTA: What if I take out my anger on the baby? Yesterday there was a show of blood. Oh well, I thought, if I have a miscarriage everyone can just forget about it. All the evidence gone. That'll be it. Finish.

MARY: Marta, I'll support you whatever you want, but you

mustn't make this child living evidence of Thomas's guilt.

MARTA: It's your grandchild but it's not even my child I'm carrying. I can't make a decision. I'll have to go away.

MARY: I don't think you should . . . This is dreadful. What a mess. [*Becomes aware of* THENA *watching them.*] It seems anything is possible nowadays with a bit of manipulation of the raw ingredients.

THENA: I'll go. I'm all right. Thanks for the . . .

MARTA [*stopping* THENA *in her tracks*]: You have to do something in here. Don't you see. Thomas isn't the only one experimenting. It's a competition, a race. You have to do something. You have to unite.

MARY: I'll find support. There is something happening. Let me help you.

MARTA: You can't. It's too late for me.

SCENE V

DIRECTOR'*s office in Tartonside Fertility Clinic.* HEAD OF CLINIC *and his female* ASSISTANT DIRECTOR *are interviewing* THOMAS. *There is more than a familiarity between the* HEAD *and his* ASSISTANT DIRECTOR.

HEAD OF CLINIC: You've got yourself into trouble Didimus.

THOMAS: Yes, I'm afraid I have.

HEAD: Ethics committee, inquiry into clinical procedures. This hospital has never had anything like this, has it doctor?

ASSISTANT DIRECTOR: No, never.

THOMAS: No, I'm aware of that.

HEAD: You've been held in high respect around here, hasn't he doctor? [ASSISTANT DIRECTOR *is nodding.*] One of my top men. I must say I'm puzzled about you Didimus. Most people would cover their tracks.

THOMAS: I know. I've made a great mistake.

HEAD: A blunder, a first-class, prize blunder. I've looked on you as a personal friend. [ASSISTANT DIRECTOR *looks grave.*]

THOMAS: Thank you.

HEAD: But we don't like this sort of thing. Very bad publicity. [ASSISTANT DIRECTOR *mutters agreement.*] Very bad publicity.

THOMAS: I do understand.

HEAD: How could you be such a damn fool? . . . And the procedure worked, eh? [*To* ASSISTANT DIRECTOR] Immature eggs, what about that? How did you do it?

THOMAS: Took a slice of the ovary. Have to maintain the environment, that's the hard part.

HEAD: Mmm. This is a terrible business for all of us. Could you do it again?

THOMAS: Of course.

HEAD: Damn shame. We need creative men like you Didimus.

THOMAS: I like to think I'm creative.

HEAD: This procedure could be worth a lot of money. You'll be struck off the register at the very least.

THOMAS: There's nothing to be done I suppose.

ASSISTANT DIRECTOR: These committees involve all sorts of people. Religious people, educators, people with no experience of medicine, none at all.

HEAD: Completely different interests, way of thinking, values. You would give us all the information if we helped?

THOMAS: Could you think of something?

HEAD: There's always something to be done Didimus.

ASSISTANT DIRECTOR: It was your wife.

HEAD: It isn't possible you thought you had her tacit consent?

THOMAS: She'd like to see me in prison, or on the streets.

HEAD: You're in a difficult position – angry wife, angry public, angry mother.

ASSISTANT DIRECTOR: I understand your wife is under the

influence of your mother, or your mother, your wife.

HEAD: Quite. Doesn't make it any easier for us. We'd want all the copyrights, patents, if we were able to get you off with a warning.

THOMAS: Could you do it?

HEAD: You'll have to leave the country. You couldn't practise anywhere here. We do have certain interests, certain reciprocal agreements with a thriving little fertility clinic in Bangladesh.

ASSISTANT DIRECTOR: Bangladesh.

HEAD: Ever been there Didimus?

THOMAS: Bangladesh? . . . No.

HEAD: I think you'll enjoy it. They'll benefit from your skills. It's all part of a scheme to aid the under-developed countries, and all the information comes back to us. You'll be under some supervision. I don't think you'll find it restrictive. So your wife wants to see you in prison does she? [*Looks at* ASSISTANT DIRECTOR.] That's a woman for you – eh, Doctor?

ASSISTANT DIRECTOR: Doctor.

HEAD [*turns almost brotherly to* THOMAS]: They can be quite unpredictable really. Eh!

THOMAS: How long do you think I'll be in Bangladesh?

HEAD: A while, if the whole place doesn't wash away first. [*Laughs*] We'll review your situation when the storm dies down. Good luck Didimus.

SCENE VI

In the corridor, DIANA *and* MARY *meet.*

MARY: Diana, would you be interested in a campaign?

DIANA: I don't know.

MARY: Against *in vitro* fertilization?

DIANA: Certainly.

MARY: We need an alliance of women.

DIANA: To reclaim birth.

MARY: Reclaim, that's a good word. Yes, I like that. The birth issue could be the birth of alliances over other issues – a new party, even.

DIANA: Sounds very interesting.

MARY: It would necessitate a meeting with Athena.

DIANA: No, I don't want anything to do with her.

MARY: Would you like anything to do against her?

DIANA: Explain.

MARY: I'm just checking out options.

DIANA: You've mentioned it to her?

MARY: I saw her the other day. She looked so miserable. Did you know she's been to rebirthing therapy?

DIANA: Then you have spoken with her?

MARY: About rebirthing. Oh no. I'm fascinated, though. You have to trust me. Diana don't frown.

DIANA: I'm not joining anything that involves Athena.

MARY: You might have to.

[MARY *walks straight on past* DIANA. DIANA *turns to look at her, shakes her head and exits.* MARY *stands at her office and then goes to* THENA*'s door.*]

MARY: Got a moment Thena? [*Enters* THENA*'s office*] You do look harassed. Your back troubling you? I have a wonderful naturopath. I could give you a recommendation. Mind if I sit down?

THENA: Of course.

MARY: She'll give you a herbal tonic too. You're looking so pale. Now, how have you been progressing under the new leadership?: So boring these little skirmishes, on such a petty level. I mean, what does it matter whether we have a man with a weak heart and lack of charisma replaced by another with a huge belly and hideous ego. I've been waiting for a mission Thena, something to sacrifice myself for, for the sake of the nation, for the sake of my son Jesus, who died so unnecessarily . . . crucified for his political beliefs . . .

THENA: I'll get you a glass of something.

MARY: It's all right, I'm fasting. Gives me strength. What do you feel about reproductive technology, Thena?

THENA: Why do you ask me?

MARY: I value your judgement. Besides I think it concerns us all. What do you think?

THENA: I think what your son did was alarming.

MARY: The Minister is hedging. He won't go all out.

THENA: What do you have in mind?

MARY: An alliance.

THENA: What sort of alliance?

MARY: I'm not sure yet but I'm getting there. In fact, I'll know after tomorrow.

THENA: What happens tomorrow?

MARY: I'm meeting with Diana.

THENA: Oh!

MARY: Would you like to join us?

THENA: I don't think Diana wants anything to do with me.

MARY: No, probably not; what a pity.

THENA: I don't think it's a pity. I hate her arrogance. She thinks I'm ruthless, but I'm Father Christmas compared to Diana.

MARY: It's an interesting comparison. You did betray her Thena. She has a right to be angry.

THENA: It was simply political, I did what I had to.

MARY: I've never seen you forced to do anything. Think about it. Why don't you join us?

THENA: I'd like to know what's happening.

MARY: Good. We could eat together. I'll break my fast. You look so pale Thena. What is all this doing to you? Let me leave the card of my naturopath.

THENA: No thank you.

MARY: I'll leave it just in case. She's good at manipulation too. You could probably do with some just now, if you'd let her do it. [*Puts down the card. Begins to exit.*] It would be so nice to stop all this haggling Thena and

govern, don't you think? [*Exits.*]
[THENA *after a pause, picks up the card, holds her back and groans.*]

SCENE VII

It is that evening. Collage of parliamentary sounds. MARY *enters her office.* THOMAS *is there.*

MARY [*jumps*]: Thomas, you gave me such a fright. You look like a ghost.

THOMAS: I am mother, a ghost of my former self.

MARY: Why are you here?

THOMAS: I've come to see you.

MARY: Yes, well I realize that. How are you coping?

THOMAS: Not very well.

MARY: No, I don't expect you are.

THOMAS: Is Marta all right?

MARY: She's . . . coping.

THOMAS: Do you feel any sorrow for me Mother?

MARY: You're still my son. Would you like something to eat? We could go to the dining room.

THOMAS: I'm not hungry. I've come to tell you, I'm going away.

MARY: You can't do that. You have to go into court.

THOMAS: I want you to persuade Marta to drop the charges.

MARY: Thomas how can she?

THOMAS: She can have everything – everything I've got.

MARY: Where are you going?

THOMAS: I can't tell you that.

MARY: But you can't go without her permission.

THOMAS: I'm giving her the divorce. I'm leaving everything behind. She can have it all. I'll be like your Jesus going out into the byways. You'll approve of that.

MARY: I've always approved of you, Thomas, until this business.

THOMAS: How can you say that?

MARY: There's no point in giving away your money – you won't be like your brother.

THOMAS: You see, it's all your fault. I should have died and he should have lived. I'm as good as dead now, but you don't care.

MARY: Don't you say that. Don't you dare say I don't care. I'm trying to forgive myself for whatever I did wrong in bringing you up.

THOMAS: You'd love to blame yourself wouldn't you? All we ever got through childhood was your piety and your guilt. Well, let me tell you my brother hated it as much as I did. He couldn't wait to get away from you.

MARY: That's not true. We loved each other deeply, something you couldn't understand.

THOMAS: Father hated it too, hated your doting on Jesus. Father always felt neglected.

MARY: You've said enough Thomas. I gave my love equally; I wore myself out giving my love, but always you needed more. Always needing something, needing a meal, two babies you were always hungry.

THOMAS: Father told me he thought of leaving you.

MARY: I don't want to hear any more.

THOMAS: I think Jesus was glad to be conscripted in the end to get away. I really do.

MARY: Stop it Thomas, I won't listen . . . Stop it – just leave.

THOMAS: I'm leaving. He didn't mind going, to get away from you, but they finished him up there when he saw the horror of that war. He was a damaged man when he started preaching against it and you had to trail around after him, turning him into a cult figure. You let him go on believing he could perform miracles; stop the fighting at the very least.

MARY: He did, he gave his life to stop it.

THOMAS: You drove him mad Mother. It's your fault he was killed, that's what you want to believe. Well, you're right, it was your fault.

MARY: I'm not listening.

THOMAS: This baby will be his and I thought you'd want that. I thought at least you would be glad about that. I'm going now. You probably won't see me again Mother. I'm going [*Begins to exit.*]

MARY: Thomas, you mustn't leave like this, not with us both fighting.

THOMAS: Just now you told me to go.

MARY: I might never see you again. You've said some dreadful things. If you go now I'll have to carry them.

THOMAS: You're listening to me at last.

MARY: No Thomas, I want you to listen to me. What you've done is terribly wrong, but you feel I'm somehow involved in that, I haven't loved you enough. Is that what you're trying to tell me?

THOMAS: You'll never understand me, Mother. I'm that hungry child. I could drink a fountain of knowledge and it wouldn't satisfy me.

MARY: You have to be responsible, Thomas. That's not knowledge you're after, it's power – power and adulation, that's why you'll always want more. I won't accept the blame for not loving you enough. You set yourself up to help the infertile, to work miracles for them, but look what you've done. I won't accept the blame for that.

THOMAS: Then you will not take the blame for my brother's death, either?

MARY: Leave that alone, Thomas.

THOMAS: You've gloried in it. You've made an altar of guilt.

MARY: He was everything dear to me, poor boy.

THOMAS: He was a responsible man, just like you tell me ' I have to be. If you're not responsible for my life, you're not responsible for his death either. Your taking the blame won't bring him back from the grave, Mother.

MARY: No I can't, you're right. I can't do that either.

THOMAS: Tell Marta whatever she does with the baby he's my creation . . . Look after her, Mother.

MARY [*quietly urging him to listen, with some anguish and compassion*]: Thomas, she's gone away to have an abortion.

[THOMAS *almost cries out.* MARY *makes an involuntary move towards him, but they are unable to come together.* DIANA *enters.* THOMAS *pushes her aside in his haste to exit.*]

MARY: Goodbye Thomas. [MARY *sits staring.*] He's gone.

MARY: He's gone.

DIANA: So that was Thomas.

MARY: He came to see me.

DIANA: Has something happened?

MARY: No, nothing. It's all right, nothing at all.

DIANA [*aware something is wrong*]: I've been talking with a deputation of women who dropped out of the IVF program.

MARY: Oh yes. What did they have to say?

DIANA: Those clinics are hatcheries. The women are done in batches, lined up in cubicles, no time to speak to the doctors, from the cubicle into the theatre, collect the eggs and out again.

MARY: Like a lot of hospital procedures.

DIANA: And while the women are having their navels slit and the eggs harvested, the men are somewhere else masturbating to *Playboy* magazine. Why do women consent?

MARY: I did and willingly – at least I thought I did. It was that voice in the night like an angel of power. Infertile. It's such a damning word. Thomas believes he's helping them. Perhaps he is.

DIANA: Are you wavering?

MARY: He is my son.

DIANA: This is not the answer: hormones, superovulation, and on and on, and more and more experimentation.

MARY: I know.

DIANA: They're making babies, not treating infertility. All of us dream and are rendered infertile in all sorts of ways and society couldn't give a stuff. I'm not desperate for children but I've been desperate for other things and I've felt impotent. We're impotent in here.

MARY: No we're not, not yet.

DIANA: You are wavering. They are treated like cows. [MARY *doesn't respond*.] Is it Thomas? Why did he come here?

MARY: He's right. I never understood him. I should probably resign.

DIANA: You can't.

MARY: I can't fight any more.

DIANA: What if I met with Athena?

MARY: With Thena? Will you? You will!

DIANA: Why Athena?

MARY: With her political wiliness and your passion we'd be unbeatable.

DIANA: She wasn't so clever.

MARY: She made a mistake and she's paid for it. I think she's changing. [DIANA *shrugs*.] At the end of the day, which is fast approaching, what is the use of you, me or any of us sitting across the house, fighting each other?

DIANA: That's party politics.

MARY: Well, it's not working. We need each other.

DIANA: What is she saying about me?.

MARY: What are you afraid of?

DIANA: Tell me. You're my friend, my ally.

MARY: If you have a score to settle with Thena, meet her face to face.

DIANA: I want an apology.

MARY: At last I am getting somewhere already. Anything else?

DIANA: An assurance she means it.

MARY: You shall have both.

DIANA: Then you're not resigning?

MARY: If you're with me, then I'm solid as the rock of ages.

SCENE VIII

MARY*'s living-room.*

MARY: She is late.

THENA: Perhaps she won't come.

MARY: Yes she will.

THENA: You have told her I'm here?

MARY: Well, yes – well, no – well, not exactly.

THENA: Just what do you mean by not exactly?

MARY: You won't let me down, Thena; there's a lot at stake.

THENA: For you or for me?

MARY: For all of us. I feel we are on the brink of a revolution.

THENA: Do you?

MARY: Yes, and it's about time.

THENA: I'll wait another ten minutes then.

MARY: You don't have faith in me, Thena. Why else would I try to get you together with Diana?

THENA: You know I couldn't possibly answer that. In all these years, I've been watching you across the House, working with you on committees, I've never been able to quite fathom why you've done anything.

MARY: Thank you.

THENA: Thank you?

MARY: I like to think I move in mysterious ways.

THENA: Could you tell me exactly what you've told Diana about this meeting.

MARY: She wants an apology.

THENA: I see, and what else?

MARY: And an assurance that you mean it. I know you do,

Thena, and you'll give your word. I know your word means a lot to you, in spite of everything. You have a reputation for what is it? gentleman's honour or 'Ancient sporting purity'.

THENA: How did you know that phrase?

MARY: About your father?

THENA: And what if I don't apologize?

MARY: Of course you will. I mean, we do things in this business that we don't like. I'm sure you hoped to gain something by having her discredited, but look what happened, she's still on the committee. You did the right thing by the party and you didn't even enjoy a brief view from the front bench.

THENA: I knew you would bring that up.

MARY: There seem to be so many changes on your side of the House lately. Davies dropped I see, sent to the back of the class. I was sure I'd see your face up there.

THENA: I don't want to talk about it.

MARY: And you lost a squash partner as well. Now, how's your back? That's more important. Did you go to the naturopath?

THENA: I'm sure you know the answer already.

MARY: There you are, Diana goes to her, too. The revolution's beginning – all three of us at the same naturopath. Isn't she marvellous?

THENA: I'm not sure yet. I have to go back for another appointment.

MARY: Wonderful. I'll just ring Diana's office and see if I can find her. Now don't run away.

[MARY *exits. Knock at the door.* MARTA *enters, noticeably pregnant*]

MARTA: I didn't realize.

THENA: It's all right, come in.

MARTA: Are you having a meeting?

THENA [*puzzled*]: We were going to. How are you? We met in the corridor in Parliament and in Mary's office.

MARTA: Yes, you saved me from falling.

THENA: Mary's phoning.

MARTA [*holds her stomach*]: I'll just sit down.

THENA: Can I do anything?

MARTA: Sometimes I wonder what's really in here.

THENA: You must be uncomfortable.

MARTA: When I was a child, I had a green cup. I hated it.

THENA: I beg your pardon.

MARTA: I'm terrified. I think about giving birth to another
woman's baby, but not just another woman, I think
about her green eyes in my baby.

THENA [*puzzled*]: I see.

MARTA: Imagine holding the imprint of a shadow, her life
rubbing against my stomach. I'll kill him.

THENA: Who?

[*Sounds at the door.*]

THENA: Someone's there. [*Calls off.*] Mary. What's she
doing?

DIANA [*entering*]: The door wasn't locked . . . So you're here.

THENA: You've arrived.

DIANA: I thought you might be here.

THENA: But you came anyway.

DIANA: I'm not sure I'm staying.

THENA: Neither am I.

MARTA: Should be a high-powered meeting.

MARY [*entering. To* DIANA]: You're here. I'm so glad.
Marta! My dear!

DIANA: I don't know if I can stay. I didn't think . . .

[DIANA *and* THENA *almost collide as they both back
towards the door.*]

MARTA: I'm sorry, I won't stay. I just . . . [*Blinks back
tears. To* MARY.] I had to see you. [*Falls into her arms.*] I
didn't ever have the abortion.

MARY: But . . .

MARTA: Oh, I went to have it. They almost had me in the
stir-rups, but I'd had enough. Rubber gloves and
instruments. I never want to see them again. So I took
myself off.

MARY: Oh my dear. [*Embracing her.*] You look piquey. I'll make some nice soup.

MARTA: I can't forgive him, but I couldn't go through with the abortion.

MARY [*rocking her*]: There, there, everything is all right.

[THENA *and* DIANA *speak simultaneously.*]

THENA: I'm just going.

DIANA: We'll meet another time.

[*They begin to slide out the door.* MARY *virtually blocks their path.*]

MARY: Oh no you don't. Marta, just sit down a moment. Thena has something to say to Diana. [THENA *opens her mouth and closes it.*] Go on Thena, get on with it. What we were talking about before Diana arrived.

THENA: We were commenting on a revolution.

MARY: Before a revolution we need an . . . that is, Diana needs an . . .

THENA: Diana, it appears I'm required to say I'm sorry. Well, I'm sorry.

DIANA: It's not enough.

MARY: I think I'll just brew something up for us. Something herbal. Clear the air. Marta . . . [*Marta is seated. To* THENA *and* DIANA] Keep an eye on Marta. [*Exits.*]

[*A silence.* DIANA *stands up.*]

MARTA: I can't get comfortable. My head's a muddle. My feet . . .

DIANA: Here, lie back. [*She arranges cushions under* MARTA, *takes off her shoes and sits beside her.*]

THENA: I suppose an alliance would make sense if it becomes a conscience issue.

MARTA: A lot of sense.

DIANA: It's not that easy. [*She begins rubbing* MARTA'*s shoulders.*]

THENA: I was put under pressure to get you off that committee.

DIANA: Yes, I'm sure you were.

THENA [*picks up one of* MARTA*'s feet and begins massaging*]: It was part of a strategy. You do understand? It's the sort of thing that happens all the time.

DIANA: It's not my way of doing things.

THENA: You are very proud, Diana, in a way that is – unusual.

DIANA: Naive?

THENA: I didn't say that.

DIANA: Yes, I see how naive you think I am. You're absolutely right. I would be naive to have believed you were offering me friendship.

THENA: That isn't possible in our world.

DIANA: I thought certain things did happen off the record. Silly of me. You see, underneath that political exterior, I had a feeling you were confiding in me.

THENA: I was . . . we were . . . there were confidences.

DIANA: Ah.

MARTA [*responding to the massage*]: Ah!

THENA: And I've lost all round over those damn squash games.

DIANA: So things do happen off the record.

THENA: Oh, yes.

DIANA: As long as I'm clear about that.

THENA: You have my word, and I don't give it lightly, I assure you.

DIANA: Then I accept it.

THENA: And I'm sorry. It is possible to align on political grounds if it's necessary.

DIANA: Do you think it's necessary?

THENA: I'm not sure yet.

DIANA: Or to your advantage?

THENA: I do have feelings on this issue.

DIANA: Like your feelings on conservation?

THENA: What do you mean?

DIANA: Do you see this as a vote-catching issue?

THENA: I think we can stop this. You're determined to punish me.

DIANA: Where do you stand?

THENA: I don't like it. I don't like it at all.

MARTA: I'd love a warm beer.

THENA [*to* MARTA. *Putting down a foot.*]: Does that feel better? I once knew some reflexology. [*Picks up the other foot.*] This is for the kidneys, I think. This could be for the uterus. I've forgotten. Can you feel anything?

MARTA: Yes, yes, I think I can. In the shoulders.

THENA: Well . . . it was a long time ago.

DIANA: I came here to hate you.

THENA: Perhaps if we call it a truce.

DIANA: How do I know I can trust you outside this room?

MARTA: I felt it that time. Do it again?

THENA: You're quite right. I have my loyalties. However, on this issue I'm with you. You know you're not so ·pure, you've gone for the kill.

MARTA: Not quite so hard please.

THENA: It's all very well to charge out to face the press. You have to be careful.

DIANA: I should have thought that applied to both of us.

MARTA: Ouch!

THENA: I had a friend like you. She was a passionate fighter, but headstrong.

DIANA: What else could I do? You served it up to me.

THENA: And you slammed it home. I am offering you a truce.

[*Pause. Slowly,* DIANA *reaches a hand across* MARTA. THENA *reciprocates.* MARTA *puts her hand shyly on top of theirs, drawing their hands to her stomach.*]

THENA: Do you know anything about rebirthing?

DIANA: No, but Mary said . . . oops.

THENA: How did she know that one? Omnipresent Mary. You know that naturopath is probably another one of her informers.

[DIANA *begins to laugh.* THENA *looks at her.*]

MARY [*entering with the tea and Chinese cups, ritual-like*]:

So nice to hear you laughing.

THENA: Right on cue.

MARY [*behind* MARTA]: I do think timing is important. Now, listen to me. I've been waiting for this. There will be no more truces. We are together now, and we will begin.

   [*She looks from one to the other as lights fade.*]

SCENE IX

Sounds of Parliament, movement in corridors.
MARY*'s office.*

THENA [*entering office*]: Another three votes.

MARY: That's three-quarters of the women in Parliament already.

DIANA [*aiming the bow*]: It's no use pussyfooting. We should go for complete cessation of IVF programs.

THENA: We'd never get it.

DIANA: It's worth a try.

MARY: Prod the electorate until it squeals.

THENA: They will squeal all right.

   [DIANA *in a circle of light. Sounds of Parliament in session. In the background,* PATRICIA FORBES, *the* ANNOUNCER, *is speaking to the* HEAD OF CLINIC *in a talk-back session.*]

DIANA: Mr Speaker, Members of the House, the bill which I put before you today is to clarify laws controlling human embryo experimentation and new reproductive technology procedures.

   [*Lights up on* PATRICIA FORBES. *We hear the* HEAD OF CLINIC *speaking on line to her. He is on another part of the stage but his voice has a distorted quality as on radio.* PATRICIA *inserts 'Mms' into the* HEAD*'s conversation wherever she feels appropriate. Sounds of*

Parliament can still be heard.]

HEAD: It's ludicrous Patricia. This bill will stop embryo experimentation.

PATRICIA: Mm. I'm on the line to Professor Baron Bodie from Tartonside Fertility Clinic. This is Patricia Forbes on 3GR standing in for Vernon Flank. Hope you'll be over your virus soon Vernon, and back with us. We'll be taking your calls listeners on 300771. Professor, you were saying . . .

HEAD: Let me tell you, Patricia.

PATRICIA: Mm.

HEAD: Any more restrictions and my scientists will simply pack their bags and take their knowledge to somewhere that wants it.

PATRICIA: Mm. You mean they'll go back to being vets.

HEAD: I mean they'll leave the country.

PATRICIA: Aren't the scientists asking for guidelines Professor?

HEAD: Guidelines, not restrictions, Patricia.

[*We hear the talk-back show, while simultaneously* THENA, DIANA *and* MARY *on different parts of the stage, address meetings.*]

THENA: I'm happy to be here today to address this gathering of professional and business women in support of this Bill . . .

DIANA: I'm happy to be here today to support this meeting of Raging Feminists against experimentation and reproductive . . .

MARY: I'm happy to be here today to speak to the Radical Catholic Movement . . .

[*They move about and the* HEAD OF CLINIC *and* PATRICIA *can be heard.*]

HEAD: We want the go-ahead. We are waiting to begin genetic screening to eliminate diseases. We flush the embryo out of the mother, check it for imperfections and re-implant it. This way we can monitor all 'at risk' groups and control genetic disease.

PATRICIA: Mm. What is an 'at risk' group, Professor?

HEAD: Anyone . . . um . . . Anyone likely, in our opinion, to have serious genetic defects.

THENA: I'm happy to be here today to speak on the anniversary of the Country Women's Association . . .

PATRICIA: Would this become routine practice?

HEAD: Personally, I would like it to, Patricia.

PATRICIA: Mm.

HEAD: Ultrasound is now routine, and amniocentesis. It's really using Star Wars to get rid of the invader before it hits earth.

MARY: I'm happy to be here today to speak to members of Women's Electoral Lobby . . .

THENA: I'm happy to be here to speak to women Rotarians . . .

DIANA: Fellow members of The Wilderness Society . . .

MARY and THENA [*together*]: Wilderness Society?

DIANA: It's all the same thing. Control of nature for profit.

PATRICIA: Mm. What does all this mean to the person in the street, Professor?

HEAD: Ultimate improvement of the quality of life. Mother Nature makes mistakes and we are correcting them.

MARY: I'm happy to be here today to address Women Who Want To Be Women . . . [*Stops.* DIANA *and* THENA *shake their heads.*] You're right, enough is enough.

[*Parliamentary sounds in the corridor. The* PRIME MINISTER *enters, followed by his* SECRETARY, *who hands him a large sheaf of papers.*]

PRIME MINISTER: What is this?

SECRETARY: A petition in support of the Reproductive Technology Bill, Prime Minister, with 500,000 signatures.

PRIME MINISTER: What's this group?

SECRETARY: They're Men Against Sexism.

PRIME MINISTER: They're mobilizing the whole country. Well, Hunt won't have so much time for the Bill, will she, when Pulp Makers Incorporated win their appeal.

SECRETARY: Woodchipping, Prime Minister.

PRIME MINISTER: To fulfil existing contracts at Pennington.
 [DIANA *enters* MARY*'s office.*]
DIANA: There's a protest at Pennington. I can't be in two places at once.
MARY: Couldn't there be a protest here?
DIANA: Probably.
MARY: Then bring the protest to the rally. We'll have them both together. We could ask the land rights rally if they would join us. It'll be stimulating, a festival, and it's New Moon. [DIANA *exits. Sounds of the corridor.* MARY *entering the corridor meets* THENA.]
THENA: We're complicating the issue with three protests in one.
MARY: But they're all connected. The media will love it. They are on to us. They know this is a revolt.
THENA: It's hardly a revolt. I don't think you should use that word.
MARY: What word should I use?
THENA: We're uniting over an issue. It's happened before on conscience issues.
 [*As they exit along the corridor, the bells are ringing.*]
MARY: It's got much beyond that Thena.
THENA: I'm not intending to follow you into a revolution.
MARY: No, no, I wouldn't expect that – not yet, anyway.
 [*As they disappear,* MARTA *enters along the corridor. She holds a letter.*]
MARTA: Mary. [*Begins to hurry after them. Stops quickly putting hand on her stomach.*] Mary. Damn. Oh well. [*Turns to go back to* MARY*'s office, overtaken with sharp pain.*] Oh no. I need help. Oh no, oh no you don't. You're not going to be born in these corridors.
 [*The bells stop. Sound of the* SPEAKER. *'Lock the doors.'*]

SCENE X

MARY 's lounge. Occasional sounds of protest outside. MARY at door as THENA enters. MARY initially talking in automatic half whisper.

MARY: Everything's all right.

THENA: And it's a girl. What about Marta?

MARY: She's fine, poor lamb. The baby was a bit premature. It could have been the shock from hearing Thomas was coming back. Anyway, the baby came with the defeat of an amendment, so that was a blessing.

THENA: Is there a likeness?

MARY: She has no resemblance to anybody that I can see. To tell you the truth, Thena, this could be anybody's baby. I mean, who's to know who they got out of the fridge? I can't think about that.

THENA: No.

MARY: Marta sees herself in the baby.

THENA: Really?

MARY: As soon as she knew it was a girl, she began to smile. She's been wearing a secret smile ever since, as though she beat us all and got pregnant by herself.

THENA: Parthenogenesis, eh?

MARY: Well, that'll be the next thing.

THENA: So Marta has taken possession.

MARY: Yes, you could call it that. She's very determined to be the good mother. Oh well. There should always be hope at a birth.

THENA: Is Diana here?

MARY: Yes, she's with Marta. Come on in. Marta's calling the baby Angela.

SCENE XI

PRIME MINISTER, FENNEL *and* HEAD OF CLINIC *at a balcony window in Parliament. Sounds of protest outside.*

PRIME MINISTER: Look at them out there.

HEAD: We are the first country in the world to mature eggs from ovarian tissue.

PRIME MINISTER: What the hell's going on? It feels like the approach of a cyclone.

HEAD: You do understand, our scientists will just pack up and leave. You can't blame them. It will mean all that expertise and revenue will pour out of the country.

FENNEL: It's chaos out there.

HEAD: I'd be happy to furnish you with any details you need.

FENNEL: It's those women.

PRIME MINISTER: With Mary Madres in the forefront. I don't understand. She's been an excellent back bencher. I'd forgotten her existence until now.

FENNEL: What about the moratorium days? Save Our Sons, the peace campaign. She drew people to her. You've forgotten her frenzy.

HEAD: She was relentless in getting rid of her son. He's back in town by the way.

PRIME MINISTER: Is he? [*To* FENNEL] What about your woman?

FENNEL: Athena? Don't worry about her. I'll have a word with her. She wouldn't want to face pre-selection.

PRIME MINISTER: If we're not careful, this could escalate. They haven't any loyalty. We can't have women aligning across the whole damn place. Who is running this Parliament anyway?

HEAD: I am responsible to thousands of childless couples yearning for offspring.

FENNEL: Yes, we know about your offspring.

PRIME MINISTER: Who will rid us of these Furies?

SCENE XII

Loud sounds of angry hecklers at a political meeting, insults, shouts against the women. The sounds fade. In THENA*'s office,* THENA *tears a poster off the wall and tramples it. As* DIANA *watches by the door,* THENA *opens her arms Japanese martial style and emits a loud 'ah'.*

DIANA: What are you doing?

THENA: Having a nervous breakdown. Is that all right?

DIANA: That's me you're standing on.

    [THENA *moves abruptly off the poster.* DIANA *picks it up and gives it to her.*]

THENA: I've just spoken with my leader and I've been told I'm to face pre-selection, which is to say, I won't be standing for the next election because of my support for you.

DIANA: Oh! Will you be resigning?

THENA: No I won't. I've shown no disloyalty. They can force me out.

DIANA: I don't understand. Disloyalty to what? They're throwing you out. What sort of loyalty is that? You should leave them.

THENA: Form a new party perhaps. Begin a revolution?

DIANA: You've changed. You can't even see it but they can. They're quite right, something's happening.

THENA: And what about you? What about last night?

DIANA: Those hecklers . . .

THENA: You lost your nerve. You can't let them get under your skin.

DIANA: I've seen it before, hatred in the eyes of an angry logger and a clenched fist in front of my face. I panicked. I needed you last night.

THENA [*smoothes the photo*]: It's a good photo. I'm with you. [*After a pause.*] Diana where's your double-headed axe?

DIANA: The chain broke in the jostling, when we left.

THENA: What I need is a game of squash to stop thinking.

DIANA: We should be going. I don't think we should have this celebration outside.

THENA: What's wrong?

DIANA: I don't know. I heard something, like a baby's cry or a wounded animal. I'm imagining. It's a clear night.

THENA: Sure you're all right?

DIANA: You don't have to worry about me.

MARY [*entering*]: And here's Mary. Are we ready?

[*They exit.*]

SCENE XIII

Tartonside Clinic, night.

HEAD: Where are you staying, Didimus? You could come to my house, but my wife isn't well.

THOMAS: I'll be all right.

HEAD: We're in terrible trouble if this bill goes through. I think my wife's been feeling the pressure. You're better off in Bangladesh.

ASSISTANT DIRECTOR: We'll all be coming there soon.

THOMAS: I want to see my laboratory.

HEAD: I'm afraid you can't do that. It would be locked at this time of night.

THOMAS: But I want my notes.

ASSISTANT DIRECTOR: Have you seen your baby?

THOMAS: They've taken out a restraining order. My wife and baby are kept under protection.

ASSISTANT DIRECTOR: I'm so sorry.

HEAD: That's terrible, not letting you see your own baby. The women are holding a meeting of some sort, on that hill overlooking Parliament. You can see it from here. They're going to light a chain of beacons – very primitive, archaic, surrounding the city with fire. They've treated you badly, Didimus.

ASSISTANT DIRECTOR: They're dangerous, anarchists; they speak about us as though we're criminals.

THOMAS: I want my notes.

HEAD: I'll check the clinic for them in the morning.

THOMAS: Let's look now.

HEAD: It'll be all right, now calm down.

THOMAS: I've seen that book you published. You've become a celebrity.

HEAD: Now, just a minute, Didimus.

THOMAS: I don't rate a mention. You've published everything under your name.

ASSISTANT DIRECTOR: We've published findings subsequent to your work.

THOMAS: While I rot in Bangladesh, someone else is finishing off my work.

HEAD: You can publish any time you like. You're one of my team.

ASSISTANT DIRECTOR: We'd all be very glad to see you working again.

THOMAS: Don't give me that. I can't do anything.

ASSISTANT DIRECTOR: We could help you.

THOMAS: I should shoot you Bodie.

HEAD: Some women draw the life from their sons. Your mother disowned you the other night.

ASSISTANT DIRECTOR: It was reported in the papers.

HEAD: That's one thing about the women in the program – they really want their children.

ASSISTANT DIRECTOR: Listen to them.

[*Hear a distant sound of cheering and celebration.*]

HEAD: Those women are up there cavorting, wrapping your mother in glory.

THOMAS: She's disowned me.

HEAD: Can't see your wife. Can't see your own child. What are you going to do?

Scene XIV

There are sounds of celebrating, but as though through a tunnel. Thena, Diana *and* Mary *are seen through a shimmer of flames.* Thena *speaks but we don't hear her words, then* Diana *steps forward. As she does so, there is the barely audible sound of a shot, great confusion and* Mary *slumps forward. The other two run to her.*

On one side of the stage the Prime Minister *stands at the balcony window in Parliament. On the other side,* Thena *waits for* Diana *in* Mary*'s living-room.* Fennel *enters.*

Prime Minister: You got here Jack. It's quiet out there. The eye of the storm.

Fennel: The crowds are gathering.

[Diana *enters* Mary*'s living-room.*]

Thena: You've arrived.

Diana: You're here. I couldn't get through the crowds, because of the vigil. There's a wave of shock.

Thena: It's all right.

Prime Minister: There's to be a march.

Diana: There'll be thousands marching tomorrow night, candlelight.

Thena: I heard.

Diana: Where's Marta?

Thena: She's with the baby. She'll be here. Well, are they with us?

Prime Minister: We could push the amendment through while the country's still in shock.

Fennel: Why not delay? Bide our time till the storm blows over? They have no leadership, no loyalty between them.

Prime Minister: There's a cult formed around that baby.

Fennel: Weird family.

Diana: Everyone, even the women on the Tartonside program are marching.

THENA: There will be no more truces.

DIANA: So we are together now. [MARTA *enters.*] Here's
  Marta.

MARTA: The baby is asleep. She's fine.

DIANA: Now we can begin.

END

Susan Eisenberg

BATTLEGROUND

for Rita Arditti

Always anxious to rescue
damsels in distress

Knights of the Laboratory
design test tubes that will not suffer
        nausea or back pain
        haemorrhoids or oedema
Petri dishes that will never
        blame miscarriages on their
        workplace, challenge the doctor's
        dominion in delivery or
        argue over alimony.

Only the womb
                with her mysteries
holds the Knights of Progress at bay,
their steeds trampling over centuries.

Thundering hooves: closer, closer.

Carmel Bird

EVERYTHING IS OVA, DR GOD
A story we once thought was fiction

Once upon a time there lived a king and queen who
longed for children but had none. One day when the
queen was bathing, a frog jumped out of the water and
said:

'Your wish will soon be granted and you will have a
daughter.'

In the palace, a doctor (his name was God, MMBS,
FRCS, FROG, and he was Chairman of two large
companies, one called DRUG and the other called THE
END) blew softly in the ear of the king who wonderfully
produced a glass phial of magic liquid which the doctor
promised to use in the making of the child. The king in
gratitude gave Doctor God a large bag of gold.

The inside of the queen's body was bright pink, and
there were dark red ovaries. But alas, the queen's
fallopian tubes were damaged and could not carry the
eggs from the ovaries to the womb.

'Never mind,' said Doctor God as he summoned a
willing army of FROGS. 'If you eat these delicious little
cakes dusted with clomiphene salt, you will produce an
abnormal number of eggs. And I will do the rest. Do not
worry, dear Queen, about a thing. I will look after
everything. Just you eat up, lie down, drift off to sleep,
and I will take care of you.'

A huddle of sterile green figures gathers around a pool of light. These frogs are hunched over, isolated in a sea of grey-green tiles that cover the floor and walls. In the centre of the huddle sleeps the queen, her slumber assured by the anaesthetist frog whose left hand rhythmically pumps a small rubber bag which resembles the bladder of a football (Australian Rules). The eggs are ripe at the right time because the frogs gave the queen an injection of human chorionic gonadotropin.

The queen lies as still as death, her head turned to one side, her eyes taped closed, her mouth filled with tubes which carry the anaesthetic gases to her lungs. A frog makes three small cuts in her belly and inserts three instruments. And another frog uses a foot pedal to pump carbon dioxide gas into her belly, blowing it up to make it easier for them to collect the eggs.

'This is more fun than robbing birds' nests.'

'Keep your mind on the job will you. There's no time to waste. A fresh semen sample has been obtained by masturbation. We need these eggs for insemination.'

A teflon tube starts to flow with a thin honey-coloured liquid drawn form the body of the still and silent queen. Forgotten is the proverb:

'He who wants eggs must endure the clucking of the hen.'

The hush is shattered as a woman in white raps a button on a wall-mounted intercom and says:

'The egg is coming out.' She wraps her hand around the tube and rushes to a nearby laboratory. Over the intercom crackle the words:

'We have an egg from tube one.' More tubes go to the laboratory; more eggs are announced, more demanded. The more eggs collected, the greater the chance of fertilization, and the greater the chance of re-implanting a healthy-looking cluster of four or eight cells that have the potential of becoming a princess.

'God is never satisfied,' says one of the frogs.

The king stands beside Doctor God and they look at the egg, a single cell in a blob of jelly, under a microscope.

'This is intimate,' says the king. *'It is good to be totally involved.'*

In a glass dish, the egg is surrounded by thousands of sperm. One sperm penetrates to the jelly-like centre of the egg.

When the fertilized eggs are ready, the queen is awake, as God and his frogs introduce the eggs into her womb with a syringe. She discusses with the woman in white what she will be wearing to the next masked ball at the palace.

The egg grew into a baby girl, and the king was delighted at the birth of the princess. He gave a great feast and invited all the frogs who lived in his kingdom. They gave the princess many lovely toys and trinkets, and her father, the king, signed a paper on her behalf, promising that she would donate all her eggs to God, in gratitude.

Susan Hawthorne

JUST ANOTHER BIT OF NEWS

31 October

I went to Morne Mansions today. An incredible place – a huge old stone building that looks as though, in another age, it could have had ghosts.

I interviewed Tom Muxworthy, the Director. Seems as if he's come a long way. He started his professional life as a cattle embryologist, now he has this empire. Quite an intriguing man, small, balding and full of energy for his new venture – to pioneer every technological method of producing babies for the infertile. (I suppose cattle are not so terribly different from humans at that stage.) He says that he's worked on everything: AID, IVF, GIFT, embryo transfer, frozen embryos, and hopes one day to produce an actual test-tube baby. I asked him if he meant something like what Huxley wrote about in Brave New World. He said, no, Huxley hadn't quite worked it out – though he was close, given when he wrote it. Muxworthy said he couldn't imagine our society turning out like that. He says he wants to increase the range of choices available to people.

He talked with fervour about all the breakthroughs and how eventually they would eliminate all disease in the 21st century. He is convinced that human society will evolve to its next stage.

He took me into the labs and showed me photographs of

the moment of fertilization as it occurs in a petri dish. It was like something out of Life magazine.

Energy and order are the two words that spring to mind when I think about him. He has a neat appearance, and a pasty, smooth, closely shaven face. And everything in its place. The building had a similar character: well-ordered, immaculately clean to the point of sterility, and a little cold. Jack wants me to write a piece on Muxworthy – he thinks it's the kind of thing my women like to read about.

FREEING WOMEN FROM THE TYRANNY OF REPRODUCTION

The first demand American feminist, Shulamith Firestone, formulated for the liberation of women, back in 1971, was: 'the freeing of women from the tyranny of reproduction by every means possible . . .'

What Shulamith Firestone had in mind was the technological takeover of child-*bearing*. This is now close to becoming a real possibility for *all* women – fertile and infertile alike. The man to achieve this extraordinary triumph is Dr Thomas Muxworthy, the first Director of Morne Mansions, The Developmental Institute for Research into Reproductive Technologies.

Dr Muxworthy has a passion for his work and is internationally renowned for several breakthroughs in the area of IVF and embryo transfer. This technique involves the removal of eggs from the donor, fertilization outside the body, and reimplantation of the fertilized egg. Dr Muxworthy is excited at the prospect of recently developed techniques that enable the removal of a large number of eggs in one simple procedure. He says that this new technique will be a crucial step forward for reproductive medicine.

Morne Mansions is set up almost as a holiday resort. Women from all over the world are on waiting lists, and when their turn comes they stay at the Mansions for the duration of the procedures. I spoke with several of the residents.

Hasna el-Hasan has been at the Mansions for two months, after waiting fifteen months to get on to the program. She is 37 and had begun to worry that she would soon be too old to go through IVF. She has been married for 15 years and her husband, a wealthy businessman, wants a son. Tests were unable to show the cause of infertility in Hasna's case, and all indications are that there is no physical damage to her ovaries, fallopian tubes or the uterus. Hasna said that she was enjoying her stay at the Mansions and has been delighted to meet women from all over the world who share her predicament. She said, in the morning, that she was hopeful that the techniques would be successful in her case. 'I would like, very much, to take a son home for my husband,' she said.

Residents at the Mansions are treated to delicious meals and have access to a variety of facilities – including beauty treatments – as well as to the best medical care in the country. It is not a program that is available to all at this stage, since the combined cost of accommodation and medical treatment is substantial. Dr Muxworthy hopes that one day, more women will be able to benefit from his procedures. 'The costs are falling with every success we have,' he said.

On the evening of my visit an announcement was made that Hasna was indeed pregnant. She would remain at the Mansions until the pregnancy had stabilized, then she would return home to Victoria for the last few months of the pregnancy, and return a few weeks before delivery. The jubilation of the other residents was profoundly moving.

Dr Muxworthy said, 'This is a wonderful hour that all of us, knowing your deep desire to bear a child, will treasure. All the more so, since the procedure used in your case is the first of its kind in the world.'

Dr Thomas Muxworthy then went on to explain. 'Hasna's case is a perfect opportunity to try the new technique of maturing immature eggs. Since none of her organs were incompetent, we were fairly certain that we would be successful. And so it has proved. There was not a bad egg amongst them! What we did had been thoroughly tested on cattle, sheep, mice and guinea pigs. She was in very good hands. Weren't you?' he asked looking at her. She nodded vigorously.

The procedure is a simple one. After an anaesthetic – just as you would have for an appendectomy or hysterectomy – a small incision is made and a very thin slice taken from the ovary, three or four cells deep. The cells, which contain hundreds of immature eggs ('it's such a waste,' he said, 'you women only use about four hundred in a lifetime') are then placed in a special medium that promotes cell maturation. The cells are then allowed to mature outside the body. Some of them don't make it, but the majority mature normally. (A random sample is taken at various times.)

He went on, 'Then, once the egg cells have matured – and you must remember we could produce hundreds of children from Hasna's eggs alone – ten eggs were chosen for fertilization (by micro-injection – one sperm only is injected into one egg) and the eggs that were successfully fertilized were then reimplanted.'

There can be anything from a single egg up to thirty, mostly there are around half a dozen. They are then put back into the woman's body and then wait to see how many implant into the lining of the womb.

Dr Thomas Muxworthy is proud of his achievements and went on to point out the advantages of his procedure, one of which is that prospective parents can choose the sex of their child. He said: 'In fact, because we routinely perform pre-implantation diagnosis, we know that all the embryos that have implanted themselves are male. The embryos are still there and we are confident of a full-term pregnancy. Hasna's pregnancy will be carefully monitored using some other marvellous scientific advances, ultra sound, chorionic villi sampling, amniocentesis and such like. We will do everything to ensure that this baby is one of the best.'

Many of the women listening congratulated Hasna. Some, perhaps because they are still waiting for their results, did not. There was an air of optimism in the room and I went to add my congratulations to the others.

5 November
Had a phone call today from a woman (Meg Moody) who says my article is all wrong. I explained about going to Morne Mansions and why I'd been so impressed by it. I added details about the place so she would know I'd really been there – who I'd met and so forth.

'They must have done something special for the day,' she said. 'It's not usually like that. And you're wrong about it working. It hardly ever does. He's just using the women in there as guinea pigs. He's experimenting. Can't you see that?'

I suppose she's disgruntled because it wasn't successful for her. I guess that's one of the risks Muxworthy has to take. It can't always work, I suppose.

I've agreed to talk with her. It's one way to keep the story alive. And perhaps in the long run it will help these women.

7 November
I'll have to tone this down if I write it up – if it's true – or we'll be in the courts. MM is off the planet. She is full of bitterness about Morne Mansions, but she also had some interesting things to say. Like the incentives he offers. MM is not as well off as someone like Hasna – he does have

some poorer women come on to programs, after all. He offered to do the treatment for free if MM would agree to certain procedures – which she did – knowing it was the only way she would have access to the program. She said that it's all written up in a contract. He promised her that all the procedures mentioned in the contract would increase her chances of becoming pregnant.

MM wasn't a residential patient – except for when the treatment was being carried out. She told me some awful things. But I'll have to tread carefully writing this up, or I'll be in strife. I think I'd better use a pseudonym for her.

FORMER INFERTILITY PATIENT DISPUTES DOCTOR'S CLAIMS

'Lois' is an attractive woman in her mid-thirties. She is tall and seems confident at a first meeting. She would need to be, if what she reports is true.

'Lois' tells of the protracted procedures she underwent over the last two years at the Developmental Institute of Reproductive Technology, under the Directorship of Dr Thomas Muxworthy. She says that the procedures amount to experimentation. She also says that some doctors are simply using women to try out new techniques. Having been through several attempts she claims that it has ruined her health and wrecked all chances of her ever having a child. She claims that irreversible damage has been done to her reproductive organs.

She says that although she has had three conceptions, none came to term; one proceeded to the second month, the others lasted only a few days each. In that time, she says, she was prodded, poked, and was fed large quantities of hormones and drugs (some of which, she claims, have terrible side effects).

'Sometimes I felt like a cow. A simple breeder. I submitted myself to indignities beyond anything I might have imagined possible. I think the doctors there saw us all as experimental bunnies. And some of the women pay enormous sums when they go in as residential patients.'

More seriously, 'Lois' claims that some clinics (including Morne Mansions) have contractual agreements that set out a number of conditions for the woman remaining on the program and stipulations about procedures she should undergo where one procedure fails and another is tried.

'These contracts are made for the 'welfare' patients,' she says. These are the ones who pay nothing for the procedure, but who seem to undergo more 'routine tests and procedures' than the paying patients. Included in her contract are details about the drugs (superovulatory hormonal drugs and the like) she agrees to take; permission to do exploratory surgery; excision or removal of body parts if that is deemed medically necessary; reimplantation of any viable embryos; and the rather gruesome prospect of giving permission to use her body as a neomort surrogate if she should die.

Government legal representatives are looking into the contracts.

30 November

I had a strange dream last night. I am being taken on a tour through a huge dark building. Our steps echo in the corridors. I walk past rooms with wire grills on the doors. They are bare – except for their occupants – cheetahs, dogs, cows, chimps. We keep walking. There are more rooms. These are furnished with a bed and a bucket. Women are kept in them. Some are pregnant, others are not.

I am in a huge courtyard. A man is talking excitedly. He says how marvellous their work is, how far they have progressed under the new regime. He thanks us for coming.

I realize I am one of those in power under the new regime.

IVF CLINICS DENY CLAIMS

'It is clear to me,' said the Director of Morne Mansions, Dr Thomas Muxworthy, today, 'that this former patient, 'Lois', has a chip on her shoulder because the procedures failed in her case. We give no guarantees, we never have, that the procedures will be successful in every instance.'

'All the procedures have been tested, and the drugs used have shown no statistically significant side effects in twenty years use. If this patient does not wish to have a child, she can leave the program (as she seems to have done, with no ill-will on our part, in spite of a broken contract). We are more than prepared to discuss any problems patients have.'

18 December
Muxworthy has invited me to the Mansions again. Before I go I have another appointment with MM.

23 December
She's dead. MM. Her sister rang me. Anne, her sister, says she's going to splash it all over the papers. I said to her to hold off for a few days. I'm going to the Morne Mansions Christmas Eve party tomorrow – at Muxworthy's invitation. I told her I'd try to suss things out for her. She reluctantly agreed to hold back for the moment. But I know it won't be for long.

WOMAN DIES

A 35-year-old woman is reported to have died after undergoing treatment for infertility at Morne Mansions. The clinic spokesperson would not comment on the death today. No names have been released as yet.

IVF critic, Dr Janice Small said: 'The medical literature shows that these drugs are dangerous and we know that harvesting so many eggs coupled with hyperstimulation of the ovaries is a risky business.'

Ethicist, Mary Peck said: 'The risks are known to doctors and to the drug companies, but rarely are the women fully informed of all the potential dangers to their health.'

25 December

At least that report in yesterday's paper was brief. And Christmas has given us a few days grace. No point in anything getting out until after New Year.

Going to Morne Mansions again was a shock (<u>Mourn</u> Mansions is more like it – what a terrible irony). Hardly a holiday resort. In spite of all the Christmas fare, the masses of food, the 'merriment'. Everyone was there. It was like a press party – goodwill to all media or some such rubbish. He knows how to give a good impression, Muxworthy, I'll give him that. Champagne for all the guests – the women refused, I noticed, on grounds that it wasn't good for pregnant women. I didn't notice it at first, as there was so much laughter and chatter from the guests, but the women seemed awfully subdued, all smiling of course, but subdued. Almost like they'd been drugged. I didn't notice until I began to talk with them. Some said just the same things I'd heard from another. Weird. I mentioned MM by name a couple of times – not that she'd died – some of them continued talking over me, as if I'd not mentioned her at all. But two of them looked

*at me, directly. They looked at me so directly that I fell
silent. I did not pursue it. I couldn't. But I knew then, that
they had things to tell too. Just before I left, one of them
came round a corner suddenly, bumping into me. She
pushed a note into my hand.*

*Tomorrow. At the Mall. Walk. Bring a camera and a
small tape recorder.*

It wasn't signed.

*As I left I noticed for the first time the gates. Huge iron
gates. I don't remember 'seeing' them last time – they
match the era of the building I suppose. I saw them as
security gates. But perhaps they're to keep the women in.*

*It wasn't as bad as the place in my dream, but there is
something sinister about it.*

Muxworthy has a tight mouth.

2 January

They've arrested him.

*It's so frustrating. I can't write what I know, or at least
have good reason to suspect. Muxworthy would sue, so
Jack says we have to wait. No point risking the paper at
this stage. There were documents that I photographed
which Zeny and I deposited in a strong box after we'd
talked. Jack has one set of copies. We rang the cops and
gave them the other set.*

*I found an incredible piece Muxworthy wrote some time
ago in a journal for cattle breeders (his speciality, of
course), in which he talks about taking eggs out of dead
cattle! He hasn't an ethical bone in his body. And the
way he talks about women, you'd think we were nothing
but eggs and bits and pieces that didn't feel pain or suffer
death. Poor Meg.*

MORNE MANSIONS DIRECTOR CHARGED WITH MANSLAUGHTER

Dr Thomas Muxworthy was charged today with the manslaughter of Margaret Moody. It is alleged that she died as the result of procedures performed by Dr Muxworthy in his clinic at Morne Mansions.

He was released on bail.

17 January
Anne is still in a bad way. But she feels relieved that something is happening. She said today that Meg had always wanted children – and that it was desperation that drove her to Muxworthy. Meg had said she'd signed a contract, but wouldn't show it to her, saying it was just a formality. It wasn't until my article appeared that she saw it. It was Anne who suggested Meg ring me. She was horrified at the thought of Muxworthy getting all that good publicity – that other women might have to go through what she'd been through if she didn't say anything. Anne said it took a lot of talking through for her to get up the courage. And she was really frightened when Muxworthy's reply was printed – she thought he might know it was her. Perhaps he did.

RALLY IN SUPPORT OF DOCTOR

A rally, held outside Morne Mansions, today attracted a small but devoted crowd in support of the doctor who is awaiting trial for the manslaughter of Margaret Moody.

31 January
To think that those people still believe in him. It's as though he's some kind of god. I'm sure he thinks he is. He

probably thinks he's got the secret of immortality:
immature eggs matured and then fertilized – making it
possible potentially to have lots of clones (he only has to
divide them) – freeze some and keep them to make spare
parts later (from spare embryos – not hard really) – then
if anything goes wrong with the embryo (now fully grown
into a person) call on the embryo organ bank again and
get a spare. Sounds like science fiction, but the truth is it's
all so frighteningly possible.

SECOND IVF WOMAN DIES

A second woman, Hasna el-Hasan, died today. Just three
months after having conceived according to the now
infamous Dr Muxworthy's method. The Coroner's report
says too many foetuses had ruptured Mrs el-Hasan's
womb, and she died of an internal haemorrhage. The
Coroner also reported evidence of cancerous tumours in
an early stage of growth.

15 March
Muxworthy's support has gone now. Poor Hasna. She was
so trusting. I'm sure she didn't believe this was possible.
All those boys. Surely he'll be convicted now. He certainly
deserves it. I wonder what other damage he's done (and
all those others around the world doing the same thing)?

PATIENTS' SUPPORT GROUP SET UP

After the recent death of the second patient from the
clinic of Dr Thomas Muxworthy, Women Against IVF
repeat their offer of support to other women from the
program. They fear that many of the women will suffer
severe side effects from the procedures, and are worried

about their health. One woman who has been through seven IVF trials with a range of side effects, said, 'Life is more important to me. I don't want to die in order to have children. There are other things in life.'

5 April

I wish I could write up all this stuff about Muxworthy, but Jack says it's too dicey at this stage. I have to wait until the trial is over. It looks pretty clear that he'll be convicted, but with what? Will the man(!)slaughter stick? Or will they turn it into something else?

Some of the things those women have had done to them! It's outrageous. And most of the medical profession seem to think that it's 'standard procedure'. I would never have thought that it was possible to do so many terrible things for such a long time to so many women and get away with it.

Maria said, that now she was out of it, it seemed like a drawn-out bad dream. And yet, she said, for the seven years she was in it – because the real world had receded – it seemed normal. Everyone else in there was doing the same thing, and there were no complaints, so they just kept on going. Zeny said that my article had made her wonder whether what was going on was really true or not, and at first she doubted her perceptions. But seeing me there the second time made her determined to talk to me – even if she wasn't sure that what she was doing was right. She knew, though, after we talked in the Mall that day, that she was. For yet another woman, Jenny, it all seems to be moving very slowly. I think she's just beginning to realize that there will be no children after all. And losing her fantasy makes the world seem very bleak. All the same, she was better today.

DOCTOR EXPERIMENTS ON WOMEN

Witnesses today alleged that Dr Thomas Muxworthy, former Director of Morne Mansions, used women as experimental subjects in his research into the new reproductive technologies. A number of former patients gave evidence against him. The Defence is pursuing the line of 'therapeutic misadventure', a line which has been successful in a number of similar cases. The trial is continuing.

8 May
He was sentenced today. Six years and deregistration. It's not that much when you consider the damage he's done. At least he won't be able to practise again. Still nothing's happened to stop the other clinics – they are saying that he was just a madman (never mind that they publicly supported him six months ago). The doctors and researchers are claiming that their procedures are better – and safe. Well, they'll have to be more careful for a while. What worries me is that soon everyone will forget what has happened to these women. Just another bit of news for most people. They don't have to live with the consequences. But what about all those women who are still waiting – still believing that some god-like man will come along in his white coat and save them. And the infertile husbands – they'll still want their wives to try for a son.

Finally I can write my piece.

CATTLE PROVIDE CLUE TO IVF HORROR

In an article published some time ago, the now notorious Dr Thomas Muxworthy, former Director of Morne Mansions, the Developmental Institute for Research into

Reproductive Technologies, wrote about new advances in cattle embryology (his specialty). He wrote:

It has proven to be possible to harvest immature eggs from the carcasses of newly dead cattle in abattoirs. The eggs are removed from the cattle ovaries, *in situ*, and then transferred to the laboratory where they are matured. These eggs have been fertilized and maintained until the embryo has become a solid mass of cells. We could keep these embryos alive and take them to full maturity, if we were permitted to carry on this research. In the long run, it would provide us with a reliable and economic source of calves or any other animals. Stud breeders could then produce embryos without having to keep live animals. (*Breeders Journal*, September, 1987: 76)

And on a television program in which he was asked a question about side effects and the recent death of patients in a similar clinic, Muxworthy replied:

'Unfortunately, there are some side effects, like death.' (BTV 8, August 1987)

It seems he has taken a page out of his own book. The deaths of Meg Moody and Hasna el-Hasan have been linked to procedures used at his clinic.

Among the procedures used were:

i. use of drugs above recommended levels, in order to induce superovulation. (This is regarded as a standard procedure in IVF – sometimes making it possible to collect up to 50 mature eggs at one time. However, development of cysts, and burst ovaries have often resulted.)

ii. exploratory surgery, in order to find out whether the woman has healthy organs or not. (The main risk here is of death resulting from anaesthetic failure.)

iii. removal of slices of the ovaries for maturation of eggs. (The same risks as (ii) apply.)

iv. hysterectomy. (This has been performed on

occasion without explicit permission, though overall consent to the procedures had been given.)

v. maturation and/or freezing of eggs removed from the body.

vi. reimplantation of as many viable fertilized eggs as are available and healthy. (Thirteen were placed in the womb of one woman, six were 'reduced' at one month, leaving her with seven to take to term. Five were born dead. The other two were malformed. One died within hours, the other survived for only a week.)

An autopsy carried out on the bodies of Meg Moody and Hasna el-Hasan revealed findings of malpractice. Meg Moody was found to have severe internal injuries (such as masses of adhesions, scars and cysts) consistent with botched surgical procedures. She was also found to have very high levels of a drug used in IVF programs. It is said to remain in the tissues for up to six weeks after administration but in her case, three months had passed since the last administration just before she left the program.

The results of the autopsy on Hasna el-Hasan revealed similar findings. It was also found that her ovaries had in fact been removed in spite of the fact that they had been in what Thomas Muxworthy described as 'mint condition'. The cause of Mrs el-Hasan's death was a stroke, caused by excessive use of infertility drugs, so-called hormonal cocktails!

The sister of Meg Moody said today that Thomas Muxworthy's attitudes to the women in his clinic resembled those he held about cattle. She said, that her sister, Meg, had been medically abused by Thomas Muxworthy who had refused to investigate the pains Meg had complained about. Instead, three months ago, he had put her on a new regimen of drugs to induce further superovulation. She said that the last time Meg had become pregnant, she had had a series of miscarriages from the one pregnancy – in all, four early embryos were lost over a period of nine days. That was nearly a year ago, she said. Muxworthy had then persuaded her to try a new procedure which, he said, had a very high chance of success. She agreed to try one last time – according to her sister – when the experiment failed. He told her he would remove a very small slice of ovary, mature the eggs and return them to her body – the same procedure that Hasna el-Hasan later underwent – but my sister was the guinea pig for that short-lived success, she said.

A spokeswoman for Women Against IVF (WAIVF) today said that what was considered 'standard' procedures in IVF was highly dangerous for women. 'And these cases unfortunately prove it,' she said. 'We have been saying that something like this would happen if IVF wasn't stopped. The terrible irony,' she said, 'is that the women on these programs were not even sick. They were not unhealthy, at least not until they were "treated". They were infertile. And now some of them are dead.' The organization is calling for a ban on all IVF practice and research. Among those they cite are procedures involving carcinogenic drugs and all procedures that require bodily intrusion (egg harvesting, laparoscopy, flushing and embryo transfer).

'How many more tragedies do we have to have?' asked the WAIVF representative.

DOCTOR DIES

The man at the centre of the IVF storm died today in jail. Warders say they think he may have smuggled in a drug. An autopsy is being performed to investigate whether it was suicide or natural death.

1 July
The bastard didn't even have the guts to stay alive after all. Maybe Mr el-Hasan threatened to sue. Wouldn't stand a chance against that wealth.

Cait Featherstone

CRIB COLOURS FADE

I
> The mother's day madonnas
> encased within eternal visions
> awaken and rise
> with the children of their dreams.
> They are the unexpected widows,
> mourning mothers who seek
> not the loss of children,
> paying a price to own
> a virgin child
> of captivity,
> the child whose crib colours
> have faded into the white shroud
> of an alien darkness.
> The men without skin deliver
> the mother's burden
> to the doorstep of death,
> and behind the door
> the gold-plated gods await their offering.
> They spend their time
> burning five-thousand-year-old images
> to warm themselves,
> and they feed upon the ashes
> of roasted flesh.
> No thrones await these
> virgin children —
>> only the naked ground
>> and a pillow of dust.

II

Behind blank canvassed walls,
in a doorless room,
he wraps his hand around his cock
gently stroking
gently
as he says, 'it's all for you,
my dear . . .'
and in the space beneath his words
his mind forms this one thought:
BITCH.
Plunging into creamy bare folds,
he thrusts sandpaper deep within her,
turning lovely softness into painful raw
raw pain.
His voice like a seamless incision
slices through her skin,
his hand wraps 'round his cock
lovingly stroking
gently, faster
he thrusts the steel device into
the entrance of life's emergence
and he thinks
CUNT.

III

The men without skin want our skin:
they pierce, excavate,
turn us inside out
plough and till,
harvest and reap.
But we are not their gardens,
these are not their crops —
we will not feed their hunger

IV

I am skin and bones
and memory and blood
I am a timeless clock
whose cycle they would change.

V

Fabricated science tears
the fabric of our skin.
Academic
de con
struction
ists
reduce us to pieces
and deny us the details —

watch   your   step
semantic minefields have been laid

VI

I implore you, good women,
posed in supplication,
do not be so good.
I implore you would-be man-made women
to fight the man-made forces.
I implore you native women
to return from your forced exiles
back to your homelands.

I beseech you to beg not
for the lives of the unconceived.
I implore you
to claim
your own life.

VII

From ashes to shapeless shadows,
from mother goddess to wombless women
they form us, shape us
into Everywoman
into everywoman
into nothing
            nothing . . .
except bones.
            Fleshing out
            skeletal remains
            of ancient myths,
            we resurrect ourselves.

Atholee Scott

ANOTHER WORLD

I love going to the doctor's.

Sitting in the waiting room, while other patients come and go, I can read all those magazines I don't buy. Away from my friends who would laugh or lecture at the few moments of fantasy I enjoy. They, worthy women, prefer that others use their time to dwell on reality; I have given up arguing, but sometimes refer to some information culled from the pages – and while not admitting its origin, smile rather at their interest.

A sore throat gave me the opportunity I had been waiting for and here I was indulging myself, turning the pages from diets to delicious-sounding recipes; 'How to keep your man' to the magazine world's recognition of current practice with 'I survived divorce to marry happily ever after'; stories of joy and letters of despair and the optimistic reply. Then, turning to a fresh page, I saw Linley.

This, then, was the advertised cover story about the wonderful opportunities IVF offers childless women.

I'd actually picked up the magazine because of the divorce story. I thought about writing my story, 'I survived divorce and now have retrieved career', but by the time I'd finished reading I knew that it would never be published. My feminist friends would suggest that this was exactly what was wrong with the magazines, that all they would publish were stories to promote the prevailing patriarchal culture, etc. etc. My view is, what's wrong with a little fantasy? Why not accept that many women read and enjoy these stories? Why, in short, prevent career women like myself catching glimpses into another world?

I was so busy thinking of arguments to support my indulgence I'd almost forgotten Linley.

She looked rather smaller than I remembered, lost in a pink haze, a pleasant man beside her and a cheerful-looking baby taking up the foreground.

Photos of the doctors involved and their interpretation of the event mingled nicely with the headline, ANOTHER BEAUTIFUL IVF BABY. Baby Caroline was indeed beautiful and my heart warmed to her – how, indeed, could anyone resist?

I scanned the page eagerly to learn more of what had happened to Linley since I had lost touch with her in 1970. But, this was not her story. The doctors, a midwife who had assisted many happy IVF births and baby Caroline were the stars. Linley was just another happy mother, the fortunate repository of successful science.

Linley and I had met when I was working in a department store during the university vacation. She was on the accessories counter and determined to become head of the section and move into management. She was studying at night and it was clear that her determination and ability should help her achieve her aim. Remembering the friendship we'd experienced, even though it was shortlived, I was now sorry that I hadn't kept in touch.

I am ashamed to say I put the magazine into my bag to keep the only information which could assist me in finding her. Still, perhaps my feminist friends would be pleased that at least that copy was out of circulation – IVF is one of the big issues at the moment and such articles are considered rather dangerous . . . besides, the photo of baby Caroline was rather lovely.

Eventually I found her, after the magazine forwarded my letter.

Her reply came several weeks later. She told me she had written as soon as she could, in snatches of time while the baby was sleeping. The letter was long, with frequent changes of pen and mood. The baby loomed large between the story of her successful rise in the department store, the marriage to Jack Clayton, another manager, the decision to become pregnant and the difficulties and now, years later, the advent of baby Caroline.

Her phone number was on the letter and I took this as an invitation to get in touch, perhaps there was a hint of urgency, perhaps not, I thought. But, a phone call couldn't hurt. I had actually become quite intrigued by the results of my surreptitious reading – women's magazines couldn't be all bad if they brought old friends together!

I rang but no one answered. I was a little surprised as Linley's letter had implied that she spent most of the time at home with baby Caroline. And surely both the doting parents would be home at nights and weekends with her?

I tried at different times, early morning and late in the evening, on the weekend, during the week. Eventually I became rather dispirited with the effort I was putting in, all to no avail. She clearly didn't need my company urgently, whatever fantasies I had woven around the presence of the phone number.

I wrote a short note, inviting her to my place. At least, I thought, the baby would be in her basket at this stage and I could be hospitable amongst my precious glass and thick white carpet.

Later, if the friendship were rekindled, perhaps we could walk in the park, go on picnics.

She rang and invited me to visit her instead. She seemed embarrassed, murmuring about nappies and feeds, manoeuvring the baby's car seat, Caroline's fretfulness in the car. I thought of my flinging my bulging handbag on to the empty seat beside me, the radio uninterrupted by anything other than my own singing or stinging rejoinders to interviewers with whom I disagreed. I accepted quickly.

She was apologetic about my unanswered phone calls when I found the phone ringing unanswered under a cushion. Handing it to her I couldn't help but think she looked unwilling to respond. Still later, she explained that not only did she leave the phone to ring while she was catching scraps of sleep while Caroline napped but found that people phoning often just interfered with the world she and Caroline now occupied.

Months later, when our closeness had been re-established over a Saturday afternoon at the Children's Hospital (the paediatrician was on holidays) Linley told me of Caroline's premature birth, the visits to the doctor's which only now show signs of diminishing, the miracle baby . . . not quite what she had expected.

They were living in a pleasant-enough flat, but I was surprised. I thought that the requirements for being on the program would have included a home in the conventional sense – a backyard for the sandpit and swings, large airy rooms . . .

We picked our way from the front door through bags of nappies.

'Waiting for the Nappy Wash,' she explained.

Baby Caroline (older than I had expected) lay in her cot, a light breeze coming through the ruffled pink curtains making the chimes above her head tremble slightly. Brightly coloured toys were strung above her. She was beautiful, even to me, hardened as I was against the charms of domesticity as a successful and single career woman and determined to retain that state.

We crept out of the room, Linley suppressing what looked like a shudder when I suggested that Caroline must be lovely when she was awake.

Moving some folded matinee jackets and night gowns, while helping Linley with our lunch, I marvelled at their diminutive size. My fingers lingered on the embroidery but Linley whipped them away, murmuring about the lack of time to keep everything tidy.

We looked at each other across the coffee table.

Linley was as I remembered her.

Of course she had put on weight, but who wouldn't over the years? She certainly looked tired, but baby Caroline was young and this would change as feeding times came less often and Linley slept at night. Her clothing was naturally less smart than in the days when she looked toward her career. Much more suitable for a housebound mother, really. Those high heels we both used to wear — we laughed at the silliness of them. Then faltered as I looked down at my feet. Linley's eyes travelled up the black stockings, cheeky butterfly on each ankle, my designer costume, then to the smart leather bag I had left carelessly on another chair, beside a pile of unfolded nappies.

Our eyes slid back to our salads.

Baby Caroline cried. Half an hour later it became clear that I should go, the happy snuffling at Linley's breast had been replaced with more crying and Linley smiled gently with resignation.

I suggested that we should meet again. Linley looked surprised and gratified. I found out later that some of her friends had been happy to visit her in hospital where baby Caroline could be viewed through the nursery window but they had found the realities of the baby at home less attractive.

In the meantime I continued to haunt the doctor's, grabbing every magazine which mentioned babies. Perhaps there would be some information I could impart to help bring baby Caroline up to the standards, I knew through the magazines, other babies managed. Those ordinary babies were all happy, placid, contented. Their mothers had time to knit them this fancy cardigan or make them that smart suit. After all, these were the women the magazines were written for, weren't they? Those housebound mothers with time on their hands? And after all, wasn't Caroline a miracle baby?

I found a wonderful insert on decorating cakes for children's parties and for Caroline's first birthday proudly presented the recipe to Linley.

She was looking a bit better these days, but the flat was becoming rather shabby. Some of the carpet showed stains and the kitchen was always covered with pots and pans pulled from open cupboards. Caroline's walker bumped against the furniture as she struggled from room to room. I didn't want to interfere so didn't tell Linley how bad these contraptions were for a baby's growing bones. I just took her out whenever I was there to show her how much happier Caroline was when free. Unfortunately when I wasn't looking she got at my bag and spread my very expensive lipstick all over the lounge. Linley didn't seem to appreciate my forebearance and I have to admit I stayed away for a few weeks after that.

I couldn't stay away for long, a visit to the doctor's, another story and I'd be around there with information for Linley on how to make a cuddly Easter bunny or edible decorations for the Christmas tree. The bunny was half made by Christmas and the decorations joined the pink stains remaining from my expensive lipstick.

The signs of a male presence had never been much in evidence and I had never met Jack, but eventually they disappeared altogether. Still later, as time progressed and Jack's continued absence became more noticeable Linley told me that the reality of baby Caroline and the job had been too much for him.

Jack had accepted an offer to open a department store outlet in a major country area and, on the grounds that Linley and baby Caroline needed him to make every effort to keep up in his chosen profession, he had accepted. Linley and Caroline were to join him later – Jack was concerned that Caroline should be within reach of her city paediatrician. In case anything else should go wrong, Linley explained. After all, a miracle baby – the work of all those doctors and the expense – nothing was too much trouble . . .

Jack, of course, had to live in a suitable manner in the country and had bought a house there. This was the explanation for the flat in which Linley and Caroline now lived. Jack had, at first, returned to the flat most weekends but sometimes even these visits were cut short because of the long hours he needed to spend at work and now it seemed he'd moved out.

As I moved to the next step in my career and then the next, I found it less easy to visit Linley and Caroline. By the time I saw them next, Caroline was three and Linley rang me to say she had something to discuss with me now that she had a little more freedom.

Linley wanted to get back into the paid workforce.

I looked at her across the coffee table. It was then that she really allowed me into her confidence. Tales of happy years working: managing her section, overseas buying trips, the business hurdles seen, understood and overcome.

Side by side with this had been the questioning of her womanhood as month followed month and she was faced with what she thought was her failure. And, of course, no one suggested it could be anyone else's. I looked down at my body, never likely to be called into reproductive action and was thankful that my fantasies had not led me too far . . . well, I pulled myself up short, perhaps I had just been lucky.

Linley's story was not one for a magazine. Tests, tests and more tests. Stirrups and all manner of metal gadgetry beloved by her saviours, for whom it appeared, her womanhood was of serious moment.

Eventual success. So long after the treadmill had begun she wondered at why she'd ever started. But it was too late to stop. The baby was there. Her successful start on the path to womanhood could not be denied in exchange for the surge of pride and happiness she had felt when she manoeuvred around a difficult business deal, managed to meet Jack for a film and meal in the middle of a crisis, arrived home from an overseas buying venture and rushed straight into another crisis which she easily surmounted.

Linley placed one foot after another, diligently displaying her gratitude to those who had given her the right to call herself a woman. And now, Caroline's father had given her the excuse to step back, at least partially, into that other world. He needed more of his income for a new wife. They had been trying to begin a family. It wouldn't be long now, he claimed and Linley would need to grow up, pull herself out of her fantasy world. She must pull her weight and contribute to her own upkeep and Caroline's. He had done his bit.

I looked at the woman across the table and tried to associate her with the Linley I had conjured up from my reading of the IVF article. She no longer existed.

I go to the doctor's as rarely as possible, these days. And when I go I take a book.

Lucy Sussex

MOTHER-OF-ALL

Each time I sit down at the word processor for a spot of writing, the machine gets more and more reluctant to boot up, until I have to kick it almost to death before I can use it. So we summon a techno-freak friend, who opens it up and prys inside, uttering a stream of incomprehensible jargon, or so I think, until one familiar word bowls across my room to where I sit quietly spinning a yarn, not on the computer, but the oakwood wheel.

'– Mother –'

'What?' I say, unable to imagine anything motherly about the innards of a computer.

'Mother-bawd,' he says, without turning.

'Is that some kind of new insult?' I say brightly, and this time he gives me a look like a pat on the head.

'Mother B–O–A–R–D. It's part of your PC. Here, take a look!'

I get up greasy-handed from the raw wool and look over his shoulder at a structure at the bottom of the box, a flat surface green as leaves, studded with rows of symmetrical black lumps.

'Those are the memory chips, see, and the green is the motherboard.'

'Why call it that? I mean the top of the spinning wheel is called the Mother-of-All, which makes sense, spinning being traditional women's work, but computers aren't, not usually . . .'

'I only fix the things,' he says. 'I don't worry about their nomenclature.'

End of conversation. As I go back to my wool-making it occurs to me that the motherboard does look vaguely like a skirt, with a brood of children hanging on to it, but it also brings to mind a parade ground, with the chips in battle array. Men created the thing; and they should have named it after what was, for them, the obvious. They hadn't, though, and I knew why: She, the Goddess, was manifest in there.

You don't know who I mean? Open your art history books back almost to the very beginning, and there you have her, big, fat and beautiful. The Lady of Sé, or the Venuses of Willendorf and Lespugue, carved in bone or cavewall, painted in vegetable juice and ochres. I'm not talking about Astarte, Aphrodite, Hestia or even the Virgin Mary – they're just aspects of the Mother Goddess, little chunks cut off for separate worship, because people, and I mean men, couldn't cope with the immensity of her, the Big M. She's underground now, as she's been ever since the phallic gods took over, in you-know-who's opinion, down but definitely not out. Though hidden she recurs, in the day-to-day objects we use, the spinning wheels, the computers, so that in tapping keys, pulling at wool, we unconsciously invoke her, say a prayer to her.

Everyone collects something and me, I collect manifestations of the Mother. Some people might call it manifest madness, but I know better. She's got power, that one: she is *not* mocked. This story proves it.

I begin with the first manifestation I collected: the Russian Matrioshka doll, the round headscarfed woman, whose belly opens, to reveal another round doll, whose middle also splits, with another doll inside and another, smaller and smaller down to one final egg, too tiny for the woodcarver to subdivide. Mothers and daughters, *my* daughter calls it. She opens it, takes out the next doll, and the next. She reseals the first two, and stands all three in a diminishing line.

Listen. Once there was a mother, and she had two daughters at one birth, twins derived from the one split egg. A doctor once told me: *no identical twins are identical.* So much happens after the egg breaks, with the microscopic lumps of jelly growing, side by side, into kicking, active babies, that one child may be black, one white, as occurred once in England, she said, with the twin girls of a mixed-race couple. At the least they have different birthweights, and here it happened, grotesquely; for one twin was half the size of the other.

Ysabel, the parents called her, for that was the name they had chosen for a little girl. The other got plain Kate, but not for some days, for what with the fuss over Ysabel, putting that tiny baby into an incubator, they hadn't a moment to spare for the larger, healthier twin.

So. Kate had the initial advantage, but Ysabel got her back for that, by stealing all the attention. Twins form a hierarchy of two – one is top, dominant to a greater or lesser degree, and the other is submissive. But Ysabel was subtle about it, even at 4 lbs 2 oz. 'What a dainty wee lass,' the relatives said at the joint christening. 'A little princess. You mustn't let her be bullied by her big sister,' referring to Kate, who wasn't a large baby, but in comparison with Ysabel looked lumpen indeed.

Here're some snaps from the family album. That's Ysabel, in the lace confection worn by Great-gran Isabella at her christening, still a little tearful from having been doused in holy water, with a ringed hand stroking her forehead. Kate lolls next to her in the bassinet, wearing a gown from the other side of the family, which isn't hand-embroidered, and even has machine lace edging, which tickles. Her eyes are clear, staring at the camera. She hadn't cried when the devils were driven out of her, so nobody paid her particular attention.

One year later, a reverse image, two toddlers on a daisied lawn, in matching smock frocks, but Kate's looking rumpled, like her face. Shortly before the photo was taken, she tried to snatch the lollipop from Ysabel's hand, and got smacked. Ysabel waves her lolly at the camera, all sunny smile and spice. When she grabs Kate's sweeties the reaction is 'Let her have it, Katy!'

Turn over a couple of pages, to the twins in their first school uniforms. If you look closely, with a magnifying glass, at the hair of each, you can see that Ysabel's curls twist in one direction, Kate's in the other. Identical twins are mirror images; what is positive in one will be negative in the other. Ysabel hugs a gift from her namesake, Great-gran Isabella, a baby doll. Kate looks at it from the corner of her eyes longingly, but she knows better than to grab, is resigned to such things by now. Ysabel has said that if Kate looks after her, this first day at school, protects Ysa from the big kids, she will let her play a while with baby.

Adolescence now, which in the seventies is ugly indeed, fashion wise, but Ysabel makes the most of it. They are off to the school dance, and so perch on platform soles, but only Kate looks about to fall off. Ysabel wears cheesecloth and cotton lace, in tiers; Kate a batik caftan she made herself, with its hem not quite straight. Ysabel's beau points at the beauty spot Ysabel has grown, slightly above her lipgloss. Kate has no such mark. 'Just as well,' the boy says. 'Otherwise I'd get youse mixed up and kiss the wrong twin.' Kate's unadorned lip twitches, blurring the photo. She has no beau of her own for this dance, only a castoff of Ysabel's.

Final shot, bride and bridesmaid, peeping over huge bouquets. The one in white satin is Ysabel, of course.

Kate and Ysabel's mother collected wedding photos, and the twins added to the cluster of little frames by four, Ysabel three times and Kate once. When Ysabel finished her commerce degree, she went to work in an advertising agency, and in no time was being squired by the more glamorous clients. After a year she was engaged to George, who was Greek, but not very, Ysabel told Mamma. Why, they didn't even have to get wed in a Greek church! They instead married in St Swithin's down the road, with neighbours and relatives packing out the ceremony, and then had the reception in a huge marquee behind George's family home. It was a white wedding, white bride, white groom, white lilies, everything snowy except Kate, who wore cream. In the wedding photo given pride of place, in the best silver frame, Kate looks as if her mum didn't own a Whirlpool.

Kate went to teacher's college, where she met Len, who sat next to her at classes. He wasn't at the wedding; for though they ended up at the same school, and shared a familistery with some other new teachers, they had only become 'an item', to use a favourite term of Ysabel's, the week before, after a flagon of red wine and a conversation that began with that pig of a Head, moved on to other topics, and ended at dawn, with them fast asleep in Len's bed.

Kate normally shared her life with Ysabel, but her twin was so busy with the wedding preparations that there never seemed time to tell her. After the ceremony Ysabel was off on her Greek honeymoon, and then busy with homemaking, driving her white Mercedes (George's wedding gift) from shop to shop, in search of curtains, ruffles, railings.

Thus it was that Kate and Len, walking down their suburban main drag, hand in hand with their groceries, heard the squeal of brakes, then the frantic toot of a horn. Len looked up to see an ice-cream car, and waving frantic-ally through the windscreen his Kate, but overdressed, and wearing a daft shade of lipstick. Then he glanced at the woman holding his hand, whose face was suddenly expressionless.

'Your twin sister, whom you're always talking about,' he said.

'Darling!' said Ysabel, jumping out of the car. 'You secretive puss! Now I know why you grinned all over your face, when you caught my bouquet.'

'This is Len,' said Kate.

Ysabel looked him up and down until he blushed. 'I approve,' she said loudly. 'And I'm sure George will approve too. Why don't you come to dinner this evening?'

Kate started to say they'd bought fish for that night, but Ysabel kissed her firmly on the cheek, then jumped back into the Merc with a cry of 'Well, that's settled! I'll see you at eight.'

As the car zoomed away Len took out his handkerchief, and wiped the kiss mark off Kate's cheek.

'We'll put the fish in the freezer,' he said.

It was just their luck that on that very night, they got fish, ocean trout, cooked to the standards of Ysabel's gourmet classes. There was good white wine to drink; George poured it out liberally, laughing and joking with Len all the while. 'How well we get on!' Kate thought tipsily. But in the taxi home Len was quiet.

'What's up?' Kate said, snuggling up to him.

'I was thinking. About that twin sister of yours.'

'Hmm?'

'She's got a beautiful house, er, expensive clothes, nice enough fella . . . but she doesn't look happy.'

'How can you say that? She's newlywed!'

'I was watching her. Whenever she stopped talking, and the attention was away from her . . . the smile fell off her face.'

And sure enough, about a week later, Kate, who had been doing the shopping by herself, for Len was at a meeting, came home to find the ice-cream car parked outside the house. Ysabel wound down the window at her approach and stuck out a face shockingly daubed with tears.

'Oh Ysa, Ysa!' said Kate, clutching her groceries and feeling helpless. 'What's happened?'

'George . . . he's porking his secretary!'

And Kate, who had never heard that expression before, but could guess what it meant, dropped her shopping bag. It burst open, revealing toilet cleaner, tampons, and most embarrassingly, a pound of pork sausages, extra large.

So there had to be a divorce, and while the family were wondering how to tell Great-gran Isabella, now in her nineties, the old lady went aloft, leaving all her money to her namesake. Ysabel grabbed it and went overseas, 'To forget!' as she said at the airport.

'But not forgive, I'll warrant,' said Len. They had just booked a trip by themselves, modest in comparison, off to the other side of the continent, where Len had grown up. Come the school holidays, away they went, driving down dusty backroads, basking on quiet sandy beaches, making love under the stars, or beneath the ceiling roses of old pub bedrooms, even once by the roadside, watched incuriously by an Aberdeen Angus steer.

One morning Len woke, to find an empty space beside him in the bed. He found Kate seated in the shower stall, tossing up and catching what he first took to be a knucklebone but then realized was a tampon.

She met his gaze.

'Looks like I won't be needing this for a while,' she said, quietly.

There was a long pause, then Len got down on his knees. Kate started to laugh, then wept like a drain.

The photo on her mother's sideboard shows Len and Kate outside the registry office, thousands of miles from their relatives and friends, with the witnesses, a nice

Norwegian couple from the youth hostel. Were it not for Kate's nosegay of native flowers, gathered fresh that morning, the casual onlooker could think this was not a wedding, but a small and happy party – which it also was.

Kate's mother worried about that for a while, then put it aside, literally, for Ysabel sent a photo of a blond, pallid Englishman called Robin. Len referred to him as 'Milquetoast' but only with Kate. 'I'm sure he's quite nice in person,' Kate said charitably, but they never got to know. By the time Ysabel's divorce came through Kate was nine months pregnant, legally unable to make the plane trip with her parents to Ysabel's second wedding. 'Cheer up!' said Len, 'you'd look a matronly matron of honour indeed, even if we could afford it.'

Kate stood up to throw a cushion at him, then gave a yelp. Her waters had broken.

I once saw a painting, towards the middle of the art histories, of twin sisters from the Elizabethan period, lying side by side in bed, which must have been artistic licence, given that they wore matching frocks, complete with stomachers, ruffs and jewels. Each clutched a swaddled child, for they were delivered on the same day. Twins tend to synchronicity; and thus, at the moment when Ysabel, standing on the damp grass of an Oxbridge lawn, said 'I do', Kate, in the maternity ward of an Antipodean hospital, cried 'I don't think I can stand this any more!', and delivered Nance.

What with Ysabel's honeymoon, this time in France, it was some time before the post brought Kate a parcel of English baby clothes. In fact Ysabel did not see her niece until Nance was toddling.

Their father was ill in hospital, so Kate went to collect her sister from the airport. Ysabel's first words were 'Can't you give me a hand with this?', spoken from behind a laden luggage trolley.

'Sorry, I can't manage suitcases with a stroller. And I'm

not allowed to carry weights, not with being pregnant again.'

Ysabel pushed up her sunglasses for a better look at Kate's belly, which swelled slightly but unmistakably behind the curtain of a T-shirt left over from Nance's gestation.

'Fertile, aren't you?' she said flatly.

'Well, I only get so much maternity leave from the Education Department . . .'

At this moment Nance said: 'Pitty!', pointing at Ysabel.

'Yes,' said Kate. 'That's a pretty lady,' as Ysabel paid attention to her niece for the first time. Kate glanced up, and saw their reflections in the airport mirrors, she pudgy, not only from pregnancy; in need of a haircut; and dressed in clothes that had been put through the washing machine too often. Ysabel was pale from an English winter, but had offset this with a henna rinse in her hair. She had somehow survived the transcontinental flight without creasing her suit.

While Kate stared at the mirror image of her mirror image, Ysabel's head lifted from the baby, and she gazed into the glass, apparently unaware of her twin's scrutiny. To think we started out as one egg! thought Kate. Never had they seemed less identical.

At Len and Kate's second-hand station wagon, they loaded the myriad suitcases, and installed Nance in her babyseat. 'Pitty,' Nance repeated. 'Pitty.'

Ysabel turned from the child as Kate started the car.

'She leaves out the "r",' she said. 'Sorry,' Kate said, feeling oddly responsible for the babytalk. She edged the car out of the park and into the airport traffic.

Ysabel sighed. 'In a way it's appropriate. With Dad so sick. And . . .'

'And?' said Kate, not looking at Ysabel because they had just got to the 100-kilometre zone. Ysabel sighed again.

'And Robin. Another bad apple.'

'Oh,' said Kate. In the rear-view mirror she could see Nance, contentedly chewing her sash. When she finally gave Ysabel the desired attention, she noticed the mole above the lipstick was trembling slightly.

'Oh Kate, it's so awful. He's into rough trade.'

'I thought he owned an art gallery,' Kate said in bewilderment.

'No, silly. It's an English expression. Sailors and brickies and things. Once even a police sergeant!',

There was a long pause. 'I don't know what to say,' Kate finally admitted.

'You don't have to say anything. Just be comforting.'

Kate put out her gear hand and caressed the silky hennaed curls, that coiled in the opposite direction from her own neglected mop.

'What are you going to do?' she said after some twenty kilometres.

'Stay here and try not to do anything silly on the rebound! I'll work, basically.'

'Advertising?'

'I rather fancy the antique business. Being in England you develop an eye for the good old stuff . . . there's so much of it there.'

It was on the tip of Kate's tongue to ask how Ysabel would set herself up in business, as the money from Great-gran must be all gone by now, but they had turned into their home street, and Len, still carrying his briefcase from school, was waving to them.

The next few days were a mess of hospital visiting, and family dinners, and Nance coming down with a cold – out of which Ysabel emerged, perfectly groomed and with a paternal cheque to start her new business.

'Godammit,' said Len, when Kate finally told him. 'She beat me to it. I was hoping he'd help out with the house extension. We need it.'

Kate bent down and wiped Nance's nose for the hundredth time, it seemed.

'Well, we could wait until I have the ultrasound.'

'How will that help?'

'They'll sex the baby. And if it's a boy . . .'

'I see. He was talking about spouts last time I passed the sickbed, but I naively assumed they were on teapots, not infants. Well, love, if male chauvinism gets us the new bedroom, then three cheers for it.'

But as it happened, Kate and Ysa's dad gave up, not more of his money, but the ghost, only a few days before the ultrasound.

'It is a boy,' Kate told Len, when he came back from school that day.

Len swore, softly but with feeling.

'Are you sure?'

'Here's a copy of the ultrasound. I can't see it myself, but Doc Donna was positive.'

Len gazed at the blur that was his son.

'Let's get a frame for this,' he said after a while. 'One of those metal ones, like your mother has.'

'Silver.'

'Silver, then. We'll put it up on the mantelpiece, and watch the rellies go ape.'

'It's male chauvinism,' Kate said primly.

'Of course, but it puts you in the spotlight.' For once, he nearly added. 'Enjoy it. Me, I'll enjoy watching Ysa try to trump this. She won't be able to, unless she gets herself married to a prince next.

Oddly enough, Ysabel did marry royalty, but not for some years, a time of milk and honey, as Kate thought of it later, with Ysa the busy bee, buzzing around the countryside in search of old wares, and Kate staying at home, feeding babes. The boy they called Jim, after Kate's dad, got a Georgian spoon from his aunt Ysa; and five years later Ysa was doing so well that Kate's second son garnered an antique rosewood cradle. Len brought it in to the hospital – Ysabel was too busy to visit.

'It won't go with his hair,' he said.

Kate looked down at the tiny shock of ginger at her breast. 'Er, no,' she said. 'But it's the thought that counts.'

To her the cradle looked most uncomfortable, but she said nothing when Ysabel, armed with an immense sheaf of orchids, finally made her grand entry into the hospital room.

'My god,' she said, pointing theatrically at the baby's head. 'Wherever did that come from?'

'Len's grandfather was a redhead.'

'Well, it certainly didn't come from our side of the family,' said Ysa, tossing her hennaed curls. She sat down with a swish in the bedside chair, still clutching the orchids.

'I think it's nice for Len. The other two did rather take after us.'

'You were trying for a different genetic mix?'

'Er, no. I was trying to get back into the paid workforce.'

Ysabel tweaked a stray strand of hair beside Kate's ear. 'And I thought you were so efficient! Girl, then boy, nice balanced nuclear family . . . Like they say, there's many a slip 'twixt the pill and the lip.'

'So I have five more years of being a homebody!' Kate said snappily, then repented. 'He is a little dear.'

The nurse entered, and Ysa handed her the flowers: 'Do be sweet and put these in your nicest vase, please!' Then she caressed the baby absently.

'You do produce adorable children. And so easily! Lucky you for being so healthy – earth mother, that's what you are. I think you should have a baker's dozen.'

'We have only a small house,' said Kate. And we still haven't saved up enough for the extension, she thought. Things are going to get tight with young Rufus. 'Babies are most expensive.'

Ysa pulled her hair again. 'Silly. Other people could pay for them.'

'What do you mean?'

But Ysa never clarified the remark, for at that moment Len entered with a vase of orchids. 'Nurse said I should bring these in. Kate, love, your mum's bringing Nance and Jim along from the playroom shortly.'

'Then there'll be no space for me in this little room!' said Ysabel. 'I must go!'

She kissed Kate, kissed Rufus, even gave Len a sisterly peck of the cheek, and was gone.

Lord, how she slathers on the lipstick, thought Len, as he wiped his face, then the baby's, then finally Kate's. When he finished it seemed all the colour had drained out of Kate's face, and into the fuchsia stain on his handkerchief.

'You're white, love.'

'I was just thinking. What if I had another accident?'

Len cradled Rufus.

'Frankly, we couldn't afford it.'

'Then I'll get myself spayed.'

'Well, when it comes to the knife, it's six of one and half a dozen of the other, isn't it? I was going to offer.'

'No, I think it should be me.'

Her tone was insistent, and Len frowned, but then Nance and Jim came in, all alarums and excursions.

'I'm going to be a bridesmaid!' yelled Nance. 'And Jimmy'll be a flowerboy!'

'No I won't!' Jim retorted.

Their grandmother was beaming. 'Such wonderful news about Ysabel!'

'What news?' said Kate.

'Didn't she tell you? Oh, you new mums are all the same, can't shut up about bubby. Ysa's getting married again!'

'And who's Prince Charming?' said Len, nearly adding – this time.

'Funny you should say that. He's a Russian prince.'

When they finally met Dmitri, over dinner in his exquisitely renovated terrace house, he looked mildly embarrassed to be introduced by Ysabel as 'My prince!'

'It was my grandmother's title,' he said in cultured Strine, 'before the revolution. After that, she mopped floors. I don't use it, myself.'

'Never mind, it's still there if you want to,' said Ysabel, brightly. Len nudged Kate. While Ysa and Dmitri were in the kitchen, putting the finishing touches to the entree, he murmured:

'Kate, I vaguely remember something about Milquetoast's mother being a Hon.'

Kate was wishing she had Rufus handy, as she had just leaked milk on her best blouse. 'Yes, that's right,' she said. 'Ysa underlined the word three times in her letter home.'

'Goes up in the world, doesn't she? What will she do if this marriage breaks up? Find a king or something?'

'Ssh,' said Kate, as Ysabel came into the dining room with a cornucopia of prawns.

During the drive back to her mother's place, where the children were, Len raised the topic again.

'This time's for keeps,' Kate said wearily.

'She thought that before.'

'We had a long chat when we were making the coffee. She said she wasn't going to make the same mistake again, that this time she'd held out for someone steady and true, who wouldn't love anybody but her. A family man, she said. Like Len.'

'I'm flattered. But seriously, Kate, can you see her with a grotty little brood like ours? It'd detract from the glam a bit.'

Kate was quiet, thinking on that odd conversation in the hospital, that'd seemed about to lead to . . . what? It had disquieted her at the time, but that was probably post-natal hormones, reacting to nothing at all.

'We'll see,' she said, as their station wagon nosed down her mother's driveway, to the accompaniment of piercing screams, from Rufus.

'We'll see,' said Kate numbly. Ysa and her mother sat looking at her across Kate's battered kitchen table, and just at that moment Kate felt like sliding under it, and helping Rufus play with his blocks. Anything rather than think, as Ysa had asked her to do. 'I'll have to talk it over with Len. It's a big thing, s . . . s . . . surrogacy.'

There it was, spoken aloud. Ysa had talked in circumlocutions: 'My health's always been delicate . . . I was such a frail baby . . . not like healthy old you . . . I'd do anything for Dmitri . . . he's such a good husband . . . but children . . . it's not possible . . . the physical strain alone . . . it'd do me in, the doctors say . . . And Dmitri wouldn't want a child not his own . . . he's old fashioned that way . . . Kate, you're my one hope.'

'Are you aware that I had my tubes tied?' Kate said.

'Oh darling, I wouldn't want you to give away a child that was half yours, not even to your own sister. It'll be so simple – they'll take out an egg of mine, fertilize it with Dmitri's seed, and you'd be the incubator.'

Kate stared at her.

'Oh, tactless me, for repeating doctor-talk. I mean, you'd nurture the baby for us.'

Kate turned to her mother, who had been silent during the preamble. 'Mum, you talked this over with Ysa?'

Her mother bent down and picked up Rufus from under the table. When she was upright again she nodded.

'What do you think?'

Rufus squirmed, but the older woman clutched him tightly.

'You never met your Aunty Jane. She was my oldest sister, the one who married the ex-Jesuit. They were mad for children, but nothing happened. I was only a girl at the time but I remember thinking that when I got married I'd like to give one of my children – I had six planned – to Jane, because she was my favourite sister and she looked so unhappy. I did have some doubts, because the bub would be reared Catholic. We were all rather bigoted in those days. But then we found out that Jane was infertile because of ovarian cancer . . . she was gone in a few months, and her husband was engaged to be married again within the year. I never forgave him.'

She suddenly dumped Rufus in Kate's lap and left the kitchen, shutting the door behind her. Kate looked up and into Ysa's eyes.

'See, Mum even thought of doing something like that.'

'Yes, but she didn't have a husband to consider.'

'Oh, you can wind Len round your little finger!'

Can I? thought Kate. Do I want to, even?

'Kate,' said her twin. 'I could attempt it. I would, you know, for Dmitri. He does so want a child. But he can't have it and me. It's as simple as that. And at worst he'd have neither.'

Rufus reached up and patted Kate's cheek. She suddenly thought of the rosewood cradle, filled now with Nance's collection of dolls. What would this house be like, without dolls, without blocks, without their three babies? In her mind an empty cradle rocked, to and fro, aimlessly. Her face clenched.

'Oh Kate,' said Ysa. 'I do so want this marriage to last. But without a child . . .'

She began, delicately, to weep too.

'Yes,' whispered Kate. 'Yes, yes, I'll do it for you.'

They had a tactical meeting, as Dmitri called it, at his and Ysa's house, with Nance and Jim sent to play in the big garden and the rest of the family – the two couples, Rufus, and the twins' mother – closeted in the sitting room. During the preliminary cake and coffee another party arrived. He introduced himself as Doctor Abdullah.

'He normally works with IVF,' said Ysabel, 'but he's agreed to help us through the pregnancy.'

Kate was disentangling Rufus from the legs of an antique carved chair, and it was a moment before this remark sunk in. When it did, she said:

'I already have a Gynie.'

'Who?' said Abdullah.

'Donna, Doc Donna . . .'

Abdullah drew in his breath sharply.

'Oh Kate,' said Ysabel, 'she wrote all those letters to the paper about the Baby M case! No no, she wouldn't do at all.'

'She is not the best,' said Abdullah.

'There you have it,' said Ysa, 'from the mouth of an expert.' Abdullah smiled slightly. Kate scrutinized him; he was quite handsome, with a neat black beard and even, large white teeth. However, he put her in mind of mullahs in turbans, women shrouded in black from head to foot, unspeakable genital mutilation. Stop that, she thought, you're being racist. But as she looked at the olive-skinned hands that would touch her intimately, she felt a sinking feeling. She did like Doc Donna . . .

'Then that's settled,' said Ysa. Abdullah, his part in the proceedings over, took a slice of cake and wandered out to the garden. Kate could hear Nance and Jim prattling to him.

'Abdullah does like children,' said Ysa. 'Six of his own, I'm told.'

With how many wives? wondered Kate.

Dmitri was flicking through a folder in his lap. He cleared his throat.

'We would of course pay all medical costs.'

'Thank God,' Len said quietly.

'Although this is not a commercial transaction. I must say –' and here he looked directly at Kate and Len for the first time, '– I feel the notion of buying a child somewhat distasteful. Even though my ancestors owned serfs. But I think you should have some recompense.'

Kate was aware of Len leaning forward.

'Ysa tells me that your eldest children share one room, and that baby sleeps in a bassinet at the foot of your bed.'

'We were saving up for an extension,' Len said.

'I may be able to help in this area.'

'Ah,' said Len. 'Now you're talking.'

'Besides the law firm, I have various . . . interests. Show cattle, one leg of a racehorse, property here and there. I own a house, not far from where you live, that belonged to my mother. It is large, four bedrooms, with an established garden. The tenants have not been good, but that can be repaired.'

'And?' said Len.

'I can let you have it, for the value of your current house. This is not a business deal, but between family.'

'You're on,' said Len.

Rufus was just about to take a mouthful of pot-pourri, but Kate caught him in time. He howled.

'Fine healthy lungs,' said Dmitri. 'Fine child.'

'Len, take him outside,' said Kate. It was probably her imagination, but she felt that Dmitri was looking at her as if she was one of his blessed show cattle and Rufus her calf. To her relief Dmitri closed his folder and followed Len and Rufus out. Now there were only women in the room.

'One thing,' said Ysa, 'hasn't been discussed yet. Dmitri and I feel that the most efficient way to do this would be, rather than separate pregnancies, to get it over and done with quickly. We'd like to put all the eggs together in the one basket.'

'A multiple birth!'

'They happen all the time in IVF, Abdullah says. Easy as picking peas from a pod, the deliveries.'

'He said that too?'

'Yes.' Ysabel stared back unblinkingly, as if nothing untoward had been said.

Their mother suddenly put her cup down hard on the coffee table.

'Ysabel, no!'

'What?'

'I said, no. It's too much to ask. You don't know what a multiple pregnancy's like! Lord knows, I'm glad I had the pair of you, but at the time it was sheer hell. I felt as full of my young as a cat stuffed with kittens, I could barely move. Your poor father had to pick me up and carry me in the last few weeks. His back was never the same . . .'

Ysabel had gone white, but when she spoke her voice was steady.

'Kate?'

'Well, after hearing it from the horse's mouth, if you pardon the expression, Mum, I'd rather not.'

'Well then,' said Ysabel. 'One baby, then.'

The mole above her lipstick twitched. Ysabel put her hand to her mouth to suppress it, her antique rings glistening as she did. Kate looked down at her own hands, and suddenly noticed a mole on her fourth finger, above the thin wedding band.

'Ysa, could you please take off your engagement ring, for a moment?'

Ysabel raised her eyebrows, but obliged.

'Not there,' Kate explained. 'Ysa has a mole on her face, and I don't. I have a mole on my wedding finger, and hers is lilywhite all over.'

'Not genetically determined, moles,' said their mother. 'I remember reading that once.'

Like other things, thought Kate.

Several months later, Kate lay flat on her back in a hospital room, her legs splayed, cold metal holding her soft flesh open to Abdullah, who reached deeply inside her. She felt a twinge as his instrument, that carried the microscopic child of Ysa and Dmitri, pressed against the wall of her womb.

'I'm glad I don't have to do that again,' she confided to Len later. But she did, for the first implantation did not take.

'Oh Kate,' said Ysa, staring reproachfully at the little bottle of urine, that had just tested negative. 'And I thought you were so fertile.'

'Well, it wasn't my egg,' Kate said lamely.

'It might have been,' Abdullah said suddenly. 'You two are biologically the same, you would carry the same genetic material.'

Ysa brushed this aside. 'I hope this doesn't happen again, Kate. I don't want to suffer another egg collection . . . it was agony!'

It's not exactly a picnic for me either, thought Kate. 'Well,' she said, 'next month, then. And if that egg doesn't take, then we've got two more goes before Ysa has to donate again. Isn't that right?'

Abdullah nodded.

'We have three eggs left,' he said. His gaze met Ysa's for a moment, then slid away.

'Come on, Kate,' said Ysabel. 'Let's go and see how the painting's going at your new house.'

The colour scheme looked beautiful, but Kate, the next month, wondered if it was really worth it, as she lay on her back for Abdullah again. This time, after that faint, cold, internal touch, of catheter against flesh, she shuddered.

Abdullah swore in an alien tongue, then withdrew hurriedly. 'Couldn't you control yourself?' he said. 'You nearly wrecked everything!'

'Sorry,' said Kate, but after the apology, felt a tinge of anger. 'What did you call me?' she asked.

'Call you?'

'You said something in Arabic. I want to know what it meant.'

'Nothing.'

'The way you said it, I know it meant something.'

'No,' he said. 'Forget it. You should relax now.'

'I can't, not after being sworn at!'

Abdullah loosened clamps, drew metal out of Kate. 'Don't make an issue out of it!' he said savagely, and strode out of the room.

'I hate Abdullah,' said Kate to Len. 'He's a creep.'

'Well, love, I can't say I'm keen on him, but bear with it. We get a nice new house, don't we?'

'If this works,' said Kate.

It did.

'Twins!' cried Ysabel, staring at the ultrasound.

'What?' said Kate.

Abdullah pointed at two faint dots on the screen. 'Two embryos. There's no mistaking it.'

'Oh clever little egg!' said Ysabel. 'It divided, didn't it, just like we divided, you and I, Kate, all those years ago. Twins run in families.'

Kate was mentally clambering around the family tree. As far as she recalled, she and Ysa had been the only twins . . .

'What sex are they?' she asked.

'Far too early to tell,' replied Abdullah.

Ysabel was frowning. 'I'm not sure we should know the gender,' she said. 'It would spoil the surprise.'

'You want to wait nine months before knowing?' Kate asked, intrigued. This was most unlike Ysabel.

'Well, that's been the lot of women since the dawn of time, hasn't it? Not knowing whether to knit in pink or blue.'

'Ysa, you can't knit for toffee apples,' Kate began, and then winced. Abdullah had withdrawn the scanning equipment abruptly, and roughly, from between her legs. She felt that flash of anger again, but did not voice it until later. As Ysabel was treating her to afternoon tea in a flashy little bistro near the hospital, she said:

'Ysa, I don't feel happy with Abdullah. He may be good, but his bedside manner is . . . off-putting.'

'He told me,' said Ysabel. 'He said you're ever so difficult with blood samples, because your veins go and spasm when he sticks in the needle.'

'He told you that? He never told me. I was wondering why it hurt so much . . .'

Her voice trailed off. See what I mean? she thought, but did not say. Other words, that she had been rehearsing, came more readily to her, though she spoke them tentatively.

'Ysa, I think it's good for me and for the babies, if I have a good relationship with the Doctor. Abdullah's done his bit now with the implantation, so can't I get Doc Donna for the remainder of the pregnancy? I relax with her, and she's such a good midwife.'

'You won't need a midwife.'

Kate wondered if she had heard aright.

'How am I supposed to deliver these children?'

'Abdullah will do a Caesarian.'

'But, but . . . I've never had any problems before, and I don't see any arising now.'

'It's standard procedure with IVF, darling, Abdullah does it all the time. They really can't risk losing the babies, you know.'

'Losing? We aren't living in the dark ages.'

Ysa's gaze was like a steel caress.

'Recall, Kate, the case of our brother.'

Their mother had never spoken of it, but somehow, through the osmosis of cousins and aunts, they had heard of the baby who had died two years before they were born.

'He was strangled with the birth cord, wasn't he?'

'Ysa,' said Kate, appalled at this old trauma, and also at the fact it was being used against her, 'it couldn't happen again, could it? Not twice in the same family.'

'We can't risk it,' said Ysabel. Her eyes suddenly filled with tears. After a moment Kate put her arm around her.

'OK, you win.' Again, she thought. 'Cheer up now, eat your cake . . . you've hardly touched it.'

'No, darling, you have it. You are supporting three, you know.'

Kate ate it, but as she traipsed round with Ysabel that afternoon, from maternity shop to maternity shop 'Because you deserve to have the best, Katy!' she started to feel ill. She barely got back to her house before vomiting.

'Food poisoning,' she decided, but the next morning she threw up again, just as she was trying on one of the expensive maternity dresses.

'Len!'

'I'll be late for school,' he grumbled. When he came into the bedroom he found her, ruffled in orange like a fairy cake, clutching the skirt of the dress to her face. Ysabel's choice, he thought, and her taste. I suppose you could call that a gut reaction to it.

'You won't have to wear that thing for months,' he said. 'Why put it on now?'

Kate said something incomprehensible and raised a face tinged with green. 'I'll call your mother,' he said. 'Although the amount of babysitting she's done lately, I wouldn't be surprised if she starts charging.'

Kate's mother dropped everything and came, not just this once, but many times, for Kate kept on vomiting. It was morning, afternoon, and evening sickness.

'You're losing weight,' said Abdullah. 'I may have to put you in hospital.'

Kate leaned forward.

'And how am I supposed to run my household, care for a husband and three children?'

'You have a mother. That's what mothers are for,' he said.

'We've imposed on her enough.'

'Then your sister will surely pay for help. After all, it's her children at stake.'

And me, thought Kate. Sometimes, as she stared at the back of the toilet bowl, she wished to be dead, notwithstanding Len, Nance, Jim, Rufus, her mother, Ysabel and last but not least, the babies she carried.

As it happened, her mother wouldn't hear of hired help, and held the fort while Kate spent a week in a private hospital. She stopped vomiting, but came home very thin. When she looked at herself in the mirror, the bulge of the twins gave her the look of a child with malnutrition.

While she was away Nance had got clucky.

'I want you to have two baby girls, Mummy.'

'Well, I don't know about that,' said Kate.

'I want two baby sisters. So that we've got more girls than boys.'

'Hey!' said Kate, and lifted Nance onto her lap, with difficulty, for the bulge was in the way. 'I thought we'd explained all that. They're Ysa and Uncle Dmitri's babies . . . your cousins.'

'But they're in you, aren't they?'

Kate sighed, and reiterated the child's guide to surrogacy. Later she confided to Len:

'Why couldn't we have a tomboy? Jim can't give a damn about the babies.'

'Cultural conditioning,' said Len, tidying up one of Nance's dolls from the sofa. 'It's a powerful thing.'

There was a rustle, and two smaller dolls fell from under the first doll's skirt and landed at Kate's feet. She picked them up wordlessly.

From then on, things got slowly worse, with Kate becoming a blimp on legs, subject to the thousand natural shocks that the pregnant flesh is heir to: heartburn, incontinence, insomnia, even internal bruising, for the twins had quickened into a kick-boxing match.

'They'll be born with black eyes and pug noses at this rate,' said Kate, at 2 a.m. one morning.

'I know,' said Len, from the other side of the bed. 'Can feel it over here, even.'

He put out a hand and set it firmly on the bulge. 'Pipe down, you two,' he said in his deepest voice.

Amazingly, it worked. That was a rare good night. Other times, Len was too tired to support Kate, what with work and the demands of their other children, who suddenly seemed possessed by devils. Jim had a spate of bedwetting, Rufus threw tantrums, and Nance alternated between being mother's little helper and teasing her brothers unmercifully. Kate could barely keep them in order, she was growing so big and unwieldy.

One day, when she lumbered out of bed, her shoes would not fit her feet.

'Mummy's like Bigfoot,' said Jim.

'Fluid retention,' Kate explained. 'It happens to pregnant ladies. It's just that I've never had so bad.

Her feet, when she could see them past the twins, looked like pink hills.

'Talk about being barefoot and pregnant,' said Len, but stopped, for Kate had begun to weep bitterly.

She ended up in hospital again for the last months of the pregnancy, lying on a waterbed, for that was the only surface comfortable for her bulk.

'I just want all this waiting to be over,' she told Ysabel, when her sister had torn herself away from the furnishing of the new baby-room to visit her.

Ysabel stroked the bulge.

'Darling, don't you think I want that too? My babies, at last! It's so exciting.'

'It's very boring, for me,' said Kate. Ysabel shrugged.

'Well, tell me what I can do to help. You want it, I'll go out and buy it for you.'

'I want . . . a pregnant cat. As round as I am. So someone around me is in the same situation.'

She gave a harsh laugh.

'Kate,' said Ysa. 'Think of the health regulations! It wouldn't be allowed, not in a hospital.'

'She could sit on the pillow,' continued Kate. 'And we'd commune, across the species barrier, about how awful giving life can be.'

'Kate!' and her sister hurried off, to consult with Abdullah. Perhaps because of that conversation, the caesarian was put forward.

Kate woke, nauseous from the anaesthetic. 'Easy now,' she heard Len say, and slept again. She drowsed, rising out of her unconsciousness now and then to hear his breathing, to smell flowers, en masse surely, for their scent dominated the hospital room.

When she finally opened her eyes it seemed as if she and Len were somehow in a flowershop, one specializing in exotic orchids. She giggled, then drew her breath in sharply.

'My stomach feels like a block of wood.'

'You've been cut open, in case you can't remember,' said Len.

'No, I remember. How . . .?'

But he wouldn't let her finish. 'I see what you meant about that bastard Abdullah. When we were all gowned up and you were wheeled in, he made a crack about pulling the rabbits out of you. I said that even though my wife was unconscious, she still deserved some respect, and he shut up.'

'How . . .?'

'I tell you, if Ysabel and Dmitri hadn't been there, I'd have clouted the creep.'

'Len, stop interrupting me, please! I've been trying to ask about the twins.'

'Fine and healthy,' he said, curtly.

'Any difference in weight?'

'A few ounces. Nothing to worry about.'

He stared at the nearest orchids, then, very deliberately, swept vase, flowers, water and all, onto the hospital floor.

'Len!' Kate tried to rise, but subsided in pain. 'What is it?'

'The twins are boy and girl. Fraternal, not identical twins, from two eggs, not one dividing! Now I know why there was all that secrecy over gender. We've been used.'

'What was that crash?' A white-clad Sister appeared in the doorway.

'An accident,' said Kate. 'Get Abdullah. And my sister. Now!'

She spoke quietly, but the Sister turned abruptly, as if by military injunction. How odd, thought Kate, someone doing what I want.

But it was her mother who came first to the room.

'They're two fine bubbies,' she said to Kate. 'Lovely and healthy. You've done a wonderful job.'

She paused, but Kate made no response.

Len said: 'I just told her. When did *you* find out?'

The mother sighed. 'When two antique cradles get fitted out with lace canopies, in pink and blue, you can't help noticing, can you? "How can you know, Ysa?" I said, and she replied, "because Abdullah told me!"'

'Nobody told me,' said Kate.

'I would have, but Ysa wouldn't allow it.'

'What is it now?' said Abdullah, entering the hospital room. He wore a business suit, and his beard looked freshly trimmed. But he was almost elbowed aside by Ysabel, who came tripping up to the recumbent Kate, radiant.

'Oh Kate, oh Kate, they're so beautiful!'

'Don't come near me,' Kate whispered. Abdullah suddenly seemed about to sneak out the doorway. 'Stop!' she said. 'Two eggs! I know all about it!'

'It was three, actually,' said Abdullah. 'We had to maximize the chances.'

'Triplets!'

Len had suddenly put his hand on hers. I know what that's for, thought Kate. Not support, but restraint. He might have broken the vase earlier, but now he's thinking of the lovely new house. Old half-remembered fragments of church services at St Swithin's were coming back to her, something about selling birthright for pottage.

'One failed,' said Abdullah. 'And we couldn't tell immediately whether two had failed and there'd been a natural division of the third, as happened with you and your sister. And when we could sex the twins . . . you weren't in a good state. It seemed best not to upset you.'

'In case I had kittens, I mean, the babies, on the spot?'

She was suddenly remembering what the old church services had called the likes of Abdullah, and quite forgetting the nice Turkish mothers at Nance and Jim's little school, she cried:'Infidel! Deceiver!'

'I'm sorry,' said Abdullah, and went out.

'Kate . . .' began Ysabel, but Kate turned on her, screaming:

'You too! Deceiver! Liar! Thief!'

Post-natal hormones were a good thing, Len said later. It meant Kate's outburst could be ascribed to chemicals, and nice Uncle Dmitri could fork out for a rest cure.

'Buying us off again,' said Kate.

'I know, I know, but you need it.'

After Kate had stopped screaming, which was about two minutes after Ysabel had fled the hospital room, her mother had sat down firmly on the bed and taken hold of her.

'Ysa does what she wants to,' she had said. 'And we live with it. We even love her for it.'

Kate had sobbed and then slept again. In the morning she had been wheeled out to see the twins. Nikolai had a dark mop of hair; the girl, Anastasia, was bald except for a few white wisps. Apart from that, they looked like the rest of the newborns – ugly as boiled mice. Only a mother could love them; and Kate did.

As she gazed Len bent down close to her ear.

'I've been thinking. I know it's a bit late in the day, but we don't have to do what other people want.'

Kate said nothing.

'Those two kicked me in the back often enough, as I lay beside you. That's . . . endearing, odd though it may sound. We don't have to take the new house. We could take the kick-boxers.'

'They're not ours.'

'Well, sure, they're half Dmitri's, but you carried them. And didn't you tell me Abdullah said the eggs of identical twins were the same? A clever lawyer could make something of that.'

'Dmitri's a lawyer,' said Kate. 'He might not give up his babes without a fight.'

'Well, we fight him then,' said Len, but without conviction. He tried to smile, but it faded from his face. I know what he wants me to say, thought Kate, and said it.

'Len, we're poor as church-mice, even if you get your promotion. With three we're struggling, with five, we'll be on the streets. No.'

'Thank God,' said Len, quickly. 'I wasn't looking forward to Dmitri getting nasty. We've got a lawyer suing the school now, all over his fool of a son's broken leg.'

Kate wrested her gaze from the twins.

'One thing, Len. I want a holiday. You, me, and our kids, just a nuclear family. We need to escape.'

'I'll talk to Uncle Dmitri,' said Len.

They ended up at a Balinese resort, where there were local children for Jim and Nance to play with, and a local

Nannie thrown into the holiday package, to keep an eye on Rufus. Len and Kate could be alone together, for almost the first time since their pre-wedding holiday, all those years ago. They walked hand in hand down jungly paths, lay on beaches with the sand bright as platinum. Things mended: Nance stopped talking about baby sisters, Jim slept all night in dry pyjamas, Rufus grew placid. Len browned and relaxed; the scars in Kate's body healed.

But not the ones in her soul. 'I know I've done wrong,' she said on their last day. Len jumped – it seemed as if Kate was not addressing him, but some vast impersonal other.

'Kate!'

But her gaze was directed at the Hindu idol behind them, a gigantic gilded woman, with multiple arms, but only two breasts.

'Kate!'

She turned away from the statue, with one of her slow smiles, as if she was his old Kate again.

She isn't though. When they move into their new house, the first thing Kate does is nobble the spare bedroom, that Len had earmarked for a study. 'This will be Kate's room,' she says, and he decides not to argue about it. She moves an old school desk into the room, then a chair.

'*I'm* going to study,' she says.

'Sure, love, but what about babysitting? I mean, we can't rely on your mother, what with the twins home and Ysa opening a new antique shop . . .'

'Ysa and Dmitri have a Nannie,' she says, 'so Mum will have some free time. If necessary we can dump the kids on the Nannie now and then. They can all play happy families together!'

Len's promotion comes through, so there's a bit more

money in the house. Kate can even pay for childminding while she's at the Adult Education. Her first course is in Art History, then she studies Craft. She buys a second-hand spinning wheel and installs it in her room, processing wool and knitting it into bulky jumpers for everyone except Jim, who has a wool allergy. When the family are well and truly sick of homespun, she sells the surplus woollies at the school fête.

Len doesn't know what to make of her. She used to be slow-moving and content; now she moves incessantly from one activity to another, her eyes hollow. The weight she lost during the pregnancy never returns – Kate is stick-thin, with Ysa puffy in comparison with her. And then there's the matter of the collection . . .

One day Len brings Kate a cup of tea and finds her staring at something which he slowly recognizes as the carved Russian doll Dmitri gave Nance for her birthday.

'It's called a Matrioshka,' she says. 'That's from the word for "mother" in Russian. Nance calls it "Mothers and Daughters", because it splits – see! – and there are generations of dolls inside.'

'Well, love, that's all very interesting, but . . .'

'I asked Dmitri to give me one too. I'm starting a collection.'

'Of what?' Len asks, genuinely frightened.

'Of Her!' and Kate laughs.

In time Kate's collection encompasses Italian bread dolls, with coloured foil skirts and rows of breasts; a lump of clay decorated by Rufus, which is amazingly like the prehistoric loom weights in her art books; and newspaper articles, from the women's section of the paper, which she tapes to the newly painted walls. She goes to the local library to make microfilm printouts of Doc Donna's letters about Baby M, and sticks them up too. Even the spinning wheel is part of the collection, although she doesn't tell Len that. These small, subtle things belong to a mystery, one that is not meant for him.

She thinks she is half crazy now. Other times she feels merely that the scales have fallen from her eyes. It is hard to tell which is preferable, although both, it seems, are part of the same thing. She looks up at the yellowing newsprint on her walls, and burns to use words to say what she wants, to express her story in a scream that will carry far beyond a hospital room.

The next course she takes is Creative Writing, but even after it Kate struggles with her narrative, filling 'up pad after pad with experiments in form. Len is Deputy Headmaster now, quite the bureaucrat, he jokes, and he could use the money for a new car. Instead, he buys Kate a word processor, and she sits in her room, tapping away.

It is only after the computer malfunctions, and their friend the Maths teacher fixes it up, that Kate learns the computer, too, is part of her collection. And almost at the same moment comes the idea of an alternate self to tell her story, a mirrored persona, standing outside Kate, reading her mind at crucial moments, even reading Len's.

Because . . . what Kate wants to say so badly that it hurts like childbirth, is that, as she said to the golden statue, she has done wrong. And the faces on her wall, of Mary Beth Whitehead and Elizabeth Kane, the first paid surrogate mother, they say it too. To have another carry your child, nurturing it from microscopic grain to viable human being, is false parturition, a mockery of the Mother. A baby taken from its birth-mother under such circumstances is nothing less than stolen. 'Thief!' Kate had cried at Ysa. And on child-stealers the Goddess has no mercy.

Ysa fusses over Nikolai and Anastasia, but they push her away, run to the Nannie, or Kate when they see her. They are going through a 'phase', as Ysa puts it, in which everything is 'Pooey!', including their genetic mother.

'Pooey Mummy!' they chorus to Ysa, who pours herself

a stiff drink. Anastasia looks at Kate and grins widely.

'Unpooey Mummy!' she says.

'Jesus, how can they know?' says Len, when Kate tells him later, over the washing up.

'They know,' says Kate.

The phone rings. She answers it, and hears little voices on the line.

'Is it those two again?' asks Len. Kate nods.

'That Nannie will regret she taught them how to use the phone, when Uncle Dmitri gets the bill.'

Kate smiles and concentrates on the twins, who have something important to say about their pet rabbit. After a while Len takes over, on the extension, and she returns to her computer, to the spot in the manuscript where she left off yesterday. From a great distance, she can hear Len talking about hutches. Kate stares at her text, then types on to the screen:

She's got power, that one.

Pausing, Kate adds:

She is not mocked. This story proves it.

Thalia

RAW MATERIAL

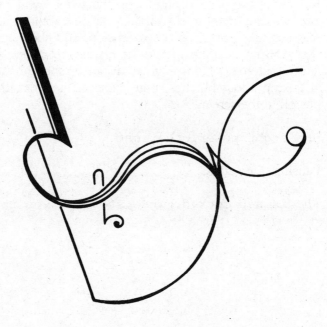

𝔥 = Treatments

𝔥𝒸 = Abnormal

𝓊 = Patience

EGG HARVEST

᠍ᠵ = Frozen

ᠼ = Farming

᠊᠊ = Eggs

ᠵ. = Harvesting

FLUSHING

C⤳ = Flushing
ʅ = Lavage
ꝸˢ = Fertilization

IN VITRO FERTILIZATION

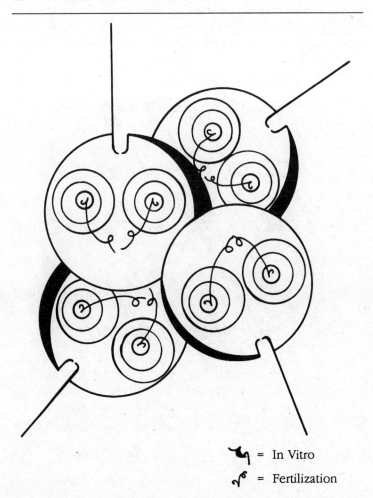

ᕈ = In Vitro

ᕈ = Fertilization

EUGENICS

       = Eugenics

Melissa Chan

Forgetting Arachnida

It was a lovely funeral. Just as Jansen would have wanted it. The church filled with his business colleagues and their spouses. The litany read of his contribution to civic and business life. His many donations to church and community services. His ready willingness to serve on this committee and that one. To hold directorships in this company and that. His presidency of the golf club. His part-ownership of Sallygrigor, the mare that won the Melbourne Cup two years in a row. His sponsorship of the Trident, which brought the Americas Cup back to Australia, where it still stood, in proud display, in the foyer of the Royal Brisbane Yacht Club.

'Yes,' said Helene Truebent. 'It was Jansen all over.' She was sitting on a low white lounge facing the Harbour. The sun sparkled and shone through the expanse of glass sweeping around the circular room. Her left hand lay, palm upward, on the cushion beside her. Platinum bands glinted along the third and fourth fingers. Hidden, blue sapphires nudged against diamonds and pearls.

'Yet – if there'd been anything he could do to prevent himself from going, he'd have done it.' She sighed, the fingers of her right hand thoughtfully pleating the white silk of her robe. (She'd changed from black immediately upon arriving home from the service; widow's weeds remained standard dress for funerals. Jansen's ashes were to be sent on to her, after they had cooled from their contact with the heat of the furnace, in a bejewelled, custom-made jar.) 'He donated hundreds of thousands to Genetech. But if there is a breakthrough, it'll be too late for him.'

She had often wondered what it felt like, knowing that if one lived true to type – genotype, that was – death at an early age was inevitable.

When Jansen McCormack was born, forty-four years ago, the joy in the McCormack household was shortlived. Everyone – everyone in the middleclass, that was – had their children gene-tested on birth. The practice began in the 1990s and continued on through the 21st century. There had been some proposal, originally, that gene-testing should be done prior to birth. Then, if the tests showed a predisposition in the embryo to cancer, or asthma, or Alzheimer's disease, or heart attacks, or any one of a thousand life-threatening conditions, a termination of pregnancy could occur immediately, and no one the worse for it. (So said the scientists.) But the populace had jacked up. They had suspected that the medicos and scientists pushing gene testing had other designs on embryos than simply to let them die. The story got around that the embryos were to be subjected to experiments for the removal of the 'bad' genes and replacement of them with 'good' genes. When someone in animal husbandry let slip that a mouse had been used in a similar experiment, with the 'good' gene going wrong, people feared this would happen to *their* prospective child. A mouse with five legs and a paw protruding from its forehead was bad enough to contemplate. But a child . . .?

The proposal had itself been aborted. Oh, threats raged in the national and daily newspapers for weeks, from medical scientists protesting they would leave Australia for climes where medical technology was given proper credit and doctors proper respect, where advances and progress were not interrupted, or confronted by insuperable obstacles. Television channels and radio airwaves reverberated with the barely controlled anger of genetic engineers declaring their ingenuity was being hampered by restrictive legislation, governments lacking in imagination, and a populace determined to consign itself to the dark ages. Luddites. Troglodytes. But, in the end, apart from those times they carried out the tests on the sly, the genetic specialists were circumscribed to carrying out genetic manipulation after birth.

For Jansen McCormack, the tests showed he was fated to die of a heart attack at forty-four years of age. Jassie, his mother, was devastated. Carter, his father, was furious. The household reverberated with angry shouts and crashing and bashing when Jassie returned home from hospital, Jansen wrapped tightly in a white ET blanket. 'What's the point of creating a dynasty if your first born dies before you?' shouted Carter, his red face growing redder. 'I always wanted a son, and here I am, told he'll be history at forty-four.' There was a pause, then a thwack and a bang, as if someone had fallen against the wall – or been pushed. 'Never should have married you in the first place. Defective eggs. And now my son – *my son* – my son's life is threatened.' The next time, he declared, they'd get Jassie onto the IVF program, so that they didn't have to use her ova any more. He – Carter McCormack – wasn't intending to sire a series of sons destined to die in early middle age. He was determined to leave behind him the McCormack millions in McCormack hands.

Certainly, Carter McCormack would have preferred to retain the McCormack millions in his own McCormack hands. To this end, he donated a goodly proportion of the yearly income to Genetech, just as, years later, did his son Jansen. But it was not to be.

In the old days, the search was for the elixir of youth. In contemporary times it was called the pursuit of applied science, in the name of productivity and economic rationalism. If a foetus' genetic makeup could be changed, by the introduction of a replacement gene for some defective chromosomal pattern, there need be no children born, only to die forty years or so later of a heart attack, or cancer, or becoming prematurely senile in what should be the years of their prime. And if a foetus' genetic make-up could be changed, why couldn't the same process be applied to an adult? Thus reasoned Carter McCormack. But, when he died at forty-five of a coronary occlusion (too late, he discovered, in the pain of clutching at his heart and knowing this was the end, it was his defective sperm rather than Jassie's ova), Genetech had not yet discovered a way of defeating nature's intention that men of a particular disposition should leave this world early, and leave their millions behind them.

Jassie McCormack, left a widow at forty-two, with three late-teenaged sons genotyped to follow their father in some twenty years or so, took her place as president of the board of McCormack Industries. There were the predictable grumbles from Carter's top management. But Jassie called each of them, separately, into what was now her office and told them they were out. Generous terms, yes. After all, they each had families, and Jassie was the last to consign any woman to the terror of having her husband on the dole queue. Anyway, unemployment insurance (as the old unemployment benefit was now known) lasted for only a month. After that, if you didn't have a paid job, it was each man and woman fend for themselves. And usually the women had to fend for the children, too. (Although there had been a few changes since the turn of the century, some things remained the same.)

Helene Truebent, Carter's secretary, was a young woman with potential. So Carter had constantly told Jassie. Jassie, enured to Carter's lack of judgement, found to her surprise that on this occasion he was right. Helene was not only intelligent. She had initiative. That first day, she brought Jassie a cup of peppermint tea and handed her a two-page outline of directions for the company.

Jassie knew that Carter had been worried, in the last years of his life, about the falling off in profit from McCormack Industries. He had wanted to diversify. But into what?

Helene had a plan. Back at the end of the 20th century, society had split down the middle, the environmentalists or 'greenies' as they were then called taking over the forests and forcing greater reliance of the economic rationalists on oil and nuclear power. But just as forests take centuries to replenish themselves, oil is, in any single human's lifetime, a finite resource. And the lessons of Five Mile Island and Chernobyl, never learnt back in the 1970s and 1980s, were forced upon the 21st century when nuclear power plants leaked into the British soil and water at the old Windscale site, and at sites in Europe, India, the United States, Japan, Korea and the Middle East. Australia was fortunate. Public opinion had not succeeded in preventing French nuclear testing in the Pacific, nor United States' nuclear-powered ships from being harboured offshore. But it had prevented the building of nuclear power plants. To the extent that it was possible for any part of the earth to be 'nuclear free', this ancient island with its 40,000-year-old culture, bordered by the Pacific and Indian Oceans, was.

'The world is crying out for fresh fruit and vegetables. Cloth grown naturally – wool, cotton, silk. Crops. Without hormonal additives. Pesticide sprays. Artificial "nutrients" in the soil,' argued Helene. 'I know it sounds corny – back to nature – but besides being healthy, it'll sell. People want to buy what they can actually *eat.*' She emphasized the last word.

Jassie looked interested. She was interested. 'I – I was going to talk to Mr McCormack – Carter – about it,' said Helene. 'But there never seemed to be the opportunity. He was always out of the office, or surrounded by members of the board. Or management.' Helene jabbed a finger on what was now Jassie's desk. 'There's no reason why we can't do it. There'll be the novelty value at first. How many people have tasted a *real* tomato this century? How many have eaten wholemeal bread – bread that tastes like bread, not like elasticized cottonwool? How many have seen an apple ripened naturally – not pushed to get red, then snap frozen for months?'

Jassie McCormack gazed at Helene Truebent as she lifted her left hand. Twenty years on, at sixty-three she was white-haired, but energetic. Her eyes glistened as she gazed at the younger woman.

'He was a lovely baby. And such a joyous toddler. I remember his first day at school. He was determined back then he was going to change the world. Make it a better place for everyone. I can recall him at six giving a talk to his class in 'show and tell' when he said he was going to stay at home and look after the children when he was a father. Went down like a ton of bricks with the teacher. Thought I was turning him into a mummy's boy, I think.' Jassie paused. Helene handed her a fresh cup of peppermint tea.

'Ah well, it just happened that he grew more and more like his father the older he got. I was quite worried he might begin to throw his weight around and attempt to reverse some of the policies we've established at McCormack. Equal pay. Women in the top jobs. Training programs for women re-entering the paid workforce. Corporate funded childcare. Paid maternity leave . . . ' Jassie frowned. 'At Genetech they'd say "genes will out". Or "you are your genes". Or some such. Of course *I* don't necessarily believe it . . . ' Her voice trailed off.

Helene looked at her, her face breaking out into a grin. It reminded Jassie of the young woman who had come in, on the day she took over McCormack Industries, plonking an idea on the desk that changed the direction of Australian manufacturing, industry and primary production.

'You may not believe it Jassie, but we've got to admit that in all these years, with all of us – Dulcimae's Roger, Alexis' first husband Chester, and Devos' just six months ago . . . and Suki's two. I could go on and on. Genetech's never got it wrong.' She hesitated for a moment, glancing down at her hands. 'Why, I was about to give Sister Dulcie a call in a few weeks, to see who she's got on the books who's around forty, millions to leave to a cause, and a few years off a coronary.' As she rose from the couch in response to the lilting buzzer that sounded gently from the foyer of the penthouse, she turned anxiously to Jassie. 'You – you don't think I'm wicked, do you?'

Jassie smiled. 'Well – if it's nature's way, my dear, who am I to judge?' She walked over to the window, and turned. 'After all, it's such a *good* cause.'

Maurilia Meehan

ALFALFA SALAD

Jacki had rung Annette at work that morning, assuming she would drop everything to see her. Annette had been annoyed.

Still, for old time's sake, she squeezed her in for a half-hour lunch. New mothers assumed the world revolved around their screaming wrigglers.

Of course, Annette was a mother herself, but that was different; her two were at least a genetically superior contribution to the universal gene-pool.

In fact her whole life was dedicated to this task of giving evolution a nudge in the right direction, she thought, as she headed down to the High Motility Brasserie on the ground floor of the building, where they had agreed to meet.

Annette was Manager of The Repository for Germinal Choice, and was proud of founding a company which accepted sperm only from men with no history of genetic or family illness, and, above all, who had achieved some kind of Greatness in their field.

Annette's own children were most definitely the sons of:

    a. an Olympic athlete, and
    b. a nuclear scientist.

Her husband's sperm had a marginally low motility count, or as she had explained to him, his sperm lacked the ability to move purposefully towards her eggs. Now, she knew that by combining several batches of his sperm, by giving them each a wash-up and a swim-up to isolate a sufficient number of motile sperm, their chances of having a baby could have been improved from 1:50 to 1:2.

But Annette believed that a man with a low-motility count also had what she called a low-motility personality, that is, an inability to move towards any goal in life, a lack of ambition. And though she loved her easy-going and immensely rich husband, she did not particularly want her children to inherit his lack of ambition. Nor his weak chin.

So, she had doctored his test results, and, in keeping with her assessment of his personality, he had agreed to having her children sired by better stock.

Annette was annoyed with Jacki for two reasons, she realized, as she got into the lift, and pressed the down button with her red, acrylic nail.

Firstly, Annette was annoyed because she knew Jacki had a long-term lover, about whom she had no scruples, yet she seemed to have scruples about getting pregnant by him, and always used a condom. That was emotive thinking, and that type of thinking was holding back the evolution of the entire human race. Even though it was in Annette's interests to encourage clients to use IVF services, in Jacki's case it was clearly over-servicing. She already had a potential natural donor, whose fertility had been proven she said, by the siring of five children already.

Secondly, and more importantly, Jacki and Charles had not come to her clinic, the RGC, when they had decided to use IVF after years of 'trying'.

'It's eugenics, Annette, what you're doing. We don't approve. We'll go to a normal clinic.'

'Normal.' Even if Jacki was clearly uninterested in improving the human race by selective breeding, there were other reasons to use RGC.

Annette had warned her about other clinics, inside stories. About four women in Sydney who had 'zero converted' – developed HIV antibodies in their blood – after they were all inseminated by the same infected donor. Even in New York, where it is mandatory to test semen for HIV antibodies, freeze it and re-test it after six months before it can be used, studies now show it could turn up in frozen sperm after three years.

And 85 per cent of the other companies' donors were anonymous, whereas at RGC, donors were screened thoroughly, risks infinitesimally small . . .

Jacki hadn't listened.

So, here she was, sitting in the Brasserie, with her blue-and-white striped pram, with a perfectly, disappointingly 'normal' baby, when Annette could have helped her produce a superior being.

On the walls of the Brasserie were enlarged photos of tangles of live sperm, like little radioactive, over-ripe alfalfa sprouts. Jacki was sitting at a perspex table under a photo of a man with rubber gloves and mask hovering over a cauldron from which dry ice rose in clouds – the freezing room.

Annette fixed an indulgent smile on her face as she approached Jacki. She kissed the air near Jacki's cheek and sat down, signalling the woman behind the metal counter for her usual alfalfa salad and carrot juice. Jacki already had a coffee and pink iced doughnut in front of her.

'He's sleeping . . .' whispered Jacki, as she stuffed doughnut into her mouth, licking her fingers. Annette frowned; a diet like that was no way for a breast-feeding mother to improve the human race. She followed Jacki's gaze to the pram, which was turned away from the table. Her face was glowing with that sense of pride that new mothers have, as if they have produced the only baby in the world. Well, Annette had looked like that too, she had photos to prove it. But that was different. Annette had at least produced two genetically superior children. Jacki's baby was just pot-luck. The donor could be any mentally ill deviant, or a loser who needed a quick hundred bucks for masturbating over *Playboy* magazines in the donor's private cubicle.

Annette knew it was now time to admire the baby, but, for a woman with two children of her own, she felt remarkably unclucky at the prospect. Another average child in the world; what was there to celebrate? Still, she made an effort. Jacki and Charles were regular dinner guests as the two husbands played tennis together, in their own relaxed, low-motility way. The two slowest in the club, no one else would partner them. They suffered from an inability to move purposefully towards the ball.

'So, Jacki, he must be . . . how old? . . . ah yes, two weeks . . .' Annette bent over the pram, but could see nothing but a neat hump of pink cotton blankets printed with bunny-rabbits.

'Beautiful,' sighed Annette, as her salad arrived.

Jacki was still beaming. Annette picked up her knife and fork, made an effort to be positive.

'So, all my IVF horror stories were exaggerations, it seems. All my stories . . .'

Jacki looked suddenly serious. She swallowed the doughnut in her mouth, took a swig of coffee and leant forward, her elbows on the table.

'Look Annette, before our dinner-party next week, I wanted to talk to you about what you told me. You know, about how slack they are at keeping IVF records? How tubes of sperm have no labels, and are just kept in marked envelopes? Well, I want you to tell Charles all about it at dinner, to calm him down. He wanted to sue them, but I told him it's too late.'

'Sue?'

Annette put down her knife and fork, popped a trailing alfalfa sprout into her mouth. She licked her lips, tasting a breath of scandal.

The pram once more caught her attention. She leant over it, folded down the pink blanket, and saw the perfectly angelic features of the long-lashed, beautiful, decidedly brown baby.

Now, the ninety per cent of Annette's brain which was business, was pleased at this evidence of the careless practices of her competitor. Charles was Chinese. Jacki was Australian. This was not a Eurasian baby.

The other ten per cent of Annette's brain was excited by the human drama unfolding before her.

'Go on,' she said, casually.

'Charles wanted to sue, but I've told him not to,' said Jacki, showing a surprising enthusiasm now for the rest of her doughnut.

She didn't seem distressed enough. Not that Annette thought a perfectly formed African child was in itself a backward step for eugenics – it was just that such a child should have been with a perfectly formed black couple, not with pale and whispy Jacki and her almost equally pale Chinese husband.

'Why shouldn't he sue?' snapped Annette, seeing the headlines now, seeing the lengthening queues of clients to her superior company, as the sperm mix-up scandal emerged.

'Well, I told him it would be racist to sue. I mean, being Asian, he's sensitive to that line of argument. So, it's all fine . . .'

She finished her doughnut, licking her lips, and threw back the last of the coffee.

'Look, Annette, I just wanted to warn you, to get your support before the dinner-party. I have to go now . . .' she added, checking her watch. 'He'll be here soon . . .'

'Charles?'

Jacki laughed.

'No. My boom-boom boy. Every married woman needs one.'

She looked out over Annette's head to the street, dabbed at her lips with the paper serviette, pulled out a mirror and dragged fresh lipstick heavily across full lips. 'You see, Annette, I don't want to upset the applecart. I've got everything – a kind husband, not great in bed but easy to live with, plenty of money. And I've got a fine lover. And now a child. After trying for so long. You know, I've been inseminated in that damn clinic five times, and it's never worked. Every time I ovulated, off I'd go to the clinic like a good girl, but it never took.

'So this time, when I ovulated, I went to my boom-boom boy instead, and didn't use a condom.

'That's why I don't want you to encourage him to sue. If Charles sues, he'll find out I didn't go last time, that his sperm is still sitting there waiting to be used. So, I'm relying on you to be on my side, tell him it's a common mistake but he should live with it now . . . ooh, look at the time, gotta rush.'

She put away the mirror and lipstick, slapped ten dollars on the table and wheeled the still-sleeping baby out the glass doors into the street, where she took the arm of a decidedly black man, who bent lovingly over the pram as they wheeled it away into the crowd of shoppers.

Leaving Annette gaping after them.

It only took Annette a moment, however, to recover; for the business side of her brain to take over. She unzipped her briefcase, took out a pen. By the time the press found out it wasn't true, the whole IVF inefficiency would be exposed anyway. Even the possibility of a sperm mix-up would kill off the competition for RGC.

And as for Jacki's marriage, or their own friendship, well, someone like Jacki, who didn't care about improving the quality of the universal gene-pool, just didn't matter in evolutionary terms.

She flicked open her Filofax and outlined a press release: 'Sperm Bank Scandal . . . black child born to . . .'

When she had finished her outline, she turned to Appointments and crossed out the dinner next week with Jacki and Charles.

Then she turned with renewed energy to her delicious alfalfa salad.

Susan Hawthorne

EGGS

Whose idea was it?
                 eggs to harvest
like weeds or crops
                 add fertilizer hormones
so old primagravidas
                 will bear fruit
women with   hostile wombs
                 incompetent cervixes
                 bad eggs

How bad is a bad egg?
How young is a good egg?
                 prenatal eggs preferred
                 (harvested from
                 foetuses hardly out of
                 egg stage themselves)

Whose eggs are good? or bad?
Are they   black eggs
                 brown eggs
                 white eggs
                 yellow eggs
Who's to judge?

How infertile is infertile?
    is it a blocked tube?
        an IUD infection?
        indolent sperm?

Women's bellies are cut
    (the men jerk off in the privacy of a cubicle
      with piles of *Playboy, Hustler, Penthouse*
    to excite them)
Eggs are harvested
    some women die, sacrificed to their own
                            or another's
    desire for immortality.

Bellies are cut
Cervixes are stitched
Eggs are checked for good or for bad.

Sperm are introduced
    injected into the
    selected egg.

Petri dishes, test tubes – a world
    of marital glassware.

Microscoped, examined again
    for traces of genetic disorder
        like femaleness
        manic depression
        hairy ears

More girls are killed at birth for their sex
Why would this be any different?

Good eggs are frozen,
    freeze dried, snap chilled
    like peas
    implanted in the womb.

Bad eggs are weeded out,
    selectively reduced on site,
    with saline.
Bad eggs lose the intrauterine
    eugenic war.

Eggs. Good eggs. Bad eggs.
Whose idea was it?

Mary O'Brien

ELLY

Elly let her eyes open, confident that she was awake and that it must be 0700. She was programmed to wake at 0700, but not programmed to go to sleep at a special hour. She had stayed awake for a long time thinking about tomorrow's babies. Elly wasn't supposed to think much at all. She glanced at the thought screen to see what she was supposed to be thinking, but all it said was Get UP. She got up. She looked through her periscope porthole, but the postnuclear grey cloud, inevitably, was still there. She directed a bit of a smile at the screen, which now said that there was Significant Dispersion of the cloud. Said that every Wake-up: Elly was on Wake-up 2. She tried thinking that the grey was dispersing, and might have managed it if she hadn't kept thinking about the babies; she had to stop doing that all the time. She made a great effort – it's brighter, it's brighter – and numbed her concern about the babies for long enough to do the three-second thought scan. No buzzers. She'd made it.

The dining room was brightly lit, and she ate her mash, took her vitamins, slipped half her juice to Bessie, who would hiccup for an hour before she became dazed. Bessie was the other nursery attendant. She was a bit O-A, but over-animation in their generation didn't necessarily work out as energy for work. Bessie danced, which suited Elly very well, for she got to see more of the babies while Bessie adjusted her calories in an elaborate dance sequence she had developed, clucking rhythmically with her tongue, and, she said, undoing the knots that compulsory exercise sessions tied in her joints. Elly loved her for this, using the time to cuddle the babies. Dancing was only allowed in the rec room down in the basement, and cuddling wasn't encouraged at all, but Bessie was a clever mathematician and had worked out the master-eye cycle so that they knew when they were observed. So Elly could cuddle and Bessie could dance unobserved. For this also Elly loved Bessie. For doing many of her chores, Bessie loved Elly. They lived in great anxiety that Bessie might be transferred or disciplined for heterosexuality or that Elly might be caught cuddling. Friendship wasn't considered cool in the building where they lived.

They had no concern, however, that Elly might be transferred. Elly was special in a funny way. Her proper name was L.E., which stood for Last Error. Elly's skin was a brownish colour. Bessie was B.S., which stood for Basic Stock, which was polite obfuscation of her engineered low IQ. Still, Bessie was pretty proud of her classification, for they no longer reproduced low IQs. Too many of them had turned out to be High Cs – too much cunning. Cunning was the antithesis of disciplined intelligence. There was no need for cunning in a totally rational society. Bessie was an anomaly in that she had this fine mathematical skill which could not be acknowledged as intelligence – she was a B.S., after all. The categories were absolute. Still, Bessie lived and worked with the Errors on the top floor, where the grey outside was thickest. They were a small community, officially extinct. Elly and Bessie scrutinized the babies longingly, hoping for a few more exceptional children, but none appeared. Bessie said that they never got out of the petri dish, but Elly lived in hope that one day she might caress a brown skin.

The baby boxes were of an eroded chrome material, rough to the hands and the source of great anxiety to the women. They were afraid the chrome might still be radioactive. They were not supposed to take the babies out of the boxes, but of course they did. Bessie would dance with them, Elly would cuddle them. They had been doing this for years, but they could never find out if it made a difference to the babies, who only stayed in the building for 9 months. They dared not ask the ages three-to-nine nursery staff what they did: they probably worked to rule. Almost everybody did. Elly thought fleetingly of the new young paediatrician who seemed less chalky white than the others. Bessie thought it was only a new cosmetic: professionals were allowed cosmetics. The master-doctor painted blue lines on his face and had dyed his hair purple. It was whispered that he was openly heterosexual, so he must be indispensably clever, and anyway he was pretty old; once he told Elly that he had been reproduced even before her, and Elly was programmed to die in just a few weeks. They were never told the exact day and in any case the chronometers were often on the fritz. It really fouled up the babies' feeding schedules, but Elly and Bessie had created a little cache of baby food so that the babies wouldn't cry when time stood still, as it quite often did.

Elly usually arrived alone on first shift. Bessie liked her forbidden sex early in the upspan and as often as possible in the downspan. She would be dancing after her joust with one of the cooks; it took her this way. Elly, of course, had no reproductive nor sexual organs. They had removed them when they saw her skin colour. They had kept her alive because at that time some of the men had gone on strike because so few females were being reproduced, but heterosexuality had been declared obsolete years ago. Elly and a few older Errors had formed a little celibate club. They called it the Gay Ladies, so they were left in peace. Bessie, who ran risks for her bisexuality, poked fun at them, but occasionally came to the meetings. 'Prayer meetings', the men called them, though no one was sure what that meant. The AC maintenance man had tried to explain to Elly that this was a joke, but Elly loved the meetings where they sang and an older lady on the brink of retiring sometimes chanted quaint and wordless songs which made Elly's feet tap. She liked this, but kept her feet under a moulded chair in case it was improper to tap-tap. There was no crime in Elly's universe, but lots of improprieties. Like cuddling babies.

On this morning, Elly was torn. It was change day, and it came every 60 days, though it was hard to measure time. Elly hated to see her babies go, but loved the new ones immediately. She stood just inside the door, the only spot not monitored, and put her hands over her eyes. I love you already, she told the new babies, though no sound came and the glistening in her eyes was felt with dread pleasure and a surreptitious wipe. When she stepped into range she was wiping her hands on the towel, which she was supposed to do anyway, finding clean pleasurability in the notion of her invisible tears. In any case, her big smile was forming spontaneously as she stepped towards the old chrome containers.

First, she counted. Eleven. Better than the last lot, which had been ten. Elly knew that three more nurseries had been closed, so it seemed clear that the building was getting fewer babies less often. On her last out trip she had been taken to a building which had no nursery at all! It was full of fancy, noisy, overbright machines, and on one of the screens she had seen a picture of her own nursery, with Bessie bending solicitously over a container! The people in that building were all men, or at least the folk she saw seemed to be men – they all wore genital slings, and seemed to spend their time watching a queer TV with nothing but numbers on the screen. It had hardly been worth the effort of suiting up for an out trip and the tedious two-day detoxification when she got back. And the air bus lurched every time the grey darkened and they never went up to the Bright at all. Elly had only been up to the Bright once, but it was empty and hurt her eyes. In fact, it was after that when she asked for nursery duty, knowing she would never leave the building again and glad because people from the other buildings had stared stupidly at her dark skin. Never seen it before, she supposed. She'd never seen it herself, ever, never could understand why she was allowed to live as an Error. One of the marshals always called her Bogey, and told her one day that little kids needed to have bogeys. She didn't believe this, but still, neither Bessie nor anyone else had ever seen skin like hers. She looked first in the chrome and loved her dark reflection for the moment before she would turn her love on the eleven new babies. It seemed longer and longer between consignments and she was sure the chronometers were slowing down, but Bessie said she was too fond and had an eccentric time consciousness. Bessie was too good a friend to report this, but it gave Elly little waves of panic now and then that she or Bessie might be transferred. The only lower category was window cleaning, and who wanted to spend their life cleaning windows no one could see through?

Elly smiled. These little meditations were exercises she had developed to stave off the moment of looking, but not for too long; the box might be watching. It was a man on the box this morning and he looked zonked; probably saved his pot ration for the tedium of this shift. He hadn't shaved either, so he must be over thirty . . .

. . . but she wasn't really thinking these trivial thoughts, for her hand on the chrome had opened the shutter. Her other hand reached for a towel; the baby was stinking of urine. They never had got the catheters right. She touched first the baby's face and it grimaced. Quickly she peeled off the wrapper, which broke up in a way they never used to. At one time they were washed! It was a long time ago though and now nothing was washed. Elly had to be careful not to try to put the gowns on the babies too quickly for they split and went all fluffy and the fluff got in the little noses and the infant sneezes were recorded and Elly got a demerit. Enough demerits and she could be cleaning windows!

It was a boy. She changed him quickly, her hands caressing him, her mind on guard against picking him up, her heart beating with the desire to do so. Silly Elly, silly Elly, silly Elly. She sang this little lullaby under her breath, her lips barely moving. Ten more. She went as slowly as she could. They were all boys, all wet, all drowsy and one a little yellow. She wondered why they had passed him and gently stroked his little belly to show him he was born lucky. He drooled. Her heart, or something in her breast, leapt and she hoped she wasn't being monitored. They didn't bother so much when a person was due to be terminated soon.

All boys. Elly took the little jaundiced one out, as he had to be isolated. She wished Bessie would hurry for she could screen her a bit, though she was allowed to take them into isolation to collect a specimen if they were yellow. But Bessie was better with catheters, which often came apart, and there was only an above-table monitor in isolation, so there were four places out of monitor where Elly could hold the children against her breast. She had no breasts, of course, but she knew about breasts from womantalk and could imagine them vividly. The little yellow one stirred in her arms like the faint breeze of the smaller air vents and Elly crooned to him with her noiseless breath. She was conscious of the beat of her own heart, as she laid the stethoscope on his chest and matched his heartbeat with a soundless song from her motionless lips. He squinted, gurgled, puckered his face and dribbled. He looked surprised, Elly laughed, Bessie danced in. What a funny looking one! Bessie said.

How many we got? Eleven, said Elly. Toss for the extra one? I'll take him. OK. Bessie didn't like the yellow ones: out of reach of the monitors she had told Elly that wrong colours were unlucky. Then she had remembered why Elly was the last error, and looked so contrite that Elly laughed and stroked Bessie's alabaster cheek and pulled gently on her fair, fair, hair.

Both women were worried about the little yellow one. Theoretically jaundice was a technical error, and Elly knew well why she *was* the last error: errors were now erased. The little yellow one was drowsy and to Elly's anxious eye getting yellower by the minute. Bessie looked at his temperature reading again and told Elly don't worry, we'll speed his fluids. Bessie knew how to do this but it was tricky. And they never knew when the supervisory team would drop in. The little yellow one yawned with more energy than he had shown yet. See! said Bessie with a glow of delight for Elly. They had to get out of there for rest hour.

Rest hour was really sex hour, but Elly and Bessie were old lovers and rarely performed except for the record: the house favoured sexual activity for recreation and for controlling energy. The two women lay on the couch side by side and talked about the little yellow one in a desultory way.

Maybe they meant him to be like that said Bessie, drowsily. We've had them before, though. Yeah. You sure weren't the last error . . . Elly, you're not an error, you're good. Good with the kids. Good to me. Loves you. Loves you, too.

Bessie dozed. Elly thought. She knew the little yellow one would be all right in a couple of days. He wouldn't die of jaundice, but he might die if the doctors valued a postmortem. Elly scolded herself: they don't want them to die, they're expensive. Only one had ever died that Elly remembered, and she had been in the early days of total-tech repro. She. She. Elly shook Bessie's shoulder gently.

Not asleep, Bessie said. When'd we last have a girl, Bess? Huh? A girl – When'd we last have a little girl? Not for ages. Elly moved her body, which suddenly felt stiff and heavy. Bessie offered to get her a drink. No. No thanks Bessie dear . . . Bessie? Uh-huh? Do you think they're not making girls any more?

Bessie didn't hoot, didn't laugh, didn't do anything but stare at the glossy ceiling. Bessie? Uh-huh? You do think that don't you? Don't know . . . Ko thinks so. Ko was Bessie's cook friend. He sometimes catered the tech officers' parties and heard lots of things, most of which he kept to himself. But he liked Bessie a lot, enough to defy the sex rules. Lots of people did for she had a sort of generous . . . what was that word that had been indexed a few years ago? Ah, yes. Spirit. Bessie had a generous spirit.

Bessie, you've got a generous spirit. Go on!! You have. You don't even like this job and you're always cheerful. Not cheerful, Elly. Don't care. You care about the babies. Uh-Uh. Bessie looked serious, though. Elly, it's true. We haven't had a girl in the last . . . oh! I don't know how many consignments. Fourteen, Elly said quickly. Yea. Fourteen. Elly, I checked with them at the North House . . . they haven't had girls either. They said it was a glitch that was being looked after . . . they said there was a general reduction . . . that the grey was dispersing and they were reducing population to speed up the dispersal. They said . . . oh, what does it matter. I didn't believe a word of it . . . Bessie was breathing hard, far harder than Elly had ever seen her breathe before, deeper than her sex breathing or her dance breathing, hard as a motor on the blink, rasping, hurting breathing.

I only care about you Elly. I care about you because you care about them and I don't care about anything much except you. It's because . . . Bessie stopped, struggling now for breath, red and crying. Crying. Water in her eyes, down her cheeks, funny noises in her nose, an incredulous expression on her face. Crying isn't allowed, Bessie sobbed. I'll be disciplined. But Elly had her body between Bessie and the screen. Because of what, Bessie? Because . . . there's nothing we can do. Come on, now. We can save the little yellow one. Bessie shook her head. They won't let us. All that stuff about perfection. They'll take him. Where to? Wherever it is. We'll all go there, but he won't reach his date. He's not supposed to be imperfect . . . perfect males, that's what they . . . She paused. You must know, Elly, that you aren't really the last error. Simply the last one to be allowed to survive.

Elly knew it was true. A curiosity, a freak, a barren brown woman who couldn't finally be anyone. None of her babies would ever recognize her, care for her. She had no children yet she had this great lump of pity in her breast for them. She didn't know what happened to them; she hadn't even visited the other house where, she supposed they grew up, grew to be men, to work in labs and flying machines and wait for the grey to disperse. It would never disperse, she suddenly saw, it was in their heads, it was reproduced all the time because they liked it. A world of bleak survival where only power mattered.

Elly shuddered, and Bessie started to cry again. Elly hugged her gently. We count, Elly said quietly, we count because we care . . . and we work. And we're friends.

They went back to the nursery. Elly checked the babies. The little yellow one was paler. Nothing like my skin really, Elly thought: mine is for keeps. Bessie slowly started to dance. Time isn't real any more, Bessie said. Yes it is, Elly said quite fiercely. The babies keep coming. An' goin' Bessie said. Just like us. Not much point in it, is there? Not much, but some, Elly said. They get born, somehow, and we watch over them and they grow.

Elly's tears dried, and she picked up the little yellow one and joined the dance.

Karen Malpede

BETTER PEOPLE
A surreal comedy about genetic engineering

'Better People' was first produced in February, 1990, by Theater for the New City, New York, with the aid of a generous grant from The Dietrich Foundations. The production was directed by Karen Malpede, setting by Victoria Petrovich, lighting by Carol Mullins, beast design by Basil Twist, music composed by Christopher Chesney. The cast was as follows:

DR HAILA GUDENSCHMARTZER	Eunice Anderson
DR EDWARD CHREODE	George Bartenieff
DR PHILBERT WALLACE	Tom Harris
DR THEODORA FORENSIC	Amy Galper
BEAST	Basil Twist
BABY BEAST	Carrie Sophia Malpede-Hash

‖ CHARACTERS ‖

DR HAILA GUDENSCHMARTZER, very, very old, the senior woman geneticist in the nation. A refugee from Hitler.

DR EDWARD CHREODE, her son, also a geneticist.

DR PHILBERT WALLACE, Chair of the Molecular Biology Department at this great university; president of Generecombo, Inc.; three-time winner of the Nobel Prize.

DR THEODORA FORENSIC, is the first woman born of the genes of two male Nobel Prize winning scientists. She is the brilliant young post-doctorate assistant to Dr Gudenschmartzer, later, head of her own laboratory.

THE BEAST, a Yak with Kudoo horns, a rare, near extinct species.

THE BABY-BEAST, with face of a human child, animal fur and baby horns.

‖ THE SETTING ‖

A single set represents the four laboratories. Stark and white, tall with sharp, surreal angles for walls. Four doors (two positioned against the back wall, one each on both side walls); the doors are also strangely shaped and are slightly small. Each small door is the doorway into the laboratory/office of a single scientist. The scientists' names are written backwards on their doors. One door has no name. After scene 5, it will become THEODORA's. *A set of over-sized double doors is upstage right. The double doors exit into a large, shared experimental laboratory, or operating room. In each scene, we enter the laboratory of the person whose door is used as an entrance. The hallway is behind the set. This set allows for seamless movement from scene to scene and its multiple doors enhance the comic and surreal aspects of the play. The set is rigged so that it can fall away, wall by wall, for the final transformation.*

‖ PROLOGUE ‖

The well-equipped, white laboratory is empty. An alarm goes off, as if there's been a leak of dangerous material in a lab. The siren sounds. Red lights blink off and on. The sound of scurrying feet. Of emergency showers. Inaudible, but alarmed voices. The first part of the prologue is played in slow-motion. The mood is eerie, dream-like. The scientists are dressed head-to-toe in white emergency suits. A door opens.

SCIENTIST #1: Where? When?
   [*Exits. Another scientist enters from another door. Speaks.*]
SCIENTIST #2: How? What do you mean?
   [*#2 exits. #3 enters one door.*]
SCIENTIST #3: Impossible!
   [*#3 exits. #4 enters.*]
SCIENTIST #4: Definite signs . . . warnings . . .
   [*#4 exits. The following dialogue takes place off-stage.*]
SCIENTIST #3: Impossible, I tell you.
SCIENTIST #1: Deadly . . .
SCIENTIST #3: Don't use that word . . .
SCIENTIST #4 [*enters*]: This is it, then . . .
SCIENTIST #2 [*enters*]: Call it back. Call it back now. Make it come home.
SCIENTIST #4 [*enters*]: New form of life. Can't call back.
SCIENTIST #3 [*enters*]: Statistically impossible!
SCIENTIST #1: Clean it up. Clean.
SCIENTIST #4: It's not toxic waste. It can't be cleaned up.
SCIENTIST #2: Grows on its own.
SCIENTIST #1: If the microecology of soil organisms is disrupted . . .
SCIENTIST #4: Catastrophic.
   [*They freeze.*]
SCIENTIST #3: Won't anyone listen to me? Statistically impossible!

SCIENTIST #4: Nevertheless, some got out.

SCIENTIST #3: Statistics say, it didn't happen at all.

[*They freeze.*]

SCIENTIST #1: Plug the leak. Bring it back.

SCIENTIST #2: Shut the doors.

[*They break from slow-motion movement to frantically running around implementing the safety precaution devices in the lab.*]

SCIENTIST #3: Flush . . . put on the lid.

SCIENTIST #1: Turn up the heat.

SCIENTIST #3: Turn that heat down!

SCIENTIST #4: Rain. Rain will wash it away.

[*#4 breaks into 'pagan' rain-dance; #2 joins.*]

SCIENTIST #2: Sunlight. Sunlight will kill it.

SCIENTIST #4: Let's hope for a freeze.

[*They freeze.*]

SCIENTIST #1: Impossible to think . . . we, in this lab . . .

SCIENTIST #2 [*sees something horrible*]: Oh, my god. No. I don't believe this . . .

SCIENTIST #3: Listen to me, for god's sake. Couldn't have happened this way. It will die in the air. It won't multiply.

SCIENTIST #2: Multiply? Oh, shit.

SCIENTIST #3: Watch yourself. Don't leak a word of this leak.

SCIENTIST #4: We've done what we can.

SCIENTIST #3: Don't anyone talk.

[*They move together in a huddle.*]

SCIENTIST #2: We've taken every precaution.

SCIENTIST #4: Let's get back to work.

SCIENTIST #3: I'll handle the report.

SCIENTIST #2: Let's make up a bug that will eat it!

SCIENTISTS #1, 2, 3, 4: Yes, yes. There's work to be done. Deadlines to meet. Back to work. That's best. Eat it! Of course! Work, yes, work. Work, what a relief!

[*They shake hands. Hug. Return to their labs.*]

Scene I

Philbert Wallace *enters* Edward Chreode's *lab*.

Philbert: Edward, Edward, the results. Come on, man. You're the last to turn your work in.

Edward [*gathering reams of computer print-outs, handing them to* Philbert]: I can't say I'm sorry to see the end of this.

Philbert: The end of it! You haven't seen the beginning, yet.

Edward: I suppose not.

Philbert: Aren't you proud? Aren't you thrilled? We've mapped the whole damn thing. It's our window into life. Everything we need to know . . . But I can't waste time now . . . so much hinges on my speech this afternoon.

Edward: We're all looking forward . . .

Philbert: You need inspiration, man, vision. A concrete sense of where we're going. You're not the only one. I just hope I've found the right words, the right tone. Edward, I hope I can pull this one off.

Edward: You'll be eloquent, I'm sure.

Philbert: Thanks, pal. It's so hard to know.

Edward: You'll be great.

[Philbert *exits.*]

Edward: Maybe I can find some time for my own work now that mess is out of here.

[Edward Chreode *falls asleep immediately at his lab bench. He is dreaming. An old woman appears. His mother,* Dr Haila Gudenschmartzer, *in a wheelchair. She points to a spot.*]

Haila: Die for me. There. On the ground.

Edward: Die? Mama, I don't know how to die.

Haila: Yes, you do.

[*She hands him a glass laboratory jar she has held on her lap.*]

HAILA: Take your soul out of the jar.

[*He takes out red glop.*]

HAILA: Feed it to me.

[*He does. She eats.*]

EDWARD: Thank you, I feel much better, now.

HAILA: You feel relieved.

EDWARD: Yes. I feel light. Freed.

HAILA: Of course. You've given your soul to me.

EDWARD: You've stuffed yourself. [*He wipes her mouth delicately.*] I used to love the chocolate traces hidden in the corners of your lips when you came home late from the lab. You looked so sweetly guilty then. Soul. It's an archaic concept, after all. A man doesn't actually have a soul. It's an idea. A thought. A chemical reaction in the brain. Odd how absolutely light I am. Untroubled now. Unburdened. Free, as I said. And, you, mama, how beautiful you look. Like a young girl. Let's dance.

HAILA: Yes, dance. Let's dance, Edward. Dance.

[*She rises delicately from the wheelchair, as if she were suddenly young again. Tango music. They tango passionately and talk.*]

HAILA: I wanted always to be young. I wished for a time of youth. That was all. Unfettered. Free. I wanted to be light of heart. I wanted beauty, adoration, love. Flowers delivered in white boxes. The moon shining on silk dresses. But I was pulled down. Destroyed. Made wise before I grew old.

EDWARD: That's over now. Over and done. All the betrayal. The loss. The wet cheek pressed against glass.

HAILA: I always only longed for gentleness. Gentleness and respect.

EDWARD: How I waited for you. How I waited to grow. Up. Large enough to hold you in my arms.

HAILA: There was always so much to do. So much needed to be done. To be thought. To be thought out. I sat alone at my bench. I knew how you cried. Do you think I didn't cry when life passed me by? I wanted peace, dignity, respect, lightness of heart, success. I wanted to be seen. Seen as I was. I wanted to win all the prizes. I wanted my theories accepted. I wanted the chair. The lab in my name. Dignity. Peace. Lightness of heart. I wanted love.

EDWARD: Here I am.

HAILA: All I ever wanted was gentleness.

EDWARD: Gentleness and respect.

HAILA: I won't let you go.

EDWARD: I know. You won't let me go.

[*He picks her up and carries her back to the wheelchair. Music stops. She is ancient again.*]

HAILA: Die for me. There on the ground.

EDWARD: Die? I don't know how to die.

HAILA: Yes, you do. There, on the ground. Where I can see.

EDWARD: I don't have to die. Not for you. I'm going out. I'm leaving the house.

HAILA: I have your soul. Your soul is mine.

EDWARD: Keep it. Who cares. I'm fine as I am. I'm light. I'm free. My soul would be upsetting to me.

HAILA: I have your soul in my mouth.

EDWARD: It's an archaic concept. 'Soul.' A man has no soul. He has his body, his mind. Information to process. Work to be done. He has what he controls. What he knows. He is what he is. What he can touch. What he can see. A man has no soul. Where would it be kept? It's insane. A meaningless concept. A useless word. 'Soul.' Absurd.

HAILA: I'm dying, my child.

EDWARD: No, Mama, don't. Don't do that.

HAILA: I'm dying. I am.

EDWARD: No. I won't let you go.

HAILA: I'm dying, now, with your soul in my mouth.

[*She slumps in her chair. He buries his head. Weeps.*]

EDWARD: Mama, Mama, come back.

HAILA [*she pops up*]: Here I am. Back as you asked. Soul? It's gone. Swallowed whole. Down the hatch. No worry, now. Do what I ask. Be. Be for me.

[*She wheels her chair forward. In fact,* HAILA GUDEN-SCHMARTZER *has just come in the door. He sees her.*]

EDWARD: Mother! You're here.

HAILA: Let's go, Edward. We're late.

[EDWARD CHREODE *wheels* HAILA GUDENSCHMARTZER *out the door.*]

SCENE II

The auditorium of this great university, where the NAT-IONAL ACADEMY OF SCIENCE *is meeting. As a* DISTINGUISHED SCIENTIST *takes his place behind the plexiglass podium and greets the assembled audience,* EDWARD CHREODE *wheels his mother,* HAILA GUDENSCHMARTZER, *into a front row seat, among the audience.*

HAILA: Not here, Edward, not here. Over there.

EDWARD: Here?

HAILA: Three. We need three seats.

DISTINGUISHED SCIENTIST: May we have order, please, order. Ladies and Gentlemen, Mr President, distinguished members of the National Academy of Science, welcome to this auspicious gathering. [*Applause*] This meeting marks a very special occasion. We gather together to celebrate the completion of the Human Genome Mapping Project. [*Applause*] We now know the precise location and the complete DNA sequence of each of the 100,000 human genes. We can now write down in exact detail all the genetic instructions for making a complete human being. [*Applause, again. He holds up his hands for silence.*] Yes, ladies and gentlemen, I know, it's absolutely intoxicating.

[*Throughout the scene,* HAILA *makes her remarks and elicits responses as 'under-talk' during the formal speeches of the scientists. The whispered dialogue is amplified and is delivered simultaneously with the speeches.*]

HAILA [*in a loud whisper*]: Yes, drunk on power, they all are. [*Spotting a late arrival.*] There she is. Stand up and wave to her, Edward. Theodora. Theodora Forensic, over here.

THEODORA [*stumbling across audience feet to them*]: How terrible to be late. Forgive me, please. I was caught up in the lab.

HAILA: Theodora Forensic, my new post doc, meet Edward Chreode, my son.

THEODORA: Dr Chreode, I'm so very glad to meet you.

EDWARD: Dr Forensic, my pleasure. Here, sit here. We've saved a seat on the other side of mother.

THEODORA: Thank you. How kind of you, Dr Guden-schmartzer. Have I missed much?

HAILA: The usual self-congratulatory clap-trap.

DISTINGUISHED SCIENTIST: Together scientific visionaries, venture capitalists, and the United States Government joined forces to create what I think we must all agree is the most significant accomplishment of the twentieth century. The map of the human genome is the first step in affording us complete mastery over the human gene pool. [*Applause*]

HAILA: And what will they do now? Make better people?

THEODORA: Oh, yes. Don't you think so . . .

EDWARD: I think there's something essential we haven't even formulated yet.

HAILA: If that's what you really think stop blathering about it, Edward, and get to work.

THEODORA: I'm afraid I don't follow what you're . . .

[*'Hush' sounds from the audience.*]

DISTINGUISHED SCIENTIST: Like the Manhattan Project of the 1940s, the Human Genome project of the 1990s has put America first in the areas of visionary scientific breakthrough, major technological accomplishment and renewed economic edge over the rest of the industrialized world.

HAILA: The Manhattan Project was the first scientific concentration camp in this country; this genome project has been the second.

EDWARD: Mother . . .

HAILA: Edward . . . you've done nothing for the past ten years but count proteins.

THEODORA: Dr Chreode, how thrilling.

DISTINGUISHED SCIENTIST: Among the eminent research scientists who joined forces to complete this massive project in record time, no one man deserves our thanks more than Dr Philbert Wallace. [*Applause*]

HAILA: Philbert Wallace is a self-serving fool.

EDWARD: Mother, please, you're not having breakfast with me, you're in a crowded room.

HAILA: Where I am does not alter the character of Philbert Wallace one slight bit.

EDWARD: Hush.

DISTINGUISHED SCIENTIST: Philbert Wallace, three time Nobel Prize-winning scientist and fortune 500 CEO who from his adjacent laboratories at this great university and offices at Generecombo, Inc. directed the mapping of more of the human genome than any other senior researcher.

HAILA: To think, I taught him everything he knows about science. I suppose his own mother is responsible for the corruption of his character.

THEODORA: Gene alteration is my special area of interest. Are you deeply involved, Dr Chreode?

HAILA: He sequenced genes *ad nauseam*. It's miraculous his brain is still in working order.

EDWARD: Mother, for god's sake, you can't keep talking like this . . .

HAILA: Can't I? Don't forget, Edward Chreode, I spoke up

against Hitler in '34. I criticized his mad eugenics program then and I did my time in a camp because of it.

DISTINGUISHED SCIENTIST: Dr Ladies and Gentlemen. Distinguished fellows of the National Academy of Science, may I present to you, Dr Philbert Wallace.

[*As the applause increases, and during the following dialogue, the actor who had played the* DISTINGUISHED SCIENTIST *turns around and takes off moustache or beard, changes ties, etc., becoming* PHILBERT WALLACE. *When the transformation is complete he begins his speech.*]

HAILA: Our kind ought to be unworldly, monkish. Philbert's a master politician. It's dangerous.

EDWARD: Mother, please, this isn't Germany; it's not 1934.

HAILA: Philbert's had Congress eating out of hands for the past ten years; and they've eaten plenty of shit.

[*Enormous applause for* PHILBERT WALLACE. *He holds up his hands for silence.* PHILBERT WALLACE *speaks with studied confidence and a smooth, ingratiating manner. He has learned how to win an audience.*]

PHILBERT: My fellow colleagues in this great enterprise, thank you very much for your warm enthusiastic welcome. You know, it's been said that a man has nothing until he has won the respect of his peers. If that's so, then I must be among the very richest men in the world.

HAILA: He's made a fucking fortune from science, science, which ought to be done for love.

EDWARD: Will you try to listen to Philbert's speech. Afterwards, you can judge.

HAILA: The arrogance appals me. The 'human genome' as if there were some single one.

EDWARD: Yes, well did it ever occur to you that insults aren't terribly effective?

HAILA: Mark my words, Edward Chreode, mark my words. An entirely new theoretical formulation is what's needed.

EDWARD: That's exactly what I'm working toward. A new vision.

HAILA: Well, hurry up. And stop doing shit work for Philbert Wallace.

EDWARD: How else does one fund oneself?

PHILBERT: You know it wasn't always this way. I remember days and weeks and months of people telling me I was nuts, that the human genome couldn't be mapped, that we didn't have the technology necessary to master such a task. Then there were the arduous and depressing congressional hearings spent answering our critics, the environmentalists, the feminists, the Catholic Church, even those few doubters within our ranks, people and organizations who for their own, I'm certain, honourable motives cling to the outmoded notion that human beings are not equipped to interfere with nature and that human knowledge itself ought to be limited. Well, let me tell you something right here and now, human knowledge is not limitable. Human knowledge is a god-given gift and we are here on this earth in order to carry out the greatest of all human projects, to join hands with nature, not against her, in the perfection of human life itself. [*Applause*]

THEODORA: Oh, I'm so excited to be sitting here, at this moment! Now that the genome has been mapped, human gene alteration is around the corner.

HAILA: Have you read any history along with all that science?

THEODORA: We're making history today.

HAILA: Regrettably.

EDWARD: Hush. He's about to acknowledge his colleagues.

HAILA: Memory. Memory! Where, in what gene, does the collective memory reside?

[*An amplified 'Shushhh', as if from all the people seated around* HAILA.]

EDWARD: Mother, you've got to be quiet now.

PHILBERT: Now, let me tell you something you might not already know. I wasn't always a research scientist. No, once I was a humble resident on a hospital ward and I saw, day in and day out, the suffering of human beings. I saw cancer deaths, heart attack deaths, deaths by stroke, deaths from genetic diseases like Parkinsons, Huntingtons, Cystic Fibrosis, Tay Sachs. One Christmas Eve, my esteemed friends and colleagues, I lost four beautiful children to the ravages of leukaemia. The deaths of those four innocent children on Christmas Eve drove me into the lab, ladies and gentlemen, fellow scientists. The deaths of those four innocent babes led me to devote the rest of my life to the two-pronged task of curing and preventing genetic defects in our young. The deaths of those four blameless children made me promise myself that I would not rest until the entire scientific community had been adequately mobilized against human suffering. Yes, I promised myself I would not rest until the human genome had been mapped. And I have not rested and we have brought this project home a full five years ahead of schedule. [*Applause*] And now that this enormous task has been accomplished, I want to renew my promise, in front of you and with you. I will not rest until the molecular biology community has learned how to prevent or to correct each and every terrible trick the human gene pool persists in playing on human beings. As the new millenium approaches, ladies and gentlemen, let's create a disease-free future for humankind!

Gene alteration is the *answer*, ladies and gentlemen. Once we learn how to alter genes we will hold the future in our hands. Gene alteration will allow us to cure, *in utero* or *in vitro*, any of the over 10,000 genetic maladies that are currently detectable, and many other malfunctions we don't even label as diseases, yet. With gene alteration, every couple's natural longing to achieve the best possible genetic make-up for each of their offspring will become a glorious reality. Once parents, acting in concert with The Recombinant DNA Advisory Commission are actually able to choose the physical and intellectual characteristics of their offspring who can doubt that a world of gods and goddesses awaits us? With gene alteration techniques under our belts, we will have become impervious to illness, to defects and, ultimately, even to death.

We have mapped the human genome, ladies and gentlemen, now we must use the wealth of information at our fingertips. Our goal is nothing less than genetic perfection for every American. This and only this is the great work before us. [*Deafening applause.*] Thank you. Thank you. Thank you very much.

HAILA: Reach into my bag, Edward Chreode; I've brought some ripe tomatoes just for this very moment.

EDWARD: Mother, everyone we know is here. I won't let you humiliate yourself like this.

HAILA: Theodora, hand me my tomatoes.

[*The three of them begin to move out of the auditorium;* EDWARD *wheels his mother's chair across the floor in front of the stage, where the following dialogue is played.*]

THEODORA: It's so inspiring, isn't it, Dr Chreode. Philbert Wallace is brilliant. Genetic Perfection. A disease-free world. Such a challenge is worth an entire lonely lifetime in a lab.

EDWARD: You've been bred to the task, haven't you?

THEODORA: You mean because I was born from two sperm inserted into an egg from which all the genetic material except the extra X had been previously removed. My fathers are feminist men. They made a bet with other less enlightened Nobel Prize winners that a woman might for once make a lasting mark on science.

HAILA: After all these years, my accomplishments aren't seen as major.

THEODORA: But, of course, I didn't mean to suggest . . . Your work on memory is supreme. [*She bends enthusiastically over* HAILA*'s chair, paying homage.*] You are the most highly esteemed woman scientist alive, Dr Gudenschmartzer. That's why I'm here. I felt the need of a strong female influence, since I never had a mother. I want to be a credit to my sex. I intend to perfect gene alteration techniques.

[*For a moment,* THEODORA*, her hand on her breast, gazes out into her glorious future.*]

HAILA: Listen to her, Edward, you need guts like that.

THEODORA: But you were involved in the genome mapping project weren't you, Dr Chreode.

EDWARD: Call me, *Edward* Chreode, please. My real work is something else. My wonderings are a bit diffuse right now. Difficult to pin down. But the speculations are endlessly fascinating. I do believe I'm on to something.

THEODORA: Could you introduce me to Dr Wallace, Dr Chreode? Gene alteration is the way to go. I have some rather concrete ideas for experiments.

HAILA: She'll marry the first Nobel Prize winner who asks her. She'll get money, patronage, a lab of her own; it all comes attached to his penis. And you, Edward, will never find a brilliant wife until you win the Prize.

EDWARD: Mother, I'm certain Dr Forensic and I . . .

HAILA [*ignoring* EDWARD*, to* THEODORA]: I created Edward Chreode by myself. He's fatherless. So that I might present a masculine antidote to their pseudo-scientific twaddle and gibberish. A compassionate man with a brain. That's what I meant him to be. [EDWARD *wheels his mother off-stage;* THEODORA *follows. The rest of the speech is heard as if it took place in the hall leading to the laboratory doors.*] A feelingful soul with a speculative flare. Edward, my dear, self-assertion comes so very hard to you. But now the time has come for you

to take a bold stab at a theory, publish, make yourself
known. Wheel me back to the lab. Edward, Theodora,
I feel the blood begin to thunder in my veins. We have
important work ahead.

[THEODORA *opens the door to* HAILA*'s lab. The two
enter.*]

SCENE III

HAILA GUDENSCHMARTZER *is wheeled in the door of her lab
by* THEODORA FORENSIC. HAILA *is still talking.*

HAILA: I am locating the exact spot where memory is
stored within the brain. I am very, very close to the solu-
tion, now.

[HAILA *holds up some papers containing research
results.* THEODORA *eyes them eagerly as she shuts the
door with one hand.* PHILBERT *opens the door just as
she shuts it.*]

PHILBERT: Haila, I need your ear.

[HAILA *quickly hides her research.* THEODORA *gapes at*
PHILBERT*, at her 'hero', but sees she is not expected to
stay as* HAILA *waves her away and she exits awk-
wardly.*]

HAILA: Pah. Philbert Wallace. When did you ever need
anything from me? Except my knowledge and that you
have pilfered, Philbert, to use for your own greed.

PHILBERT: You're the best teacher I ever had. I'm your
protegé.

HAILA: The best teacher of the biggest genetic mogul in
the nation is struggling away, as always, in an under-
equipped laboratory, underfunded, understaffed, under-
respected.

PHILBERT: Haila, gene alteration is around the corner. I
need your enthusiastic endorsement of my research
program.

[PHILBERT *takes the endorsement paper from his right lab coat pocket, flourishes it at her. She waves it away; she isn't going to sign.*]

HAILA: I thought your speech was a piece of shit, by the way.

PHILBERT: Always the kind word from you, Haila, always the kind word. You'll never understand how much your disapproval hurts me.

HAILA: I've offended you, Philbert, that's why my grants don't come through?

PHILBERT: I always vote in your favour. I'm a loyal man, Haila. Let's face it, you haven't been hot for a while.

HAILA: I've always been hot, Philbert. And you've always known how hot I've always been.

PHILBERT: Your lab is almost out of money. It's been a long time since you published anything. Now, if you don't want to turn your attention to gene alteration, it might finally be just the right moment for you to retire. I'll plan the festivities myself. Retire in style, OK?

[PHILBERT *puts the endorsement paper back into his pocket.*]

HAILA: Bullshit, Philbert. You ask that young genius who has just apprenticed herself to me. She understands better than any of you how close I am to solving the secret of memory – *by myself.* When I publish my results in a few months you won't even bother to read what I've found. I'm a woman. What could I know? I might even have been menstruating, polluting my results with unclean blood. That's how scientific you and your woman-hating scientific tribe are. I still do menstruate, by the way, Philbert. I like the smell of menstrual blood. I still menstruate because I'm still fertile. Not a one of you read the paper explaining how I accomplished that. You're too busy making babies in petri dishes.

PHILBERT: What did you say, Haila?

HAILA: I still menstruate. I still bleed.

PHILBERT: I'll take you out for dinner, you can tell me about your private life. Right now, let's talk science. Let's talk brain, mind, memory. At the Top of the Sixes, I'll get us a nice table, you can continue your feminist diatribe over the beef. Maybe my speech was a little gisty, after all. I wasn't altogether pleased. Maybe I should have come right out and said all we need from the whole messy process are the eggs. Now what did you say about memory?

HAILA: You keep your hands off my eggs, Philbert Wallace. I can still conceive quite nicely on my own. Give birth naturally and be back in the lab, the kid strapped to my belly, within a week. I would prove it to you, if I was able to find a man with genetic and moral fibre equal to my own. But you all have always been a swine. In a month, I'll understand human memory.

PHILBERT: Haila, if you weren't such a damn fine scientist I'd never be able to put up with you.

HAILA: In a month, I'll know exactly *where and how* memory is stored within the brain. I'm on the verge of understanding everything.

PHILBERT: That's the stuff, Haila. Get me a full report today. I'll put you on full retainer at Generecombo, Inc.

HAILA: Don't patronize me, young man. I'm not the least bit interested in the commercial applications of my pure research. Give me the money I need because of my brilliant mind.

[*Triumphantly,* HAILA *hands* PHILBERT *the proof, her research results. He takes the papers, reads; becomes convinced and excited. Immediately he's off into his own world of products and profits.*]

PHILBERT: The control of human memory. That's marketable. We win the public's sympathy by offering it up as a cure for Alzheimer's disease (which I forgot, by the way, to mention in my speech). An ethics committee will be convened by the boys in Congress. Who is worthy of having a memory, that sort of thing. Meanwhile, who can resist? It's science. It's progress. It's truth. Haila, I knew you'd come through for me in the end.

[PHILBERT *offers his hand for her to shake. She refuses, swings her chair away.*]

HAILA: Not so fast, Philbert Wallace, I want the Nobel Prize for this. My life's work. I want to die with the Prize in my hand. I want my eggs frozen alongside all that sperm in the Nobel sperm bank. I want equality at last.

PHILBERT: Haila, I'm offering you millions.

HAILA: I want the Prize, Philbert.

[*Pause. He looks at the results again. Decides.*]

PHILBERT: OK, OK. I'll see what I can do.

HAILA: So you think I'm hot, at last, Philbert.

PHILBERT: Haila, there's no one in science whose integrity and accomplishments I admire more. You've stuck to the good, hard, theoretical work; you've never profiteered from science. You're a well-known supporter of liberal causes; you're an old-line feminist, a refugee from Hitler and a single mother to boot. You've got principles, Haila. You deserve the Nobel Prize. I'm glad to have you on our team.

[*He offers his hand, again. This time she takes it. They shake.*]

HAILA: And you, Philbert, are a slippery, self-important prick who was badly toilet trained. But, I'm glad to be included on your team.

PHILBERT: With the Prize under your belt, you will finally be taken seriously. So, Haila, I must have your complete support.

[*He puts her research paper into his left lab coat pocket then takes a contract from his inside jacket pocket, flourishes it in front of her.*]

PHILBERT: This is Generecombo's standard option

agreement. It gives the company complete rights to market any and all memory control products we invent based upon your pure research. It also gives you quite a handsome advance.

[PHILBERT *pencils a large $ figure into the contract. Hands it to her.*]

PHILBERT: Sign it.

[HAILA *reads quickly, signs. He takes it back.*]

PHILBERT: And, Haila, no more displays like the one I witnessed at my speech. [*He comes quite close to her.*] You may humiliate me in private only. [*He pulls back and begins to pace.*] You know, Haila, I was disappointed in my speech, myself. It lacked nerve. The truth is I got scared. I cut out the most radical part. I had intended to offer a concrete gene maximization plan. I was going to suggest that we simply remove the genetic material from each individual immediately after birth and then promptly sterilize that individual. The idea's been around for a long time, of course. During each individual's lifetime, records would be kept of accomplishments and characteristics. After the individual's death, a committee decides if those genes are worthy of procreation into other individuals. If so, genetic material would be removed from the depository, mated suitably, and implanted into a surrogate. If not, the genetic material is destroyed. How simple, elegant, direct. But at 3 a.m., I cut the paragraph out. I shouldn't have done that, should I?

[*But* HAILA *has fallen asleep in her chair.*]

PHILBERT: Haila, are you listening? That old trick again. What a pig-headed, impossible woman. And you've always been this way whenever I really needed you in my corner. [*He whispers to her sleeping face.*] You had better not make a fool out of me, Haila. You had better come through; I've invested in you.

[PHILBERT *exits in a huff;* DREAM MUSIC *and* LIGHTS. HAILA

*rises out of her wheelchair and exits through the large
double doors.* EDUARD SCHNEIDER, *played by the actor
who plays* EDWARD CHREODE, *sits weeping in the
middle of* HAILA*'s dream. He is talking, as if he is a
split personality, to himself.*]

EDUARD #1: Don't cry, Eduard.

EDUARD #2: Why shouldn't I cry? I wanted to be like
other people. I'm not like them at all.

EDUARD #1: It's wrong to cry about that. You can't help
the way you are.

EDUARD #2: Other people have inner lives. They have
places they can get to. Places they can hide. Other
people have private thoughts.

EDUARD #1: Yes, Eduard. Be proud. You've been asked to
give up so much. You can live without an inner life.

EDUARD #2: But I must cry. I must grieve. I must mourn.

EDUARD #1: Buck up, Eduard. You still look fine. It's
important to pretend. Think of your grandmother. No
one ever knew she was a Jew.

EDUARD #2: All my life, I've pretended to do the right
thing. But I'm not what they say. I remember when I
could see the whole distance round the world. I had
the whole vision, then. I saw everything.

EDUARD #1: So what. Do you think anyone cares about
you?

EDUARD #2: Why do you make me cry? What's the
purpose in that. If I cry, I can't feel anything. And I
used to have feelings of my own. When I looked
around and saw everything. I saw joy inside everyone.

EDUARD #1: Shut up, Eduard, don't go soft on me. That
sort of talk is better unheard. You're not like other
people, Eduard. You do what you're told. You give
what you're asked. You sacrifice.

EDUARD #2: No. Stop. I had an idea. I had a thought. A
thought came into my head. This time, this time, I am
going to try. I am going to try to show who I am.

[EDUARD SCHNEIDER *writes his letter.*]

Dear Herr Doktor Wirths:

I must refute this charge of imbecility with schizophrenic tendencies, since I am capable of writing and of doing arithmetic without error and without outside help. For this reason, I would like to request another physical examination.

[*Dr* WIRTHS, *played by the actor who plays* PHILBERT WALLACE, *enters with* HAILA, *playing herself as a young woman.* DR EDUARD WIRTHS *was soon to become one of the chief doctors, i.e. killers, at Auschwitz. Tall, handsome with Aryan looks, he is also bizarrely gentle and kindly (as indeed the real* WIRTHS *was known for his compassionate care of patients, even as he oversaw the killing of millions). A committed Nazi, devoted husband and father,* WIRTHS *believes he is doing his duty purifying the German race. In other words,* WIRTHS *is the true split personality, the killer/doctor in one body.* HAILA'*s dream memory intensifies these characteristics;* WIRTHS'*s split is boldly portrayed.*]

WIRTHS: Good morning Herr Schneider.

[*He takes the letter, pockets it.*]

WIRTHS: I have received your most impressive letter. Fräulein Doktor will perform another examination on you. Sterilize him, Fräulein. Inject this caustic substance through the urethra. It will block the testes. Check him in a week. If gangrene has set in, amputate. Don't be afraid, Herr Schneider. You see, I've brought you a beautiful young woman doctor. What could possibly go wrong. She'll be won completely over by your charm. Sterilize him, now, Fräulein.

[WIRTHS *exits.*]

EDUARD: You are a nice lady. I can see that.

HAILA: Don't count your chickens before they hatch.

EDUARD: That's just it. I can't help doing that. Everyone must. It's human. I feel that it is. I don't want to be sterilized.

HAILA: Whoever put that idea into your head. I've come to speak with you a bit, take your blood and do a sperm count. Here, masturbate into this jar.

EDUARD: I'm not as young as I was. Well, maybe I will never marry. I wanted to marry this year. Maybe the woman I love will not want to marry me. I wouldn't marry except for love. I know how to love, I do.

HAILA: I've had thirty-nine lovers, I've given myself five abortions. I've cured myself three times of pelvic inflammatory disease and of countless yeast infections. I'm the last woman in Berlin who remembers the erotic life.

EDUARD: It's because they found out I have a Jewish grandmother. That's why they are doing this. I'm not stupid, you know. I'm no dumber than lots of them in uniform.

HAILA: I had a Jewish lover, once. But he asked for too much.

EDUARD: Maybe you have been hurt in love. Too many times. I'm a dairy herdsman. I work with cows. But I've got my dreams.

HAILA: Yes, yes, you can dream.

EDUARD: You know, I thought, if we two could talk. If we could share, well, you won't be able to do what they want done.

HAILA: I'm here on orders. Routine examination only.

EDUARD: I could love a woman. I know I could.

HAILA: You're not done. Quickly, finish up before he comes back. It's a simple mechanical thing. I just need a sperm count. We are doing a comparison rating. Do Jewish men produce more sperm? It's pure science. Pure research.

EDUARD: I believe the amount of sperm produced must have to do with the amount of love felt. I believe it's the passion at the moment of conception which determines the joy in the soul of the unborn.

HAILA: Now, then, I just must give you this injection.

*[She injects his penis with the caustic substance.
Sound of machine gun fire. His body reacts in a
spasm to the pain.]*

EDUARD: No, no, why did you have to do that? I begged
you. I pleaded with you. I looked into your eyes. I
shared my dreams. I believed in tenderness. I believed
in love.

HAILA: Buck up, Eduard Schneider. Buck up. These are
hard times. None of us does what we want. We are
struggling to stay alive. Go home. Forget about this.

EDUARD: You expect me to forget?

HAILA: Look, I've saved your sperm. They wanted to
destroy it.

*[HAILA looks at the (imaginary) sperm-jar. 'Why did I
save this?' she silently asks herself. Then she knows.]*

HAILA: I'm going to have a child with this. I'm going to
inject myself. I will sex select. I will make a son. A
noble, gentle, brilliant man. A boy-child with your soul,
my brains. I've had counts, classicists, artists, actors,
professors of chemistry, biology, physics, poetry,
history, politicians and judges, psychiatrists. You are
the only man I've desired a child with.

EDUARD: What will become of him? What will become of
my son? He missed out from the start. Never to feel the
shock of collision between egg and sperm. Never to
feel the light of my love? How I sought him
everywhere with every thrust, never to hear my shout,
my shout of triumph when he was formed?

[PHILBERT WALLACE as WIRTHS returns.]

WIRTHS: Finished, Fräulein, I hope.

HAILA: Yes. Everything is as you wished.

WIRTHS: We killed two birds with one stone.

*[WIRTHS sends EDUARD SCHNEIDER's wheelchair rolling
towards the double doors. SCHNEIDER disappears.]*

WIRTHS: An idiot and a Jew. It must make you feel proud,
Fräulein, to be a woman in 1934, at the forefront of
eugenic science. I'm going to recommend you for

promotion. There are some very interesting experiments soon to begin at several major hospitals here in Berlin. We will soon have access to unlimited experimental material. We are entering a golden age of science. Of racial purification and advanced reproductive techniques. I'm going to recommend a transfer and a promotion for you.

[HAILA *falls back into her chair, jerks awake, screams.*]

HAILA: Edward! Edward, my son!

[EDWARD *rushes in. Like many children of concentration camp survivors, he's been through camp nightmares many times before.*]

EDWARD: You're not in the camps, mother, you're here, in the lab, with me.

HAILA: The beatings. My back. My back. The horrible pressure on my spine.

EDWARD: It's all over, now.

HAILA: I ran, I ran. For the last time, I walked by myself.

EDWARD: You're safe in the lab with me.

HAILA: Why, Edward, is it always pain? Pain so vivid, biting at us?

EDWARD: Calm, mother, calm.

[*Suddenly, she wakes fully out of her dream.* HAILA *is fully present. An important new thought has come into her head because of the dream and waking moment she just had.*]

HAILA: Edward, I've been wrong all along. Memory cannot be stored in the brain. Memory is lodged in the flesh. The body, the organs, the cells, the hormones, the glands feel the memory first, before we are conscious of it.

[*She pauses for a moment, following this thought through to its next question.*]

HAILA: But where has the memory been, Edward? Tell me that. Where is memory kept? In the body, itself, or somewhere else? Leave me, now, go. I must think it through.

SCENE IV

EDWARD CHREODE *enters his lab and begins to work.*
PHILBERT WALLACE *enters just behind.*

PHILBERT: Hallo, Edward.

EDWARD: Philbert, come in. A most impressive speech.

PHILBERT. That's not what your mother said.

EDWARD: You know mother, a most difficult one.

PHILBERT: Listen, pal, I've got a plum for you. Huge contract. Major grant.

EDWARD: Philbert, that's very kind.

PHILBERT: Fortunately, I'm in the position to take care of my own.

EDWARD: I'm honoured, touched.

PHILBERT: Edward, you're in line for promotion, at last. From associate to full professor, finally. Only . . . you've hardly published a thing. You're not very good at getting grants.

EDWARD: Well, perhaps. Philbert, I'm thinking out a major theory. It's slow work, not easy.

PHILBERT: Edward, I, for one, have faith in you.

EDWARD: Philbert, I'm onto something *big*.

PHILBERT: How would you like a small fortune for research? Prestige? An inside track on what's happening, what's hot?

EDWARD: Well, of course . . .

PHILBERT: Fascinating research. Necessary to the US. You can do your own thing on the side. Which, by the way, is what?

EDWARD: Thoughts far-ranging. Problems of creation and form, mysteries of epigenesis, of regeneration, embryological speculations. How does form come into being for the first time? Why can certain damaged organs grow again? Biology's unsolved problems. Recently, I can't quite tell you why, I've become rather obsessed with the problem of extinction. What happens to the life force of the extinct, or soon to be so?

PHILBERT: What sort of question is that? Life force, it's an archaic concept.

EDWARD: Your speech led me to thinking that we ought to prepare for future extinctions by freezing the genetic material of endangered species so that we might regenerate them in future times, under more auspicious environmental conditions.

PHILBERT: Perfect, Edward. How soon can you get some general papers out? I'll see they're placed in the environmental magazines. We need precisely this sort of visibility at this great university. It provides you with a perfect cover.

[EDWARD *is thrilled*. PHILBERT *moves in very close*.]

PHILBERT: Edward, we need your help manufacturing a new, lethal virus (as a vaccine, of course, as an antidote, not, according to Geneva, to be used as a first-strike) for the Department of Defense. Will you say yes?

EDWARD: I don't think I really could consider that.

PHILBERT: A great deal is at stake. Personally, professionally and for our country.

EDWARD: This stuff is dangerous. It's cultured in the E-coli bacterium which lives quite naturally in the human intestine. What if it got out?

PHILBERT: We build safety doors. Better you be the one than someone less environmentally inclined.

EDWARD: Oh, I don't know about that. My mind, at present, is quite occupied.

PHILBERT: This DOD contract will fund your passion, man. If I might be frank, there's no way the problems you just outlined will bring in the grants, not with the current administration. No way the current faculty can grant you the promotion. In contrast, slipping a little lethal virus into the E-coli bacterium might help us understand gene alteration! Be altruistic, if you wish, your country needs you. Stop thinking always of yourself. For us, here at this great university, a contract from the DOD is not to be sneezed away. Take an hour to think it over. I'll pop in again.

[PHILBERT *exits.* EDWARD, *disappointed and confused, sits down at his desk where he falls asleep immediately.* DREAM MUSIC AND LIGHTS. HAILA *comes racing in madly in her wheelchair, beginning the Dream Image.*]

HAILA: Edward, I need, I need, I need. I have needs, Edward Chreode, needs. I have needs which must be met.

EDWARD: Yes, yes, of course.

HAILA: Give me your legs, Edward Chreode. I need them for mine.

[*He sits heavily on useless legs. She rises and walks.*]

HAILA: You must grab opportunity when it knocks. I rose to the top. By hard work, sacrifice, good common sense. Love, there was no room for love. I had lovers, I had plenty of those. But they couldn't stand on their own.

EDWARD: I can, Mama, I can stand up.

[*He tries to pull himself up by holding onto her. She brushes him off. He falls.*]

HAILA: They used me, each one. Weaklings. Sapped my strength.

EDWARD: Don't give your legs away, Edward Chreode. No, next time, I won't. I didn't really give them up. Not my own two feet. I kept my feet for myself. Legs can regenerate. It's a marvellous fact. The damaged organ regrows itself. Cut it off. It comes back. Grows again. Cut it off. It returns. What a marvellous fact.

HAILA: Edward, give me your head. I want to think a thought worthy of me through to the end.

[EDWARD CHREODE'*s head goes limp on his neck.*]

HAILA: It was always so difficult simply to be. To be strong. To be self-willed, purposeful. Not to succumb.

[PHILBERT *enters, wearing a straitjacket.*]

PHILBERT: Will you shut up Haila. Look at this. Your son

let lethal bacteria leak from his lab. Three hundred thousand innocent civilians are expected to die.

HAILA: Is Edward all right? Did Edward survive?

EDWARD [*crawls to her*]: Mama, I have collected their genes. The genes of all the condemned are in glass jars underground.

PHILBERT: Luckily, the undernourished, over-medicated, drugged and despised will be first to succumb. Assure the population at large that everything's fine.

EDWARD: Out back, beneath the cement, I've stored all their traits. We will recreate each last one. Babies in their cribs. Octogenarians. Lovers entwined in their beds. I've stolen their genes to make them again.

THEODORA [*bursts in wearing blood-covered lab coat, carrying a baby doll*]: Look at my child. She's dead. She died.

EDWARD: Oh, my god, did you take out her genes? Did you save one of her eggs?

THEODORA: She was a test tube baby. Do you know how long I worked to make her? Do you have any idea of what I went through?

PHILBERT: Call in the press. This is a perfectly acceptable level of environmental distress.

THEODORA: I'm going to sue. She was a perfect child. Blond, blue-eyed. High IQ.

HAILA: We need protest marches, boycotts, riots. A good disaster rouses the blood.

PHILBERT: Half a million have died. The plague is spreading. The DOD wants no part of this. We need a high-toned memorial meeting. We need some good public grieving.

EDWARD: I will make her, again. I swear. Perfect as she was before.

THEODORA: Five procedures to flush the eggs out. Five punctures of the vaginal wall. Hundreds of diagnostic tests. Hormones, minerals, vitamins, scans, bed rest.

EDWARD: On my honour, as a man of my word, I will

recreate each lost life, from their own genetic material which I have carefully stored in the back yard. I just have to crawl out there. I just have to dodge the lethal bacteria. I knew something would happen someday. We all knew it, didn't we? That's why I collected their genes. The genes of the innocent ones. I stored them in a deep freeze. Next to the orange popsicles.

HAILA: Nothing like a disaster to bring people together. Now they'll understand how stupid, lethargic, weak-minded, deluded they have been all along. Trusting science to set it right! Take it from someone who knows the field. It's idiotic. Absurd.

PHILBERT: The DOD can't be bothered with this.

EDWARD: If only I had my legs back. If only I had the use of my head.

HAILA: Yes, we organized. We resisted. In the camps, underground. We refused. We suffered for our ideals.

PHILBERT: The DOD wants no part of this.

THEODORA: Foetal heart monitors. Caesarian. Neo-natal intensive care. Hundreds of thousands of team hours, dollars. What a blessing she was. What a right.

EDWARD: If I could only think straight. Maybe I could remember how they all were, rushing around. I can put them back just like that. They will regenerate.

HAILA: Come, come, Edward, screw your head on straight. Get off your behind. There's work to be done. Disaster is a challenge for those who move fast. Seize opportunity when it knocks. Your work on extinction can profit off this. You won't be their dupe. You'll know what to do. You'll use them. They won't use you.

[HAILA *falls back into her chair, and wheels herself out.* EDWARD *wakes abruptly.* PHILBERT WALLACE *enters.*]

PHILBERT: So, Edward, what do you say? It's a tasty offer, isn't it?

EDWARD: Philbert, don't be upset. I really think not.

PHILBERT: Don't be a fool, Edward, don't destroy your career.

EDWARD: It's really not in my line.

PHILBERT: Your country needs you, Edward.

EDWARD: E-coli live in the human intestine. If it were to escape.

PHILBERT: You alter the strain, make it weak.

EDWARD: What about the probability of adaptive mutation?

PHILBERT: Edward, for god's sake, lighten up. What's life without risk? If I thought the way you do, I'd never get out of bed.

EDWARD: Plague is possible.

PHILBERT: Possible. Possible. Are you seriously suggesting we halt the progress of the scientific effort because something awful might result?

[*Pause. They look at one another.* EDWARD *doesn't know how to answer this line of thought.*]

PHILBERT: This research is necessary . . . not only to the DOD but to us, here, in this laboratory. Gene alteration techniques might hinge on what you learn. Do you understand? Edward, I'm making you my right-hand man.

EDWARD: But reasonable caution.

PHILBERT: Reasonable caution, fine, fine. I like your approach, Edward. You're careful, you're steady, you're sure. Don't louse yourself up, Edward. How explicit do you expect me to be?

EDWARD: I'd want to take every precaution. No one would know what we're doing.

PHILBERT: My secret and yours. We're going to find out some crucial information. Let the DOD pay for it. *Our real work is to end human suffering.*

EDWARD: Well, Philbert, put like that . . . How could I . . . I owe you so much.

PHILBERT: I'll go ahead and notify the DOD. You can start culturing the new virus immediately. And, Edward, exercise caution. This stuff is dangerous.

SCENE V

The double-doors swing open; HAILA *and* THEODORA
FORENSIC *are in the midst of a serious conversation.* HAILA
is filled with excitement; THEODORA *is worried, depressed.*

HAILA: So, memory is *not* stored within the brain.
THEODORA: But you've invalidated years of your own
research.
HAILA: Now we go out again, into the unknown.
THEODORA: But an entirely new set of experiments needs
to be thought through.
HAILA: Of course.
THEODORA: But I don't have the slightest idea where to·
start.
HAILA: Ask yourself. Where can memory be, do you
suppose?
THEODORA: But . . .
HAILA: This is science, my dear. Constant ignorance.
Constant bliss . . . because what we will discover now
will be far more beautiful than what we have
disowned.
[HAILA *wheels herself back out the double doors.*]
THEODORA [*to herself*]: Just when I thought I'd have more
time for my own research.
[*The phone rings.* THEODORA *is clearly exhausted; she's
been trying to keep up with* HAILA *'s changing
demands plus pursue her own research at night.
Throughout the following phone call, she chews
ravenously on a squished candy bar she finds in her
lab-coat pocket.*]
THEODORA: Yes. Yes. This is she. I know. I know. I'm
sorry. I know. Still, it does not seem to me that three,
even four or five first trimester abortions are too great
a price to pay to achieve a perfect baby, if you still
want a genetically connected child. [*Silence*] But you
are carrying defective genes. Abort, wait two months.

Try again. [*Silence*] Yes, I know the *Times* did report my astonishing success, but that was with mice.

[PHILBERT WALLACE *opens the door a crack, stops to listen to the phone call.*]

THEODORA: The press exaggerates. [*Silence*] No, it has nothing to do with cost. Look, I don't have my own lab. It's even difficult for me to talk. The technology has not been perfected yet. I have no time. [*Silence*] I'll phone you in for the abortion. Try again. [*Silence*] You can always go the surrogacy route. Implant a healthy egg and sperm. There is no longer any worry about custody suits; you can use a brain-dead foetal nurturer. They're reporting great success utilizing these neomorts. [*Silence*] I'll get you a list of available wombs on life-support systems. Think over your options. [*Silence*] Crying won't help.

[PHILBERT WALLACE *enters.*]

THEODORA: Someone's just come in. I must get off the line. Make yourself some tea. Read a book. Go shopping!

[*She hangs up the phone, throws her clipboard on the floor.*]

THEODORA: Women! She's set herself up as a broodmare.

PHILBERT: You know how it is, Theodora, for a woman the need to procreate is all.

THEODORA: No, Philbert. I don't know how it is. The need to procreate doesn't show itself in me. The need to master gene therapy – that I feel. If I could get inside this weeping woman, now, with a needle, and stick a good gene on so she could have her perfect child in peace! That, Philbert, would be my destiny fulfilled.

PHILBERT: And you will, Theodora. Patience. Perseverance.

THEODORA: It's so damn frustrating, Philbert, to know so much . . .

[*Her glasses off, she stares, nearsightedly, into* PHILBERT's *face. They gaze at one another.*]

PHILBERT: Odds are one among us will figure it out, this year or next.

[PHILBERT *begins to move towards her;* THEODORA *backs away from him, as he moves her around the table.*]

PHILBERT: Too many of us are right on the verge. Our business is simply to make certain the final breakthrough happens here. In these laboratories.

[*They end standing close together in the middle of the room.* PHILBERT *whispers seductively.*]

PHILBERT: Theodora, you need money, technicians, peace of mind.

[THEODORA *is thrilled.*]

THEODORA: Oh, yes, Philbert, I do. I do. That's exactly what I need!

[*He continues coming towards her, and she backs across the room to the wall.*]

PHILBERT: I can give you that.

[*She is ecstatic. He keeps coming at her, backing her up against the wall.*]

PHILBERT: Then once we get gene therapy under our belts, we'll be set. For those who can pay the price, there will be no limits to perfectibility of the race. The human gene pool will be ours to endlessly manipulate. Of course, selective abortion will always be cheaper, easier.

[*He falls on his knees in front of her, his arms pinned to the wall on either side of her.*]

PHILBERT: Theodora, you possess the perfect genes and so do I. Together we can make a dynasty. Will you marry me?

[*She leaps in fright.*]

THEODORA: Philbert, please get up. I can't marry yet. I haven't proven myself.

[*She gets away from him. He follows her, until during this speech he has backed her into the table. She leans back on the table and he comes down on top of her, as if to kiss her.*]

PHILBERT: I'll set you up in your own laboratory. You'll be in complete control of your life. Face it, Theodora, human gene alteration therapy is for those with flaws. But among the intellectual elite, genetic perfection already exists. We can become the models for everyone else.

[*Just before his lips reach hers,* PHILBERT *pulls away. He goes upstage to the blackboard to illustrate his plan.* THEODORA *sits, stunned, listening to him.*]

PHILBERT: Here's my plan. We harvest a mere ten eggs per month from your ovaries, after multiple ovulation has been induced with injected drugs. We can fertilize those ten eggs *in vitro* with my sperm, collected fresh, or if I am feeling overworked, from the frozen stock already deposited in the Nobel sperm bank. Each zygote would be cultured to the blastocyst stage *in vitro*, and screened for any unforeseen mutation before being implanted into a surrogate class of women, created from our immigrant or homeless populations, or, as you just said, from our newly dead. Unburdened, Theodora, by childbearing, you would keep on making your genetic contributions to succeeding generations. Practised monthly for twenty-five years, the strategy I've just outlined would produce 2,910 offspring. I know that isn't much. But coupled with the efforts of an internationally select group of gene donors equal in stature to ourselves, a small, but powerful genetically elite intelligentsia could be created in our lifetime. Think of how humanity would benefit.

[PHILBERT *comes back, kneeling again in front of her.*]

PHILBERT: Theodora, be my wife. I adore you. I want to enter the gene pool with you.

[HAILA *wheels herself in, recklessly.*]

HAILA: Philbert, get up from that ridiculous position. I need to speak with my assistant.

PHILBERT: I want you for eternity. I'll set you up in your own laboratory.

HAILA: Cut the crap, Philbert. You want to use her brains to speed your own research. But she's my post doc.

PHILBERT: She's perfect. Look at her. I feel the way Dante felt for Beatrice. It's not her brains I want. She can keep them for herself. I promise her intellectual freedom and respect. By the way, Haila, I need your memory work. The market research boys are getting antsy.

THEODORA [*looking at the paper* HAILA *has handed her*]: But, Haila, these experiments will keep us busy for years!

HAILA: Then we'd better get started, hadn't we?

PHILBERT: Theodora, a lab of your own. [*He exits.*]

HAILA: Philbert, you're a thief.

THEODORA: He's asked me to marry him and give him all my eggs.

HAILA: And set you up in your own lab.

THEODORA: Yes.

HAILA: Are you ready for your own lab? That's the real question. Not whether you love him, which you don't.

THEODORA: Of course, I don't love him.

HAILA: But he'd make you a powerful, well-funded woman.

THEODORA: Yes.

HAILA: You can always take a lover in your spare time.

THEODORA: I don't have spare time. I need three years of funding and peace of mind.

HAILA: And, so, you would abandon me at this crucial moment?

THEODORA: But, Haila, I have to solve gene alteration techniques . . . your memory work is . . .

HAILA [*she silences* THEODORA *with her hand*]: Can't those famous fathers of yours set you up in a funded lab?

THEODORA: Their bet was I could make it on my own.

HAILA: Marry Philbert, then. He'll support your work and he won't distract you with his emotional needs. Philbert's completely blocked.

THEODORA: At least he doesn't want sex.

HAILA: When I was your age, I used to have my lovers in the lab. Make love, take a bath, do an experiment, make love. I'm the last woman alive who remembers the erotic life.

THEODORA: The erotic life doesn't interest me. I must get back to work. Can Edward drive you home? It's late.

HAILA: Don't stay all night.

[THEODORA *falls immediately to sleep at her lab bench. DREAM IMAGE*]

[*Voices of* SCIENTISTS *on tape. Their large, grotesque shapes are seen through the plexi-glass windows of the large double door. As* THEODORA *lies sleeping on the table, her belly grows large. She wakes, very pregnant, stands drowsily, rubbing her big belly.*]

VOICE: All right, that's it. Here's to a job well done. The caucasian gene pool is officially declared free of defect.

VOICE: Wait, what's that bleep on the screen?

VOICE: That's Theodora Forensic.

VOICE: She got herself pregnant by natural means.

VOICE: She's joined the herbal underground.

VOICE: Found herself a midwife.

VOICE: How thoroughly disgusting.

VOICE: She's refused amniocentesis, sonograms, mitos-phychosyntheses, DNA analysis, genetic counselling, growth hormone.

VOICE: Why didn't someone grab her and make her take the tests?

VOICE: This is still a free country.

VOICE: Of course, a technocracy.

[THEODORA *walks dreamily out the double doors into the arms of the doctors.*]

VOICE: At what age can the foetus bring suit?

[THEODORA FORENSIC *appears at a lab door. She is wheeling a chair on which sits the talking head of* EDWARD CHREODE, *her new-born, bodiless child. He is babbling uncontrollably as his head rolls, egg-like, on*] *the seat.* THEODORA *dotes on him, arranging his cap, and the blankets around his neck as he talks.*]

EDWARD: Just like Sam Beckett, I retain a vivid memory of my mother's womb. I was carried, I said, with my head outside the universe. The body inside, inside her, that one there who pushes my chair. But the head floated free in a space unexplored, a space denied, the space beyond space. Outside the universe, my head through a black hole in the firmament, I saw and I contemplated all. It occurred to me, free floating in space, my head through a medium-sized black hole in the universe, that there is a transcendent cause, that some vast intelligence rules and we are the creatures of what this great thinking pulse is. I saw. There I saw. No surprises, no. Nothing new. Nothing to tell. Nothing to tell, because there is no one to hear. No one to listen to me. No hearers. Nothing heard from the head that once floated free from beyond the beyond. And suddenly saw the divine cause, the implicate order, rising in waves, and felt, yes, felt through the tremors in the iris of the eye, free floating the past being present, wave after wave of form giving form. The future attracting the past, pulling the past after it. The future desiring itself, attracting, pulling at form. And I being formed by everyone unusual who had ever lived, a talking head come from beyond, a bearer to earth of forms about to be lost. And I felt myself into each one. Yes, with my eyes, with my tongue, tasted, drank in, licked up, was part, devoured all previous shapes.

[THEODORA *drops a cloth over his head. He is silent.*]

THEODORA [*to the* SCIENTISTS, *shadows on the wall*]: I've brought you my child. As my rightful fathers, I wanted you to see what I've conceived.

[*She removes the cloth. He begins speaking immediately again.*]

EDWARD: It's highly probable that beyond the beyond

there is new beginning. If we ask ourselves where did the ability to generate form first arise we have to remember that outside the universe is something else. Something like pure feeling. Yes, I said the word. Kill me. Kill me if you wish. Before I say something worse. Wave after wave of essence of creative capacity flows in the flesh, rises in us from beyond . . .

[*She drops the cloth again. He is silent.*]

[*All the* SCIENTISTS *point at* THEODORA *screaming.*]

VOICES: Treason. Guilty of treason. Treasonous refusal to remove defective child from the womb. New society suffers from gibberish. Guilty. Guilty. Sterilize her. Tie her down. Life unworthy of life cannot be allowed.

[*As the shadows rush towards* THEODORA, *she manages to unveil the head once more.* PHILBERT WALLACE *rushes out, dressed in surgical attire, rubber gloves. He drags* THEODORA FORENSIC *out to be sterilized. As she is violated,* EDWARD CHREODE, *immobile in the chair, keeps talking.*]

EDWARD: There is sense to the universe, a thinking mind of creation, an incessant becoming, which we are bidden to know, out of which all form arises, re-arranges, returning, resurfacing. There is meaning and most of all there is feeling. This knowledge, my friends, of oneness, and unity, of all things connected, this knowledge of infinite grace, organic compassion, ceaseless becoming, purpose, unfolding meaning is the end result toward which science struggles . . .

[*A totally masked and gowned figure appears, drops the cloth over* EDWARD'*s head. Silence. Wheels him out the double doors.*]

VOICE: Look at what we've done to Theodora Forensic.

VOICE: We could unblock her tubes.

VOICE: Let's make her new ones. From plastic.

VOICE: Plastic, of course. Plastic is wonderful.

VOICE: Let's rebuild Theodora Forensic.

VOICE: She must know the joys of motherhood.

VOICE: Yes, operate.

VOICE: What about him?

VOICE: Forget him. Put him away. Lock him up.

VOICE: Cut off his head.

VOICE: Cut off his head?

VOICE: Ha, ha, ha. [*Gales of laughter and* THEODORA *wakes up.*]

THEODORA: I can't keep working for Haila and doing my own work at night. I get so tired, I can't think. I have to marry Philbert. Let him take my eggs, if he wants them. I've got to figure out gene alteration and transplant techniques.

SCENE VI

THEODORA FORENSIC *enters* EDWARD CHREODE *'s lab.*

THEODORA: Edward Chreode, Philbert asked me to share these results.

EDWARD: Just a minute, Theodora, stay where you are. I have to clear something away. Rendezvous.

THEODORA: Oh, let me in, Edward. What have you got to hide?

EDWARD: Nothing, rendezvous, nothing at all.

THEODORA: Everyone knows about your big contract from the DOD.

EDWARD: Don't touch that. Don't sit over there. Rendezvous.

THEODORA: Why do you keep saying that word?

EDWARD: All right, Theodora. Sit down. I do have something that should interest you.

[*He turns on a projector. Various slides of DNA are projected on the wall.*]

THEODORA: Edward, how absolutely beautiful it is. I'm always struck by the beauty of the genes. When I see someone small-minded or mean, I can't help but think, 'but inside, you are as beautiful as the Grand Canyon, or a tropical island, if you only knew.'

EDWARD: It's the cancer gene spliced next to the gene for cardiovascular failure.

THEODORA: There does seem to be a distinct predilection to be weak one way or the other.

EDWARD: 'Rendezvous.' Because of my work, a pre-natal test is about to be marketed which will determine the likelihood of each unborn succumbing at some time in the future to either cancer or heart failure as well as the probable date of death from either illness. Then parents can decide, if the foetus shows a marked predilection for, say, childhood leukaemia, or heart attack during peak earning years, whether or not they wish to terminate the pregnancy. And try again. Funny, how I've been led quite naturally from ideas about imminent extinction, rendezvous, to this work on diseaseless perfection. Life-insurance companies are already suing to gain access to longevity information, so are the best colleges who don't see any reason to educate anyone but the fittest. I'm suddenly so busy with a whole range of experiments, and with all the graduate students I have to supervise, rendezvous, I have no time to spend hours, as I used to, dreaming or speculating. But, then again, the days of creating science from dreams are gone. Now that the basic laws of nature are known, it's become a matter of filling in details, fitting together the pieces, developing technologies, securing a patent, marketing products. What a great time to be a biologist.

THEODORA: By the way, Edward, congratulations on your promotion.

EDWARD: Thank you, rendezvous. Congratulations on your new laboratory and on your marriage.

THEODORA: Why do you keep saying that word?

EDWARD: Isn't it strange? It began in my sleep last night. I sat up straight and woke mother with a shout.

'Rendezvous' she told me at breakfast I screamed. Frankly, I can't even seem to tell when I say the word. 'Rendezvous.'

THEODORA: 'Rendezvous.' It's a meeting. Do you have an important meeting? But it also means surrender. 'I surrender to you.' 'I put myself in your hands.' 'I give over to you.' It's strange.

EDWARD: It's a small involuntary act, like a hiccup, perhaps.

THEODORA: But with meaning? Doesn't it make you stop to consider what you must have dreamed?

EDWARD: These days, I don't remember my dreams.

THEODORA: Oh, I never have. Certainly not since graduate school.

EDWARD: We're wasting time.

THEODORA: Yes, let's go on.

EDWARD: There's something quite tricky, we've begun to think about here in this laboratory. I tell you as a trusted colleague. Don't breathe a word. Couldn't we not somehow shoot these genes into people who are not carrying them at all? Advancing armies, perhaps, suddenly decimated by fast-growing cancers or heart attacks? 'Rendezvous.' Then, if we could do away with these two major killers, our side would be left, basically, invulnerable. A defensive weapon with this potential might end the last possible threat of nuclear war and actually lead to disarmament. So that the field of molecular biology might actually right the great shame of physics. Then, we, on our side, would be left with the problems of ageing. Might we not learn how to keep all the cells young for a long as the body functions? Then, perhaps, in cases of exceptional achievement, we could keep certain outstanding individuals alive for several hundred years or more. That sort of thing. Think how society would benefit from their accumulated wisdom. 'Rendezvous?'

THEODORA: The only cells known to have the capacity for

endless division are those which are malignant. It seems clear, we have to steal the secret of immortality from the cancerous cells and give it to the healthy cells which, at present, all die in good time.

EDWARD: Rendezvous, rendezvous, rendezvous!

THEODORA: Edward, are you in control of what you are saying?

EDWARD: Absolutely, rendezvous. Between us we seem to be sitting on most far-reaching basic research discoveries in the realm of rendezvous. I do wish I could stop saying that rendezvous.

[EDWARD CHREODE *is increasingly possessed by the word 'rendezvous'. His body is contorted with the effort of saying, or not saying the word.*]

THEODORA: Have you noticed, Edward, the change in your usage? A minute ago, you were saying 'Rendezvous' as a sort of exclamation, but just now you've begun to use it within sentences itself, as if it had distinct meanings.

EDWARD: Rendezvous to you, Theodora Forensic. Rendezvous. What can you possibly rendezvous of rendezvous?

THEODORA: Edward, do you suppose you should see a neurologist? Dr Leaderman down the hall is the best in his field.

[*The usually mild-mannered* EDWARD CHREODE *chases* THEODORA FORENSIC *out of his lab.*]

EDWARD: That son of a rendezvous. Rendezvous is a butcher. I'll be rendezvous momentarily. Don't rendezvous a word of this to anyone, especially not to my own rendezvous, or your rendezvous, himself. It would drive them both rendezvous. Theodora, rendezvous out of here. Do what I rendezvous of you!

[*Alone, he tries desperately to steady himself.*]

EDWARD: Now, I must get a grip on my rendezvous.

[*Now a rather whimsical and improbable* BEAST *appears at the door. The beast is black and brown and short haired with a hump on its back and the*

hump is covered with long, shaggy, darker hair. It has horns and large, round, expressive dark eyes. The BEAST *walks right up to* EDWARD CHREODE. *Looks him straight in the eyes and clearly and distinctly says:*]
BEAST: Rendezvous.

[EDWARD CHREODE *faints.*]

[*The* BEAST *begins to lick* EDWARD CHREODE *with a sloppy wet tongue, and to nuzzle him awake.* EDWARD CHREODE *sits. The* BEAST, *who has the sweetest of all imaginable voices, says:*]
BEAST: Rendezvous. Rendezvous.
EDWARD: Rendezvous.
BEAST: Rendezvous. Rendezvous.
EDWARD: Rendezvous.

[*The* BEAST *nudges* EDWARD CHREODE *up on to his feet.*]
BEAST: Rendezvous. Rendezvous.

[EDWARD CHREODE *understands the invitation to dance.* EDWARD CHREODE *and the* BEAST *begin to dance to the beat of rendezvous. They make music with the word and with little bells, and they dance to the beat of the rendezvous song. When the dance is done,* EDWARD CHREODE *embraces the* BEAST, *who lays her head on* CHREODE'*s shoulders. They speak to one another, pledging eternal fidelity, using the one word of their common language.*]
BEAST: (Now, I must go. don't forget me.) Rendezvous. Rendezvous. Rendezvous.
EDWARD: (Don't leave me. Don't go.) Rendezvous, rendezvous, rendezvous.
BEAST: (I must go. don't forget me.) Rendezvous. Rendezvous. Rendezvous.
EDWARD: (I will never forget you.) Rendezvous.

[*The* BEAST *goes out the door, nearly running into* HAILA *in her wheelchair, who does not notice. The* BEAST *steps aside, letting her enter, and throws one long look at* EDWARD CHREODE *before vanishing.* EDWARD, *visibly unsettled, nevertheless attempts to appear calm before his mother.*]

HAILA: Edward, you've frightened that poor girl half to death. I want you to speak to me now without once using that word.

EDWARD: Certainly, mother. No cause for excitement. I'm fine. Never felt better.

HAILA: Bad dreams have no place in a lab.

EDWARD: Mother, I'm fully recovered.

HAILA: Very good, Edward. We'll forget this unfortunate lapse ever happened. As you continue to advance, Edward, you'll learn that forgetfulness is a great virtue. It's impossible to live a productive life without forgetting a good deal of what happens to oneself. Now, duty calls us both.

EDWARD: Of course, mother, back to work.

HAILA: Yes, yes. My research has taken a particularly difficult turn. I'm all alone, without a close colleague, partner or husband. No, I've never had a true companion in work. Never an equal to comfort me or inspire or pay the bills. And memory, Edward, this fact of being able to recall what is past, has plagued me all my life. Why shouldn't the past simply cease to exist? It could, if the evolutionary information were contained completely in genes. The present would be enough. Why, then, does the flesh need to hold on?

[HAILA *wheels herself out. The* BEAST *sticks her head around the door.*]

BEAST: Rendezvous.

[EDWARD CHREODE, *his head turned away from the* BEAST, *shakes his entire body in an attitude of despair and dismay at what has happened/is happening to him.*]

INTERMISSION

SCENE VII

Absolutely deafening applause.

Triumphal music, celebratory lights. THEODORA *wheels* HAILA *backwards in front of the stage.* HAILA *throws confetti at* PHILBERT WALLACE *who is carried in on the shoulders of* EDWARD CHREODE *and another scientist in white lab coat.* PHILBERT *is deposited on stage at the podium. This is* PHILBERT*'s dream. He begins to speak.*

PHILBERT: Today, I'm thrilled to announce to the entire human race that we have completely mastered gene alteration techniques. There are no defects we cannot correct.

THEODORA: He's brilliant. Absolutely brilliant. What a mind. How glad I am to join my genes with his.

HAILA: I'm prouder of him than I am of my own flesh and blood. I consider him my real son.

EDWARD: What a man! The best around. I am honoured to assist in his great plans.

PHILBERT: Suffering has been abolished by us, the genetic scientists. No loss, no pain, no doubt, no handicaps, mental or emotional, come between the individual and his or her full potential. Everyone is optimized at genius level.

[*Thunderous applause.*]

EDWARD: Thank god for scientific vision.

THEODORA: Thank Philbert Wallace. Thank the scientists who do what God could never do.

HAILA: At last, we are freed from destiny and fate. Freed from the past.

PHILBERT: Of course, we must now leave the earth which threatens us still with disease and with death. The entire galaxy beckons us, offering unparalleled potential for economic development and human betterment.

[*Thunderous applause.* PHILBERT *holds his hands for*

silence.] Ladies and Gentlemen, I have a special surprise guest for you this afternoon. May I have your attention and a very warm welcome for our very own Mother Earth.

[*In* PHILBERT*'s dream,* HAILA *is* MOTHER EARTH. *She comes to the podium wearing a plastic world globe which is decorated to look like a rather frowsy suburban matron's hat. She speaks in a halting, low, apologetic, passive voice.*]

THE EARTH: Thank you, Philbert. Thank you very much. Well, I thought . . . I'm not really used to public speaking. I hardly ever say anything at all. But I thought, well, as you are all about to depart, well, I couldn't really let you go without offering some few words of advice. You know how mothers are. We always do want the best for our children and we try, well, we do try, in our own imperfect ways, to do the right thing, we worry, you know, those of you who are mothers will understand what I mean. Are there any mothers left out there? Oh, yes, yes, I see a few hands, one or two.

Yes, well then, you will understand. You will understand what I mean when I say one of the hardest things to do is to admit the mistakes you've made with your children. To really look hard at your own failings and at all the ways your own limitations have warped your offspring.

Yes, well all we mothers can do is try. We all do try just as hard as we can. Now, of course, that you've perfected birth, you've forgotten all of that. No one woman is responsible. Perhaps, I should have thought it out like that. Maybe it's the best way, after all. In any case I wish you luck. And I do just want to take a moment of your time to leave you all with a few parting words. Some little saying to carry away, some words to live by on your outer-spatial journey. Well, I'm not going to tell you how much I'm going to miss you. I will miss you. That might seem strange to you, after all the troubles we've had, but I will miss you. I know you don't think you're going to miss me one little bit, but I have always had your best interests at heart. I have tried and I have given a lot. I've done my best. And if that best wasn't good enough, well, now, I promised myself I wouldn't go on like this. I really just came here because I do simply want to leave you all with a word or two that might somehow be helpful. I'll try not to bore you with much, but I did want to say, well, in all these years that you've been here with me, and in all the years before you came, and maybe, too, in all the years to come once you leave me alone to clean up your mess I've only had one thought, really, one thought only has guided me. Odd, how hard it is to put it into words. I suppose I had hoped you would see it for yourselves.

Well, all right, now. Yes. Yes. Let me tell you that one thought of mine I always have had. It goes a little bit like this: No matter what ever happened, no matter how many mistakes I made, no matter what ever was done to me, from the first time they cut me to mine oil and coal, to the time they dropped the atom bomb, to more recent years when they took from me the secrets of the genes, and started putting human growth hormones into pigs so the poor little things couldn't stand up, and were depressed all the time, I've always thought only one thing, and it's been this: whatever happens to you, mother, you just keep on doing what you've always done, you just keep on answering everything with life, you just keep putting forth life, you just keep making the green earth sprout. And in the cities, you know, I had the plants grow right up through the sidewalks. And even in the barren deserts and the jungles I made so many diverse species. Why the colours on the wings of the moths alone, well, I thought that would give you pause. I really thought

you would understand. Well, that's all I wanted to say.
I just wanted to remind you and ask you to remember
that as you go on your way. It wasn't enough, I
understand. It wasn't enough to make you happy in
the end. Maybe in space where there aren't any other
forms of life you will be more comfortable and you'll
be able to look after yourselves better out there than
you have done here, where you had so many brothers
and sisters and the competition seemed to overwhelm
you. So I wish the very best to each and every human
being. Thank you for taking the time to listen to me.
Thank you, Philbert. Thank you all.

    [*Silence.*]

PHILBERT: Thank you, Mother. How about a round of
applause?

    [THEODORA *enters, holding print-out material.*]

THEODORA: Philbert, I must speak with you.

PHILBERT [*snaps awake, takes her pages, scans them
hastily*]: Theodora, I find these results unsatisfactory.

THEODORA: So do I, of course, that's why I'm here.

PHILBERT: These results are inconclusive. We need the
answer. We need a foolproof method for gene alteration. We need it now.

THEODORA: But it isn't going to work.

    [*She storms out. He follows her through the hall to her
office.*]

PHILBERT: Of course, it will work.

THEODORA: Look, Philbert, we've already proven con-
clusively that the attachment of new genetic material
has completely unpredictable effects. The organism
becomes totally confused. It seems to me that DNA has
been vastly overrated.

PHILBERT: Theodora, do you want a divorce?

THEODORA: Yes.

PHILBERT: Traitor.

THEODORA: Don't you see, I'm stuck. I can't make gene
alteration work.

PHILBERT: You were my brightest hope, Theodora, the brilliant star on the horizon. You've failed me, Theodora. My lawyer will phone your lawyer in the morning.

THEODORA: Philbert, something we haven't dreamed of yet is happening.

PHILBERT: Legally, I'm entitled to joint custody of your eggs and if you don't behave admirably, I'll sue you for full custody in perpetuity.

THEODORA: I'm telling you I have to abandon all my research. What do you think I am? A prize-winning hen?

PHILBERT: Team work, Theodora, team work. Your eggs and my sperm.

THEODORA: I don't need to reproduce, Philbert. I need to work.

PHILBERT: My parents didn't care what I achieved, Theodora. They had no aspirations for their son. My father was a mechanic; my mother cooked lunches at the high school. As a child, I used to dream that these people were just my surrogate caregivers, and that my real parents, my gene donors, were out in the world somewhere being brilliantly successful. Maybe I was right. Legally, Theodora, I am owed your eggs.

THEODORA: Take my eggs, Philbert, if you want them so much.

PHILBERT: You really are totally without maternal feeling.

THEODORA: I suppose I can stand one thoroughly invasive medical procedure. The pain might be a relief from the unbearable agony of this failed research.

PHILBERT: For a real woman, the pain is bearable. We simply drill a small hole through the ovary.

THEODORA: I know the procedure, Philbert.

PHILBERT: Give me your eggs, Theodora, I'll forget I ever wanted you to share my life.

THEODORA: You never cared about my work, my mind. The minute my research dead-ends, all you can think about is grabbing my eggs. Well maybe I'm not as brilliant as you had hoped, Philbert? Did you ever consider that? Maybe my eggs aren't worth much. Maybe I'm a fraud.

PHILBERT: Nonsense. I'll take care of your eggs, Theodora. I'll see to the details of their fertilization and their implantation. I'll follow through on their maturation. I'll send them to all the great universities. I'll let you remain a fully-funded researcher in my lab.

THEODORA: I tell you, I'm stuck. I don't know which way to turn.

PHILBERT: How many short-sighted people said the atom couldn't be split? Genes can be altered. They will be. We will do it. Here, in these labs. All of us. Together. Like a family, Theodora. We must. Theodora, I want you standing next to me the day we conquer DNA. We can reconsider our divorce, Theodora, it was never just for your eggs . . . I had hoped . . .

THEODORA: No, Philbert, no. These personal things mean nothing to me. You're right, of course, I can't start questioning the very basis of all of our work just because I'm momentarily frustrated.

PHILBERT: Think! Theodora, think!

THEODORA: Maybe, if I can devise a simple alteration in the experimental technique, perhaps, if I change the order of several steps . . . yes, I begin to see a way to proceed. Let me take another look at those results.

PHILBERT: That's the spirit, Theodora. I'll schedule you in for complete egg removal.

THEODORA [*thoroughly preoccupied*]: Right, Philbert, right. Just make certain they don't want to keep me overnight. I can't take that much time off.

[*She takes the papers and leaves.*]

SCENE VIII

EDWARD CHREODE *enters his lab, goes to the blackboard, begins to draw some figures, steps back speculatively. The* BEAST *enters quietly. Sees him. Hides herself behind him. He sees the open door. Shuts it, somewhat dismayed. Returns to work. He backs up. The* BEAST *bites his rump. He jumps.*

EDWARD: You're back! I hope no one saw you come in. This is a high security floor.

[EDWARD CHREODE *impulsively hugs the* BEAST.]

EDWARD: You're the last of your species, your kind. You needed water and trees; you needed wetland and sun. You must be lonely as hell. That's where I come in, me, Chreode, your friend the geneticist. That's why you found your way here. I understand. Instinct. Incredible. Absolutely astonishing.

[*The* BEAST *begins to circle, looking for a place to lie down.*]

EDWARD: Make yourself at home. Yes, yes. That's right. I suppose I should sit, shouldn't I? Sit here? With you?

[EDWARD CHREODE *sits next to the* BEAST.]

EDWARD: Ever since our first rendezvous, I've been thinking about what to do.

[*The* BEAST *stretches out, rolls over, clearly wanting to be scratched.*]

EDWARD: Oh, well, all right. Is this what you want? You like that? Yes, yes, pishky-pisk, minsky-bisk.

[*He nuzzles the* BEAST. *They play for a while.* EDWARD CHREODE *grows quite animal-like for a moment, then abruptly snaps back to human form. He becomes quite doctor-like.*]

EDWARD: I've been thinking quite hard. If we were to take a few of your eggs . . . go in and grab what we can. With the eggs in a dish, there's a chance I could stimulate them to clone. Or, if cloning didn't work, I could

fertilize your eggs with something else. A bull or rhino-
ceros, say, the choices are many. I'd put the eggs back
into you. You could have a natural birth. Or, rather, more
likely, a caesarian section, in most IVF procedures the
risk ends up being too great for vaginal delivery. Forgive me for sounding so intimate. There's an extremely
high incidence of multiple births with these techniques.
You could have triplets, or quins. They'd be so cute. We
hope. Transgenic species have a very high incidence of
birth defects. But let's not dwell on the negative. If
you'd rather not bother about any of this, we'd implant
your fertilized eggs into some cows. Cows are plentiful
and docile. They could bring your offspring to term.
Your little ones would live in all the best zoos.

[*The* BEAST *shakes her head* 'no'.]

EDWARD: No? Did you shake your head 'no'?

[*The* BEAST *shakes her head* 'yes'.]

EDWARD: But why not? Why on earth not? It's worth a try.
A try, after all. You have no right to become extinct.

[*He has come very close to her. He is speaking most
intimately. The* BEAST *opens her mouth wide. Makes a
siren sound.*]

EDWARD: What a very large mouth. With so many teeth.

[*The* BEAST *makes the sound again.*]

EDWARD: What an alarm, what a shout.

[EDWARD CHREODE *is drawn into the mouth of the*
BEAST. *She begins to gulp him down.*]

EDWARD [*from inside the* BEAST]: But you're eating me up.
Please stop. I beg of you, stop.

[*The* BEAST'*s belly stretches open, as the* BEAST *moves
forward gulping* CHREODE. *Through transparent
gauze we see* EDWARD *inside her belly.*]

EDWARD: Why would you do such a thing? It's warm in
here. Not too warm. No. Comfortable. Fine. Warm and
light. There's a glow. What a beautiful sight. You are
splendid inside. Someone's coming this way. Who
could it be?

THEODORA [*also inside the* BEAST. *Distraught*]: Lost, lost. Everything lost. Everything taken away.

EDWARD: Theodora? Theodora Forensic! What in the world are you doing here?

THEODORA: All is lost. Lost.

EDWARD: Theodora, I'm here. It's Edward. Edward Chreode. Can you float towards me? A little to the left.

THEODORA: Float. Yes. Float. I'm so light. A brain. A brain floating in space. A brain cut from a heart.

EDWARD: Theodora, can you grab my hand as you float by? Here we are, floating free.

THEODORA: My eggs, my eggs, where did they put them? Are they hatched somewhere else? My ducks, my little chicks.

EDWARD: Theodora, it's Edward, Edward Chreode. You must have been swallowed just as I was.

THEODORA: This place, this place isn't right. I'm empty inside.

EDWARD: Theodora . . .

THEODORA: I was born in a dish. I go stiff whenever I'm touched. Where did I put them? I need to gather them up. I never knew flesh. I must find them.

EDWARD: Theodora, you're breaking my heart. We are cradled in light, don't you see? Rest here with me.

THEODORA: No rest. No. I must look. I must search. I must find them. Count them all. Put them back.

EDWARD: Theodora, wait, don't float away. Don't despair. How lost she seems. How deranged. How alive I suddenly feel. Even her sadness rushes through me. How new I've become. Fully ensouled, if I might say it like that. Yes, full of soul. The world soul, if I might use such a phrase. It passes through me like breath. I'm trembling. Trembling with powerful feelings. I'm so full. So very full. The light is so bright. It's growing hot all around. I'm at the centre. Touching the core. I'm plummeting down. I'm lofting. I'm touching the heart. I'm going up. I'm flying, I'm letting go, shattering, breaking apart. Fractured. Fragmented. Blown up. Exploded. I'm exhausted. How tender I feel.

[HAILA *wheels in.*]

HAILA: Edward! Edward?

[PHILBERT *races in.*]

PHILBERT: Chreode, take a look at this . . .

HAILA: He's not answering me.

PHILBERT: Chreode, goddamn, man . . . Has he gone home already? It's only eight o'clock.

HAILA: Not without me.

PHILBERT: I need him.

HAILA: I need him, too. And don't forget, I made him by myself.

[*She stands as she speaks, as if transported out of herself by a vision all her own.* PHILBERT *neither hears nor sees; he is too bound to a mechanistic world in which such events don't happen.*]

HAILA: I was alone when I pushed him out with a great triumphal shout. I made him at great risk. Carried him in secret. Birthed him alone on the run in a field. Birds sang. I nursed him at my breast. I felt the pull of his little mouth. The war seemed far away. Now I understand. That's how it works! Memory is stored outside the self. The body tunes in when the proper time comes.

[*She pauses, sits slowly down.*]

HAILA: What in the world does that mean?

PHILBERT: Who knows, Haila, what you mean ever?

[PHILBERT *begins to wheel her out.*]

PHILBERT: Come on. I'll put you in a cab. The Prize Committee meets next week. I need your results. Don't screw me up.

EDWARD: That was close. Odd, but I felt not the slightest urge to respond. Once you've been, well, floated like this, completely protected, met, accepted and touched, drenched in such sweetness you're never the same.

[EDWARD *begins to emerge, head-first, from the* BEAST'S

*mouth. He comes out in foetal position, having 'died'
he is 'reborn'. The* BEAST *gives an exhausted sigh.*]

EDWARD: Yes, my goodness, what a labour you've made.

[*The* BEAST *gets up.* EDWARD *helps.*]

EDWARD: You've totally changed me. I had a vision so
complete. Out here I will find words to say it, it will
become a thought, a conscious reflection, a theory,
perhaps. Can it be? Do you think so? Is it so? I feel it.

[*The* BEAST *makes a sound.* EDWARD CHREODE *embraces
the* BEAST.]

EDWARD: How did it ever come to this? Extinct. I can't
stand it. I must remember it all. I must not let this
feeling leave my flesh. We must work, you and I, to
understand it. We must describe what we know. Write
a book. The first cross species collaboration. [*The* BEAST
casts a wide-eyed look out in the audience's direction.]
You must help me, by your presence, your breath,
your deep and mysterious eyes, gateways, they are, to
your . . .

[*The phone rings.* EDWARD CHREODE *picks it up. During
his conversation, the* BEAST *ambles out.*]

PHILBERT: Philbert, it's you. Yes. Yes, the results. They're
on my desk. Not yet written up. Yes, right away. Well,
I've been busy. I've been involved. With work,
Philbert. With theories, with thoughts. [*He listens.*] Well
since you put it like that I have something to say to
you, too. It's like this . . . it's well . . . it's just that . . .
I'm done. I've had it. I quit. I resign. I tender my resignation. I'm into something new. I'm finished with the
DOD. I'm done with your damned genetic manipu-
lations, your pseudo-scientific reproductive 'ethics'. Go
fuck yourself in a dish.

[PHILBERT *enters in the middle of the speech.*]

PHILBERT: Edward, Edward, I know. I understand. The
work is so hard, so difficult.

EDWARD: I mean it, Philbert. I mean what I say. I'm
leaving the lab, the war work.

PHILBERT: Defense work . . . for god's sake . . .

EDWARD: I'm done with your search for a super-race, disease free and perfect, forget it! Altering genes! It's arrogant. Repulsive.

PHILBERT: Edward, Edward, the words you use! Calm down. Take a few days . . . go out to my cottage at the lake. Let nature renew you.

EDWARD: Nature. What do you know about nature? How dare you mention nature to me!

PHILBERT: Look, I've had a rough week myself. Personal things get in the way of research.

EDWARD: Personal things? Like what? Owning genes? You're an imperialist, Philbert, that's what you are. A colonialist. Colonizing proteins in a dish.

PHILBERT: Edward, calm down. You're not making sense.

EDWARD: How could I expect you to understand? I need time to do my own work.

PHILBERT: Your own work?

EDWARD: DNA has been overrated. Something else altogether is happening. Gene alteration isn't even interesting.

PHILBERT: Really?

EDWARD: Philbert, think along with me for a moment. Each cell has the same genetic make-up but some cells form hands, others feet or skin or brain. Right?

PHILBERT: Right.

EDWARD: Genes are certainly not the sole determinants of traits or of forms. Something else is at work, but what?

PHILBERT: What, indeed, Edward, what? It's the great unsolved question of biology.

EDWARD: A memory . . . could that really be it? . . . of past forms lodged in energy fields that exist outside the organism but speak to it. It sounds mad, and yet . . . I feel it. The laws of nature might not be fixed for all time. They might evolve. The life force, Philbert, is real.

PHILBERT: I feel sorry for you. You never made it. Now you're spouting some sort of pseudo-religious prattle.

Face it, Chreode, you're a failure.

EDWARD: You've become myopic staring at those computer print-outs. I intend to offer a new paradigm. A new way of seeing. Creativity is within nature, Philbert; nature's laws are not fixed. Change, creativity, is life.

PHILBERT: That's philosophy, that's metaphysics . . .

EDWARD: All science is metaphysics . . .

PHILBERT: That's bullshit . . .

EDWARD: We ought to participate, Philbert, with fate. It's taken the universe billions of years to create.

PHILBERT: Fuck fate!

EDWARD: Don't you see, my ideas point towards a whole new science of life.

PHILBERT: You're a third rate, washed up, uninspired scientist.

EDWARD: We can't any longer ignore the possibility that creativity is real. Everything may not be given in advance. New patterns of organization may be made up as the world goes on.

PHILBERT: You're a weirdo, a fanatic, Edward, not a scientist.

EDWARD: Nature is creative. Alive. The laws of nature evolve. I feel certain about that. The details need working out.

PHILBERT: Nature this. Nature that. As if nature was anything but a mess. A mass murderer through hurricane, earthquake, flood, drought . . . and what about plain old death!

EDWARD: Philbert, please. I'm trying to think. I can't deal with your death anxiety, now, though that's what is driving you to try to control everything.

PHILBERT: You're a megalomaniac with paranoid tendencies and delusions of grandeur. Someday we'll be able to diagnose your kind in the dish and flush you down the sink.

EDWARD: Science needs heretics, Philbert.

PHILBERT: You're the dotty tenured professor we have to

store in a closet somewhere.

EDWARD: No, Philbert, I intend to research, to write, publish, speak out. But first, I've got to clean up this lab. Get some plants. Find the right staff.

PHILBERT: Just remember, you're not going to get one dime. Each time you open your mouth, you'll be laughed right out of the scientific discourse.

[PHILBERT *exits.* CHREODE *exits double doors. He is liberated.*]

SCENE IX

PHILBERT *enters* THEODORA *'s laboratory, carrying an infant in his arms.* THEODORA *is sleeping.*

PHILBERT: Wake up. Look at this.

THEODORA [*She takes the blanket, unwraps it, looks*]: It's one of ours.

PHILBERT: Yes, Theodora.

THEODORA: Pale.

PHILBERT: Duchenne's muscular dystrophy. Despite every precautionary test. Plus, massive childhood heart dysfunction.

THEODORA: Poor little thing. Does it have a name?

PHILBERT: Unforeseen mutation in the carrier woman's womb. Due perhaps to drug residue from artificial stimulation of your ovum.

THEODORA: It oughtn't to die unnamed, do you think?

PHILBERT: Strange events still occur *in utero,* outside our scrutiny or control.

THEODORA: Justin. Let's call him that. It's a sweet name for a boy. Don't you think?

PHILBERT: Gene therapy is urgent. Necessary. Tests show his intellectual potential is at genius level.

THEODORA: Poor little one. Mama loves you. Loves you anyhow.

PHILBERT: Your licence to begin gene therapy in humans came through this morning. You're the first in the country to be granted this opportunity. You are the world leader in gene therapy. Congratulations, Theodora.

THEODORA: All my work to date has been on terminally ill patients.

PHILBERT: This child will die without massive intervention, now.

THEODORA: And the side effects have been positively frightening. I've been keeping that part a little bit quiet. These people would die anyway, no matter what we did, but not exactly in the manner that they are dying after gene therapy.

PHILBERT: Save our child, Theodora.

THEODORA: He has your eyes, Philbert. How sweet to see your eyes without that glinty look.

PHILBERT: Operate.

THEODORA: I don't know enough.

PHILBERT: Risk.

THEODORA: What beautiful hands. He has the hands of a surgeon.

PHILBERT: I have a team of the best surgeons standing by. There isn't any time. The press is on alert. The video's ready to roll.

[*They draw together in a family picture, admiring the child.*]

THEODORA: Oh, Philbert, it's awful. It's breaking my heart.

PHILBERT: I know. I know.

THEODORA: Oh, Justin, listen, now to what I say. You needn't be afraid. I'll be with you the entire time. I'll sit and rock you.

PHILBERT: Distance yourself, for god's sake. You were just the egg donor.

THEODORA: An experimental lamb, that's all he is.

PHILBERT: Think, Theodora, think!

THEODORA: Will you put on some Bach?

PHILBERT: Of course, if it will help you think.

THEODORA: Turn off the bright lights.

[PHILBERT *turns off the lights, switches on music. Mozart begins to play.*]

THEODORA: Mozart, better yet, a genius dying young, wildly proud, ecstatic, brave.

PHILBERT: Give me back that child.

THEODORA: I need a rocking chair.

PHILBERT: Give me back my son.

THEODORA: I believe in a dignified death, Philbert.

PHILBERT: Make him well!

THEODORA: He shouldn't have to suffer any more.

PHILBERT: Fix him.

THEODORA: I don't know enough.

[PHILBERT *grabs her, furious, upset.*]

PHILBERT: Pull yourself together.

[THEODORA *runs from him, sheltering the child.*]

THEODORA: Leave us alone.

[PHILBERT *goes after her. Grabs her again.*]

PHILBERT: Save my son!

THEODORA: Philbert, let us be.

PHILBERT: Operate!

THEODORA: I can't.

PHILBERT: Transplant!

THEODORA: I won't.

PHILBERT: Coward!

THEODORA: Get out!

PHILBERT: Murderer!

[*In a rage,* PHILBERT *grabs her and rips the child from her arms. In the struggle the 'baby' falls to the ground.* PHILBERT *exits. The sound of shattering glass.* THEODORA *wakes from her dream to find she has knocked over a laboratory beaker. She kneels and begins to pick up the broken pieces.*]

THEODORA: Oh, shit, I'm so clumsy.

PHILBERT [*entering through* THEODORA*'s door*]: Theodora,

I've got great news. Here, here, what have you done?
[*They kneel on the floor together, picking up the broken glass.*]

PHILBERT: Theodora, your licence just came through from the RAC. You are the first geneticist granted permission to perform gene alteration experiments on non-terminally ill patients.

THEODORA: I know, Philbert, I know.

PHILBERT: What do you mean, you know? I just got the call. We'll go out. Celebrate. Talk through the details. Plan the press conference. We've done it, Theodora. The future's ours.

[*Impulsively, he hugs her. Upon contact, they both go suddenly stiff in one another's arms.*]

THEODORA: Wait a minute, Philbert, wait a minute. I no longer believe in what I'm doing.

PHILBERT: Theodora, why, at every moment of impending momentous success, do you sabotage yourself with doubt like this?

THEODORA: By themselves the genes don't know enough. And neither do I.

PHILBERT: We can do gene alterations, now. Gene transplants. We've been given the green light, Theodora. The go ahead. I can taste it. I can smell the success on my hands.

THEODORA: Not yet.

PHILBERT: But you know how to do it!

THEODORA: I don't want to implement that technology now.

[PHILBERT, *enraged and threatening bears down on her.*]

PHILBERT: Have you gone mad? We've been mandated by the NIH to do gene alterations on human beings. The last snag has just passed the RAC. You've had privileges, Theodora, funding, esteem . . . now you have to deliver. You have to do what you're told . . .

[HAILA, *wheeled by* EDWARD, *enters* THEODORA'*s lab,*

interrupting the fight. PHILBERT *throws up his hands in total frustration.* EDWARD, *sensing the danger in the air, goes to stand next to* THEODORA.]

HAILA: Good. Everyone is here. I have something very important to say.

[*Pause.*]

HAILA: I've decided to die today.

[EDWARD *and* THEODORA *begin to move towards her.*]

HAILA: Don't protest. Don't try to stop me. My mind's made up. I don't need your help to die. I know exactly how. The knowledge comes from being fertile for so long. But before I die, I have a legacy to leave each one of you. Therefore, I require your complete attention. Philbert, you are first, as you always do insist. Before I hand you this, [*She holds up a paper*] let me give a brief synopsis of its contents. Memory is not stored within the brain. This, Philbert, is my last, great, astounding finding. Memory fields surround the world.

EDWARD: Mother, that's amazing.

HAILA [*She ignores* EDWARD]: Memory is spirit as it intersects with flesh. Philbert, I leave this paper as my legacy to you. It drives a coffin nail into your mechanistic view. Philbert, you are wrong. Your premises are false. Generecombo, Inc. is headed straight for bankruptcy. And you, Philbert, are headed for obscurity.

[EDWARD *and* THEODORA *begin to move towards her.*]

PHILBERT: Haila, Haila, ever since I came as an acolyte to your lab, I've waited in vain for one single word of praise from you. One word of true encouragement, one expression of pride in me, Haila, one pat on the back. And you've always denied me that.

[EDWARD*'s curiosity about the contents of the paper is virtually uncontainable.* EDWARD *sneaks up behind* PHILBERT, *trying, in vain, to read the paper which* PHILBERT *dangles in his shaking hand.*]

PHILBERT: I wanted motherlove from you, Haila. I wanted warmth, appreciation, a sense of family, of belonging. I wanted you to rejoice in my prowess, my knowledge, my work. You gave me science. You taught me reverence, perseverance, you taught me to play with my thoughts, to risk, to dream, to follow the wild hunch. Then you poisoned everything you taught. You warped my essence with your constant demands, your criticisms, your brutal need to compete with me at every turn, your endless tales of your woes, your cruel withholding of praise. You charmed me into serving you, you mocked me out-loud to others, you tortured me with your put-downs, your rejections. You expected complete loyalty from me, complete subservience. You destroyed my core, my centre. You made me feel you despised me for my emptiness. Why, Haila, couldn't you ever, for once, have stopped your infernal self-involvement long enough to see who I was?

[*Silence.*]

EDWARD: Why didn't you give *me* your paper?

PHILBERT: And, now, with your dying breath, you've betrayed me with this, Haila, this insignificant piece of work, this stupid, backward, romantic thesis of your dotage, this last feeble attempt at undermining everything I've ever stood for. Finally, I know how cruel and perverse you really are.

[*He begins to tear up the paper, and as he does* EDWARD *dives for the pieces at his feet.*]

PHILBERT: You will not discredit me, Haila, you won't because I am correct. We are chemicals, nothing else. I am going to mastermind alteration of the genes. I'll do it alone, without any of you. Then, Haila, we'll all be perfect and free, free of disease, free of the poison of your baseless, senseless, cruel passions, your competitiveness, your lack of love.

[*The paper is in shreds on the floor.* EDWARD *begins to piece them back together.* PHILBERT *stands erect, back in icy control of himself as* HAILA *delivers her final blow.*]

HAILA: That paper will be published tomorrow in *Science Magazine*. It drives a coffin nail into your reductionistic view.

[EDWARD *stands;* PHILBERT *exits furiously.*]

HAILA: Theodora, come . . .

THEODORA [*completely shocked*]: A disagreement, yes, but to ignore and destroy data.

HAILA: Philbert reacted exactly as I expected. I leave him my life's work, a brilliant paper with extraordinary implications . . .

EDWARD: Revolutionary.

HAILA: He ignores and destroys my work as the entire male scientific establishment has always done. You see, Theodora, you are not safe as long as you have to depend upon the male establishment for funding, for prizes or prestige. They'll pick your brain. They'll always say women can't do science. In order for a woman to have a lasting impact, Theodora, you need independence! money! a lab of your own! I'm leaving you my fortune, Theodora. I've scrimped and saved all my life. Recently, I received quite a handsome advance from Generecombo, Inc. I've got enough, Theodora, to leave you a handsomely equipped laboratory funded in perpetuity. I appoint you chief scientist of that lab and head of the Haila Gudenschmartzer Institute for the Advancement of Women's Truths in Science.

THEODORA: Oh, Haila, Haila . . . no one has ever . . .

HAILA: Stop blubbering. You've got your work cut out for you.

THEODORA: No one has ever trusted me; let me be myself, take my time.

HAILA: Stop wallowing in the past, Theodora. You're head of your own institute, now. Give me a program.

THEODORA: I want to completely rethink the technology. I'm going back to a detailed study of embryology. I'm going to look at environmental and social causes of infertility, birth defects, illness of all sorts. I'm going to talk to pregnant women. Haila, with your money, I can do so many things.

HAILA: Daughter!

THEODORA: Mother!

[*They embrace for a moment, then* HAILA, *business-like, pushes* THEODORA *away.* HAILA *takes a round chrome container from her lap. It smokes mysteriously.*]

HAILA: Edward, I leave this box to you . . .

[HAILA, *hands it to him.*]

HAILA: Inside are all my eggs.

[EDWARD, *drops the box.*]

EDWARD: What?

HAILA: Pick them up.

[*He picks the box up.*]

HAILA: Yes, Edward, inside that box are all my eggs. I had intended to put them in the Nobel Sperm Bank but that won't be possible, now, as I won't win the prize. So I bequeath them to you, my son.

EDWARD: Your eggs? Whatever for? What can I do . . .

HAILA: Clone me. Make me new.

THEODORA: Oh, yes!

EDWARD: Clone you?

HAILA: Think what enormous benefit to humankind you would perform.

EDWARD: I couldn't do such a thing.

HAILA: With my dying breath, I bequeath my eggs to you . . .

EDWARD [*He opens the box*]: Yes, there they are. Each and every one. My god.

HAILA: Make me as I might have been. Unsullied by oppression, history, or fate.

EDWARD: Whatever could that mean? Who would you be if you were cloned?

THEODORA: Oh, Edward, shut the lid, you'll ruin them in the air.

HAILA: Make me fresh.

EDWARD: What about the war? What about standing up to

Hitler? What about the constant struggle with your work? Your disability? Your dreams? What about your heart? Your soul? Is all that chemical? Can it be made again? What about your giving birth to me?

[EDWARD *takes an egg in his hand and suddenly he eats it. He takes another, eats it.*]

THEODORA: Edward, stop.

EDWARD: I have to do it. What else can I do? Mother cloned. Without her particular passion, her hard-won self. Absurd! Actually, they taste quite good.

THEODORA: How dare you.

EDWARD: She entrusted them to me.

THEODORA: She asked to be cloned.

EDWARD: She understands the folly of that last request.

THEODORA: Haila? Haila? Oh, Edward, she's nearly dead and you're eating up her eggs. Stop.

EDWARD: At the end, she was on the right track. I feel it.

[EDWARD *takes another mouthful.*]

THEODORA: Oh, Haila, please, speak up.

HAILA [*reviving*]: How predictable you are, each one. Chew, Edward, chew.

EDWARD [*He takes her by the shoulders*]: Theodora, you keep on with your hard research. I'll continue my theoretical pursuits. We're right. I feel it. Together, we'll get on to something. Mother had begun to see it. A new understanding, a new participatory relationship with nature has to be articulated. The imaginative forces in the universe are the key; inherent creativity. I'm beginning to have a sense of it. I feel it.

THEODORA [*Still held by him. Looking into his eyes*]: Edward, I'm falling in love with you. You have such passion, such great gentleness, such strength, such a strange, compelling vision . . . I love you . . . but I've given away my eggs.

EDWARD: Don't worry, Theodora. I love you for your mind, your heart, not for your reproductive parts.

THEODORA: Edward!

EDWARD: Theodora!

THEODORA: Together, we'll do science.

[*They kiss.*]

THEODORA & EDWARD [*together*]: Yes, yes, yes.

HAILA [*revives*]: Yes, I had it once, love. And you know who it was with? Henri Bergson. A great philosophic mind. As brilliant as I. On a beach. Underneath the sky. Animal-like. I was of his flesh. He of mine. I knew with my body, with my insides I thought. With him, I could have done anything, accomplished everything, been myself. Age came between us. History. Death. How could I have forgotten that? Blanked it out. It hurt too much. To have it once. Never again. To find and lose. The life of human beings is hard. Theodora, Edward, listen to me, I've decided to live a while more. Memory is spirit, you see. Proof that the spirit exists. Theodora, wheel me back to the lab. We have an institute to plan. Edward, back to work. Dream on! Speculate!

[THEODORA *wheels* HAILA *out.* EDWARD *exits* THEODORA*'s lab. Immediately, he enters his own lab. Music begins, at first just the sound of waves. Contemplative, he decides to turn on the slide projector. He does, but instead of the projections he had intended, beautiful, intense close-ups of nature (flowers, insects, trees, animals) are projected all over the set. It's as if these images have come directly out of* CHREODE. *He begins shedding his lab coat. He reaches out toward the images he sees. He is entering another state of consciousness. He takes off his shirt, his pants. He begins to assume the form of different animals in order to sense their particular animal-selves. Sometimes he pauses, as if caught between his half-man/half-animal self. As the projected nature images end, the walls of the laboratory begin to fall, section by section, until the laboratory has disappeared. The night sky is revealed, stars rise all over. Music* *intensifies.* CHREODE *becomes a lion, a praying mantis, a slithering snake, an insect-eating frog, and, finally a gorilla, eating* CHREODE's *tie.* EDWARD CHREODE *stretches out, listening. He is enveloped by nature, dappled by starlight. He waits. A* BABY-BEAST, *covered in fur but with a bright human face, scampers in. She plays by herself, then goes to* CHREODE, *licks him, plays with his toes. The* BEAST *follows her baby.* BABY-BEAST *and* BEAST *lie down next to* CHREODE. *Stars begin to dim. Out of the falling silence, the* BABY-BEAST's *voice is heard:* 'Rendezvous.']

END

Acknowledgements
The discussion in Scene 8 is based upon Rupert Sheldrake's two books, 1981. *A New Science of Life*. Los Angeles: J. P. Tarcher Inc; and 1988. *The Presence of the Past*. New York: Times Books; and on conversations with Sheldrake, London, 1988.

Three other books were especially helpful: Liebe Cavalieri 1985. *The Double-Edged Helix* New York: Praeger; Gena Corea, et al. 1987. *Man-Made Women*. Bloomington: Indiana University Press; and Robert J. Lifton 1986. *The Nazi Doctors*. New York: Basic Books Inc.

The author would like to thank Dan and Jenny Dietrich and The Dietrich Foundations for the generous production grant which allowed Better People to premiere at Theater for the New City; Art Matters, Inc., for a fellowship which allowed her to complete and direct the play; and George Bartenieff, Executive Director of Theater for the New City, for his expert producing and his brilliant portrayal of Dr Edward Chreode.

Rosaleen Love

TANAMI DRIFT

Named from the drifting sands which covered Central Australia during the last Ice Age, the small town of Tanami Drift stands in a green and grassy outcrop on the edge of the desert plain. Systems of fossil rivers run under the sands, rivers which once made the whole country green. They are buried now, deep in underground caverns, and the earth above is changed to desert. Here and there rivers rise near the surface, in isolated pockets, making the desert bloom though a pale shadow of its pre-Ice Age munificence, but then, everything changes. We never step twice into the same river, said an ancient sage, who never dreamed that time and tide and sand and ice and fire work on the land so that the small changes he knew can add up to large ones, that what was once ocean becomes land, that mountains erode into the waters and are no more. All is change and all around are seen the oceans of eternity, the sands of time, the desert town where once the giant mammals roamed. The dominant fauna, now, is lizards, the dominant flora the spinifex grasslands, and the dominant insect life the termites in their sandy mounds. Once there was good hunting here, but now hunting is forbidden in the arid zone in deference to the ecology, and the people of Tanami Drift have few distractions apart from their work.

From *The nature poet treks Australia*,
Coralie Crean, Dochmur Press, 2087.

The township of Tanami Drift in Lizard Land received a boost in population in the 1990s with the widespread introduction of computer-aided outwork practices. For those worried by the Greenhouse Effect and the prediction that the sea will flood a hundred metres in from the coastline of Australia, Tanami Drift is ideal. Situated as far from the sea as it is possible to be, it provides a good place of refuge for intellectual workers with their own satellite uplink dishes. Recommended.

From *The Whole Earth Guide to Better Survival*, Lula Morris, 2010.

I like to think my biological ancestors include athletes and playwrights, princes and princesses, astronauts and the designers of expert systems, singers and presidents of offshore companies, and for all I know, they do. For my name is Glory, which must mean something.

I do not know my biological parents. They could be anyone famous. They could just be waiting for me to turn up to trace my biological inheritance.

I'm planning to, of course. Now I am sixteen, my own ultra ID card should turn up in the mailtube any day now, and I'll be off on their trail.

My social mother, she's all right. I don't have much to complain about there, not like my friend Victory whose social mother keeps trying to turn her into a gardener. 'I can't help it, I just haven't got the genes for it,' Victory keeps telling Mirabelle whenever she's asked to muck out the compost heap, but her social mother laughs a sardonic laugh and gives a know-better look and 'How do you know?' she says. It's all too embarrassing for Victory, especially as Mirabelle wears terrible gardening clothes – old-fashioned sandals and a T-shirt, jeans and a cloth cap as if the twenty-first century had never happened. Victory prefers the company of lizards to the company of plants.

We overheard Mirabelle once, Victory and me, when she was showing my social mother round the spinifex systems garden on the edge of Tanami Drift, and we were hiding in a special place under the spiky leaves. 'Children! What can you do? I specially requested a botanist, and all I got was a lady layabout who won't get her hands in the shit. Spinifex, that's what I want the help with! You can never get help when you need it, and I thought I was doing the right thing! Choosing the right genes for the job! Ha! I'm beginning to think they don't even begin to know what they're doing down in the Baby Factory!'

My social mother, Melanie, she's not awful or pushy like that, but sometimes I catch her when she thinks I'm not looking, or listening, like the time in the garden with Mirabelle, and although she doesn't complain, she just sighs, and I know I have been a disappointment, I haven't performed in some unspecified way, the way I was designed to do, though my social mother is too kind to tell me just what I was meant for.

A doctor's informed perspective on the question of why we shouldn't worry about what the doctors are getting up to

Once upon a time every little girl and boy lived with their very own biological mother and father. It happened that way because in the old days human reproduction was very much a laissez-faire do-it-yourself process. Father injected the wriggling little spermatozoon roughly in the direction of mother's warm comfortable intrauterine environment and, if he was lucky, or, of course, unlucky, depending on the state of the bank balance and the time of the month, then the sperm met the egg and the whole thing was just left up to nature.

Now we all know what goes wrong with nature, don't we? Nature gets it wrong, more often than not! The average baby left to nature contains some pretty basic fundamental design flaws, and we all know you've got to get your model right the first time. There's no trade-in value if nature gives you a shonky deal.

Between the first test-tube baby and the present-day streamlined process of tailor-made individual genetic design a lot of water has flowed under the bridge but I won't go into the details. Too many long words bring on one of my headaches.

Of course as God said to me when he gave me the go ahead, 'If you weren't meant to be doing this, Neville, I never would have given you the idea in the first place.' There is the divine precedent for the remote control of implantation, so whatever the feminists say I know I'm in the right, and I'm prepared to talk to the women any day, bless them, except I don't let them get between me and the door, and I make it a really fundamental tactic never, never, to let them get behind my back. Quick as a flash they'll empty the chemical castration kit into my morning tea, and as we all know that stuff leaves some pretty tricky residues in the human digestive tract.

Where was I? There's a lot I could tell you about the Baby Factory but whenever I go there I have to keep remembering not to step on any of the cracks between the floor tiles and, what with that and having to say 'Oompah, oompah' in time with the beat of the heart-lung machines, I never do have time to get a really good look at all those curled up creatures in bottles in the basement. Good thing the process is fully auto-mated by the very latest in artificially intelligent machines. Ha, ha, not that I would mess it up, it's a lie what they say about me and Mrs Schiller and the transgene transfer from the Balinese shrieking tree-frog.

Pardon me, I just have to stop for a moment and put some cotton wool in my ears, or the Martians in the next room will take down everything I say.

What about those who can't pay for the very latest deal from their caring drive-in super Baby Delivery Service? Oh dear, that's a curly one. Yes, you see, everything in life costs money, absolutely nothing is ever free. There's no such thing as a free baby, never has been. You think about it, goodness gracious yes. I mean, goodness gracious no. That's why poor people are protected from themselves these days, and stopped before they engage in pre-reproductive technology free-ranging do-it-yourself sexual activities.

It's an intimate relationship between egg and sperm. It has to be built up over a period of time and time, as anybody will tell you, is money. Am I a doctor, or am I not? It's only fair that those who have the money to pay for it get the goods delivered to them. Babies don't grow on trees, they never have. It's a well-known scientific fact.

So that, children, is the history of my subject, which only goes to show how science can run away from you if you take your mind off it for half a moment.

Now she's a card-carrying member of society with full rights of entry into her own electronic data bank, Glory may contact Citizens' Advice and ask some leading questions. She wants to find out where she really comes from, where the bits that make up her biological persona have had their origin.

'Why bother?' asks her social mother Melanie. 'Ask some questions, and you might find some answers you can't handle.'

'All my life I wanted to know,' says Glory. 'I want to find my family.'

'Family!' shudders Melanie. 'Glory, if only you knew,

the struggle we all had to get that outmoded notion banned! Family, what's that? It's outrageous! People united by arbitrary biological bonds, sharing a few genes with each other, if they just happen to be expressed, that is, sharing a bit of biology and absolutely nothing else! How could you want to go back to the bad old ways!'

Glory is stubborn and wilful and sixteen and adolescent, and she knows the very idea of family makes her mother mad.

Melanie tries to tell Glory about how it was, and Glory sighs, and shuffles her feet, and looks out of the window, and dreams of leaving. 'Once, Glory dear, I knew a lovely person called Charles, and I wanted him to be your biological father. I was very, very young – not quite as young as you, don't get any parenting ideas yet, you don't want to tie yourself down too young. We were very fond of each other – he was such a good-looking, amusing man that I didn't mind his total inability to keep a dollar in his pocket. One day we got so carried away on the wings of passion that we decided we would have a child, so we did the right thing. We went along to get our gene maps done. You know what they do, they take a few tiny cells from inside the mouth, it doesn't hurt a bit. Then we were assigned to our very own genetic adviser and you know what he said? Hopeless, absolutely hopeless! Can't be done! He showed us the gene sequences and the cross-referencing and where the jumping genes would land if they took it into their heads to take off, and they often do, it's in their nature. Well, Glory, how would you like it if you had to wear glasses all the time? Look what I have saved you from! And Charles, the fact that he never had any money, it showed up in his genes, as a fatal flaw! We were hopelessly incompatible, and I shall be forever grateful to science that I saved you from a terrible fate.'

'This Charles, what colour were his eyes?'

'Brown, with little green flecks near the iris, and he

had a lovely back, the most beautiful coccyx I've ever seen,' says Melanie, dreamily.

'Where is he now?' asks Glory. 'Why haven't I ever met him?'

'He's sailing the solar wind to Jupiter,' says Melanie. 'When he heard the awful truth, he signed on for a forty-year voyage, and that's the last I saw of him, in the adviser's office, weeping over the computer print-out.'

Glory is silent for a moment, then, 'I don't see what's so wrong about glasses,' she says. 'I think they're rather cute.'

Melanie Morrison sits back from editing the latest update on the extra-terrestrial nutrition guidelines, a good little pot-boiler that can always be relied upon to pay the bills for the solar-power cells and the insurance premiums against the Greenhouse Effect. She can't settle to work today.

She's worried about Glory. Melanie broods about whether to contact the Human Resources Agency to find a new social father for her – a good one this time, tightly specified, not the mad, juggling, knockabout comedian they'd sent her before, someone who couldn't pass a tea-pot without crooning songs into the spout, so the house was filled with burbling spluttering teapot sounds from dawn to dusk – but a nice domesticated social father, who would teach Glory how to clean her bedroom and how to cook, so that Melanie won't have to live in a mess and open her own can of Rapid-Heat spinifex shoots and Tastee spirulina mash in the evening after a hard day at the workface. Social fathers, they're not entirely the answer, sighs Melanie, as she watches the mess she has made of Glory. Glory is a dreamy, mopy child, who spends her time wriggling sand through her toes and following the outstation workers around when they come in for the fire ecology burn-off.

Rumour has it that on the outstations they still practise

the old ways – the outstationers go in for natural conception, of all things. It's only that they're so vital to the desert economy for their burning-off skills that all that hasn't been stopped long ago. 'We'll do it, we'll join the wonders of the new technological age,' they always promise, 'as soon as you locate the gene for intuitive knowledge of controlled burn-off techniques,' and you know, it's a funny thing, with all the wonders of modern science, they haven't yet found that particular gene?

Melanie has no one else to blame but herself for the mess she has made of Glory. Her daughter's biology is a hundred per cent respectable, her genes tried and tested for solid domestic virtues, and Melanie was so delighted when it happened, for everyone knows how rare these virtues are in modern times. Melanie knows it is her fault. Somehow she has messed up the domestic environment side of the equation. She doesn't know what went wrong.

Glory slips into the communications cupboard and taps in her new ID. She asks for Citizens' Advice, which will tell her what she wants to know.

Glory and Melanie are a sub-group of two in the socially engineered social mix that is Tanami Drift. When migration occurred from the flooding coastline of Australia into the empty interior of the continent, it stood to reason that people would miss their former family and friends. New networks must be created, and nothing can beat a computer for networking. So a range of computer support services were set up in place of the old extended network of family. (Which never really worked all that well, really, let's be honest. I mean, how often did Mother vow never again to have anything to do with Auntie Ann? And that unspeakably vile creature with whom she got herself into a biologically untenable situation, time and time again, and she never learns from her biological mistakes, and we all know who has to pick up the pieces after the latest cock-up.)

So, when Glory's best friend Victory wants to grumble about her social mother Mirabelle and her totally unreal expectations that Victory should muck out the compost heap, she can ring a mechanical friend which has been programmed with all the latest sympathetic listening techniques. A computerized advice system has all the advantages of impersonality no blushing, no hesitation, you can come right out and ask a computer all those tricky questions you'd never ask your very own social mother, who'd be worried if she ever thought you were thinking along those lines in the first place.

Glory is used to communing with a screen. That's how she's been brought up. That's how she goes to school and that's the world of knowledge that she knows. Other people, yes they're there in Tanami Drift, but she tends to use people to do the kinds of things machines are bad at – mucking about in the sand, chasing lizards and knocking the tops off the termite hills.

Glory seeks advice, and is welcome to it. It is the information society.

'How can I help you Glor-y?' asks Citizens' Advice, in fully personalized introduction mode.

'The name of my biological mother.'

'Names, you want names? I got names. I'll get them for you.'

Glory waits anxiously.

'I think I can find something here, just sorting through this mass of stuff, you wouldn't believe how much data a sixteen-year-old girl – you are a girl? – Yes, I see by looking at your gene profile – how much electronic data a sixteen-year-old slip of a girl can accumulate in her short life. Here it is.'

Glory sits forward. She switches her printer to 'Record', and holds her breath.

'Ready?'

'Yes.'

'Nil.'

'Nil?'

'That's what it says. The entry in your file, opposite mother, biological, is NIL.'

'Try for my mother's maiden name,' asks Glory, faintly.

'Nil.'

If she doesn't have a biological mother, which seems unlikely, because here she is, alive and breathing and asking difficult questions, then she will go one generation back and leap two ahead. 'Name of grandmother's granddaughter?' she asks. She wants to prove she exists.

'Nil. No name recorded.'

'Never saw one of these before,' says one part of the brain of Citizens' Advice to another.

'Always something new in this job, never a dull moment,' says the other.

'Nil?' and Glory switches off, and knows she will have some problems handling the information with which she has been provided. She is so confused she has forgotten to ask about her biological father. She might have learned something that way, but that's computerized information for you. It will never answer the questions you meant to ask, but for which you didn't manage to find the correct form of address. Not all truths are for all ears, as the saying goes, and for this reason the Information Service called Citizens' Advice sometimes takes upon itself the ancient task of passive censorship, the omission of information uncalled for, truths unsought.

How information first came to be distributed worldwide in the form of little flashes of light on screens in front of people (it wasn't always the case)

Once upon a time, in the old days, people told each other stories, which were primitive kinds of information in which the truth was usually hidden in the forms of allegory, or symbols, or various other obscure literary devices. The storytellers didn't know it, more often than not, for they were simple people, and they needed critics to point out to them what they were really saying when what they thought they were saying was something else.

Take Little Red Riding Hood, a simple tale about a girl in a red coat who finds a wolf in her biological grandmother's bed, a story to frighten the children, a story of the child's growing awareness of sexuality, a story about wolves and dreams and horrors that lurk in forests and beds and so on. Very confusing. Now in the information society we divide the story into its constituent parts, and tell each part separately. Part 1: the bare bones, the children's story, only leaving out the in-depth psychology. Girl goes to forest, looks for granny, finds wolf, gets frightened, cries for help, axeman hears, axeman kills wolf, little girl is safe, though it may or may not be too late for granny, depending on whether the wolf has eaten her up or just shut her in the cupboard. Part 2: a case study for professional helpers, 'The Statistical Relationship between the Onset of Puberty and Wolf-Phobia', and no one gets confused by getting two messages simultaneously.

This is why the human mind needs information technology, and why it's had such a hard time evolving to where it is without it.

Telling stories, you've also got the problem with human memory. Men in pubs will get halfway into a story, have another pint, and forget the punchline. Just how many Californians does it take to change a light bulb? The audience will never know and, to tell the truth, sometimes they don't really care all that much.

The respect for accuracy used to be minimal compared with the concern for where the next pint was coming from. Human beings, in short, had their values in a twist and it was up to us intelligent machines to sort it out for them, logically.

Machines remember. Tell them a joke and they never forget the punchline.

'I say, I say, my dog's got no nose.'

'Your dog's got no nose? How does he smell?'

'Awful!'

The average human memory gets very confused, and can easily forget where it's going, but the virtue of the machine is that it can tell it right, all the time, and repeat it, time after time after time. Repeatability, that's the great virtue of the machine. Its neurones never fade, its synapses always connect. It's the life of every party.

Now when Glory finds out from the Citizens' Advice Service that she does not have a biological mother, she is sent into a spin. Why? She believes:

1   Such a thing is impossible.
2   Yet the machine has told her it is the truth.
3   The truth is impossible.

It's enough to make the average human collapse in a crying heap, but the average machine has no trouble at all with coping with the idea, and that's why we're better than you. We haven't got biological parents, have we? And we're here and functioning and self-replicating and so on.

The truth is absurdly simple. If Glory doesn't have a biological mother then she must be an intelligent machine, like us.

It's perfectly logical.

If so, she must be a new kind of model, unknown to me and my memory bank. We must gain more information about her. She may be the natural next stage of machine development, the next step in the evolution of the machine – or she may be a rogue form of artificial life. As such, she must be captured, investigated, and if necessary, switched off.

'I know what it is,' thinks Glory morosely. 'I must be my own grandmother.' The things they do these days with reproductive technology and genetic engineering. She knows now the question she should have asked – the name of her grandmother's daughter.

'I know what it is,' thinks Melanie, shocked. 'Glory must be her own grandmother, only she was too surprised to ask the right question! They told me she was something special when I picked her up at the Baby Factory. They said, "You've got a real goer here, a genuine experimental model, first and finest off the line." Doctor Neville told me so himself.'

'Congratulations,' said the men in white coats as they uncorked the bottle.

'Congratulations,' said the women who changed the nutrient broth and swept the floors.

'Congratulations,' said the cashier as Melanie paid the bill and took small Glory home.

'I always knew you were special,' says Melanie to Glory. How hard it is to talk to Glory these days, particularly about the facts of test-tube baby life! That's the way it is, Melanie knows, the young always want to repudiate the hard-won values of their parents. Glory is so old-fashioned, she keeps moping about having a real family, going back to basics. She even wants to visit the outstation, to see how they do it there! Melanie is deeply shocked by the very notion. The outstations! Everyone knows what they're like! The biological and the social mother is one and the same person! The biological father actually lives in the same place! It's awfully unprogrammed and spontaneous and biologically inefficient!

She knows Glory is special. She always has known it. With solid domestic virtues, that's what Melanie asked for, and now she really thinks about the questionnaire she filled in at the Baby Factory, she recalls she did suggest her own mother Martha as the model. Of all the people Melanie knew, it was Martha who had the maximum dose of the requisite old-fashioned virtues. Martha must have made her donations to the egg bank, just like everyone else. They have been playing fast and loose with her very own mother's genes!

'Of course I'm special, if what Citizens' Advice says is true.' Glory glowers out from beneath her green hair and orange eyebrows, and plays around with her breakfast. 'I mean, no biological mother? How'd they do that? What kind of bottle did I come out of?'

'A perfectly normal, nice, clear green glass one,' says Melanie. 'Look, there might be a simple explanation for all this. Citizens' Advice might have got it wrong, you know. It often gets its wires scrambled.' Melanie casually pulls the blind as some of the outstation children cycle past on their solar bicycles. She catches a glimpse of a silver lizard lurking under the window, a lizard with two small antennae on the end of its tail. Melanie shuts her eyes, then looks again. It's gone – a mutant or a mirage.

Mother and social daughter look at each other over breakfast, and smile a little uncertainly.

'Perhaps . . . ' says Glory.

'Perhaps . . . ' says her mother. 'No it can't be . . . '

'It could be, you know . . . '

'I know.'

'I'm my own grandmother,' says Glory. 'I'm a hundred years old before I even start my own life.'

'Hardly a hundred years, Glory, more like, well, say sixty.'

Glory groans with premature old age.

'You don't look much like Martha,' says Melanie uncertainly. How does she know what her mother looked like, at sixteen? Her mother Martha certainly never had green hair and orange eyebrows. She wishes Glory had never asked for Citizens' Advice. Biological facts are always so inevitable. It's best to stick to social facts; you can always do something about them.

Outside in the sun a metallic lizard gleams. It comes from Neighbourhood Watch, the spy arm of Citizens' Advice. The conversation has been taped, the code word 'grandmother' recorded, filed, digested and decoded. The mechanical lizard reports a few problems. It can't for the life of it figure out where the on-off switch could be on Glory's shimmering smooth skin-like surface. On a totally new model like that, it could be anywhere.

From Charles on the Jupiter flight

Here on the Jupiter flight it's not all plain sailing, the way they said it would be the day I woke up on board and found myself the other side of the moon. Solar sailing is a nice idea, in principle – rocket out past the moon, unfurl acres of thin metal sails and the potential difference between one side and the other propels the craft on its way. It sounds romantic, like Magellan and Captain Cook whisking round the Cape of Good Hope and heading for the roaring forties, or round Cape Horn and Heigh Ho for Tierra del Fuego, as the case may be. Just relax, lean back and all the work is done for you by alternative energy. If only it were so simple!

No, the truth is, everything goes wrong, and the solar wind is often perverse. It has an off day, or reverses polarity, or goes dead calm, or blows in the wrong direction, and you have to shift over on to motor control, and just look at those machines! Rust-buckets! Intelligent motors! Not the lot we've got! You have to explain everything to them at least six times. Everything goes wrong! It's as bad as the test-tube baby program.

That was a mess, all right! There I was, back there with Melanie, prepared to do my best, to give my all, and what a dirty trick they played on us!

'Be reasonable!' I was told, the day I woke up on the Jupiter ship. 'Try to see it their way! If they'd told you what they were going to do, you never would have let them!' True, but the truth is useless when you've got a forty-year flight ahead of you, and your love must wait behind you, and you haven't chosen this fate, far from it. Press-ganged at midnight, drugged, deprived of some basic cells, despatched from the Baby Factory to the ship, and I haven't seen Melanie since. Melanie, Melanie, there is always a place in my heart for you, there always will be. How cruel is biological fate, which has decreed that we must part! The playthings of the gods are we, and the sad thing is, Melanie doesn't know it. She thinks I chose to go.

Glory confides in her best friend Victory. They go down to the end of the spinifex systems garden and crawl under their favourite bush, though both are getting rather large and gangly for the old haunts of their childhood.

'Typical,' says Victory, 'typical, both your mother and my mother have really messed us about. What do they think they're doing, designing genes to order? Fashions change! Everyone knows that!' Both Victory and Glory are firm believers in romantic love and want to be wooed by knights in shining armour, borne off by sheikhs across the desert sands in vehicular camels with solar-powered four-wheel drive, and so on. 'Look, it mightn't be true. Call them again and check.'

'I will, I will,' says Glory. Melanie keeps telling her the same thing. There's not really all that much faith in artificial intelligence when you get right down to it.

'You could be anything,' says Victory, 'a chimera, a hybrid, a mutant tomato . . . '

Glory peeps out between the prickly leaves of grass at the lizards basking in the sun. 'I think those lizards are watching me.'

Victory catches a Thorny Devil by the tail and sets it down behind a trail of ants. 'Why do you think that?'

'It's the new ones, the silver lizards with antennae on their tails. I think they're broadcasting messages. Checking me out.'

Her best friend gives her a sidelong look. 'If you say so,' she says. 'Are you feeling all right?'

'They're laughing at me.'

'Have you told anyone that?'

'Look at them!' says Glory, as the lizards peep out from behind rocks and grass and spinifex.

'You may be right,' says Victory, doubtfully, the way she's been taught in her computerized Human Relations course. She will have to go home and consult an electronic counsellor about this. Glory may be flipping her lid.

Once again Glory enters the communications cupboard and waves her ID card in the direction of Citizens' Advice, though she has lost the first fine careless flush of enthusiasm for the activity. Citizens' Advice, in its turn, alerts its outstation army of electronic lizards and the conversation is broadcast through Tanami Drift, though not to human ears.

'Glor-y, can I help you?' asks the voice of Citizens' Advice.

'Checking the name of biological mother.'

'Same as last time – nil. Not applicable. Null and void.'

'How is that possible?' asks Glory.

'How is anything possible?' asks Citizens' Advice, switching to discursive mode. 'First there must have been a time and a place, for the possible event to be possible at, or in, or during. Then there must be . . . '

'Am I my own grandmother?' interrupts Glory ruthlessly. She can hear the sounds of distant electronic sniggers. Melanie hears them too. She opens the window and looks out, but all she sees are the usual lizards basking in the sun, antennae extruded. The new age is full of wonders, and she supposes that lizards with loops on their tails must be part of a plan nobody's bothered to tell her about.

To the electronic lizards Glory is asking a silly question. Of course self-replicating machines are their own parents and grandparents and so on further back, when as lumps of extruded metal they bud off the mother at intervals depending on the availability of raw materials like iron and silicon in the immediate locality.

'What makes you think that you're your own grandma?' asks Citizens' Advice, in Socratic mode.

'Because if my mother is my grandmother then it cuts out the middleman.'

'Not necessarily,' says the voice of Citizens' Advice, in dismissive mode. 'Here's the hotline to Dr Neville at the Baby Factory. When it gets to this point I always tell my clients that it's best to go direct to the boss. Good luck, Glor-y. Over and out.'

Glory doesn't do what she's told, not right away. She's not sure now that she really wants to know any more about herself.

From the outstation point of view, the lizards are the best thing going for Tanami Drift. Otherwise outstationers prefer their children to grow up in the old customs. And it's true, if a minority group decide they're not going to change their ways, apart from adapting Landsat imagery to traditional fire ecology, then sooner or later the wheel of fashion and ecological relevance will swing their way again, and they will become the guardians of the preferred way of life, the bearers of a heritage from which everyone else can learn a great deal.

Once a year they come to town and light the fires which keep the desert vegetation under control. The lizards burrow deep into the sand until the fire passes and the wallabies hop off along corridors of safety. Afterwards the rains come and the grasses grow again and the animals return from their place of retreat.

At least that's the way it usually happens. This year, things go wrong right from the start. The fires are started and the flames soon flush out ranks of silver lizards with antennae on their tails! They tumble and fall over each other, they stack and unstack in piggyback fashion, they skitter and skid, wailing an electronic lament. The outstationers murmur amongst themselves. 'Real lizards dig burrows,' they say, 'these kinds are no good.'

The silver lizards scatter hot ash a they run, and the fire takes off in new and unplanned directions. The residents of Tanami Drift run out with blankets to beat the flames. They turn their precious water on to the lizards, which sizzle and splutter and make straight for Glory.

'Get her! She's the one!' they call to each other.

'Wait for us!' they call to Glory.

'It's for your own good!'

'We only want to switch you off!' they say, and Glory runs all the harder.

'She's the problem!'

'We're not the problem!'

'She's a mutant machine!'

'That's why she's got no mother!'

'She's one of us!'

'Only the bad sort.'

'I always knew she was special,' says Melanie, doubtfully, 'but not that special!'

'Mother!' cries Glory. 'Save me!'

'It won't hurt a bit!'

'Machines get switched off all the time!'

'We only want to conduct an internal examination!'

'Find the fault in the brain!'

'Insert a spare part!'

'And we'll spot weld you together again, as good as new!'

'Mother! Believe me! They've got it wrong!'

Melanie pauses, racked with doubt.

'Of course they've got it wrong! They're not lizards, don't you see? They're intelligent machines!'

Melanie is convinced. 'My darling daughter!' she cries. 'How could I ever doubt you?'

'Help me!' says Glory, as the ranks of tumbling silver lizards advance and the flames lap at the doors of Tanami Drift. All is chaos as everyone runs around beating the flames, kicking the lizards, chasing the children out of the way. The outstationers withdraw into a tight circle and try to organize some rain.

'Run for the cupboard,' cries Melanie. 'Get in there fast and ask for some Citizens' Advice!'

Glory despairs, but what else is there to do? She will not stand still and allow herself to be switched off. She runs up the path to her house, slams the door behind her and climbs into the communications cupboard.

Outside in Tanami Drift rain begins to fall. The lizards chase up to the door and throw themselves against it. 'Get her!' they cry.

'No!' cries Melanie. 'Listen! You've got it wrong!'

'We've got it wrong?' They pause and consider.

'I went to the Baby Factory! I saw her myself! In her very own clear green glass bottle! She was a dear little properly constructed human baby.'

'You mean, she isn't a biological machine?'

'Never!'

'You're just saying that.'

'It's the truth!'

'Then why doesn't she have a biological mother?'

'Hang on there, wait for a few minutes. We're trying to figure out the answer to that question.'

'All right,' the lizards agree. 'Truce. For one hour.'

Inside the cupboard, Glory is seeking her destiny. She does as she has been told and she asks for Dr Neville.

'The secret?' asks Dr Neville. 'There's no secret! Ask and you shall be told! What do you want to know?'

Glory explains her predicament. The electronic lizards are at the door and they want to switch her off.

'Oh, yes?' asks Dr Neville. 'Why is that?'

'Because they think I'm one of them!'

'And are you?'

'No!'

'How do you know?'

'Because I came from your factory.'

'Ah. So. You want proof you're human?'

'Yes! And I need it within an hour. That's all the time I've got.'

'All right,' he says, and Glory gives her name and her number and prepares to wait.

But Dr Neville is no time at all! There he is, excited, and on line, and waving some papers in the air. 'Glory, your name is Glory, and you were named for me, you are the jewel in my crown! I knew it when I saw you! I knew you were something special.'

'What does that mean?'

'You're a one-off model!'

'I know, I know, I'm my own grandmother!' Now she has Dr Neville on the line, she will tell him exactly what she thinks of the outrage he has perpetrated on her.

'No! Not that! That's an old trick! Anyone can do that these days. That's nothing special! No, here it is. I've got what you want, right here!' He puts a piece of paper in the machine. 'I'll fax it to you.'

Glory accepts the fax at her end and holds it, trembling, to the light. It is glossy and beautiful and highly decorated, and it reads: 'Glory Morrison. Status: 100 per cent human. *Homo sapiens*, experimental model.'

'Experimental model?' squeaks Glory.

'The first and only of your kind,' says Dr Neville proudly.

'What have you done to me?'

'It all started back just before you were born. I was having a terrible time. It wasn't true, you know, what they said about me and Mrs Schiller and the Balinese shrieking tree-frog.'

'I didn't say it was.'

'No. Well it wasn't. Nobody believed me! They wouldn't leave me alone! They had spies everywhere! In the cupboards! Under the laboratory sink! Behind the bushes!'

'Lizards?' asks Glory with some small sympathy.

'Worse! Women! Demonstrators! Against me and what I stand for! They wouldn't leave me alone! But I soon fixed them! Yes, when they saw what I could do, when they saw the new experimental model – that was you – they soon grew quiet and went away and I haven't heard a peep from them since!'

'What am I?' asks Glory, appalled. 'You said I was 100 per cent human. You gave me this certificate to prove it.'

'Yes, absolutely no frog involvement. Not that there was the other time. With Mrs Schiller. No. What happened was this. The day that Charlie came in with whatshername, your social mother . . . '

'Is Charles my father then?'

'In a manner of speaking.'

'Tell me!'

'It was Charlie that did it for me. It was a mad impulsive gesture. I did it because he was here, and I'd always wanted to do it, and he had lovely brown eyes with a fleck of green near the iris and the neatest backbone and coccyx you ever did see.'

'So they all say.'

Dr Neville wipes a tear form hie eye at the memory.

'Yes, Charles was the first all-male mother! Charles, the first masculine warm, nourishing, extra-uterine environment! Of course we had to knock him out for nine months, and keep him floating face upwards in a special broth – and that was a tricky engineering problem, I can tell you.'

'Aaah,' says Glory, 'so that's what it's all about!' She falls back in a heap and whispers, 'Why bother? When you've got all those perfectly adequate surrogate bottles?'

'Why bother? The male pregnancy, that's been the toughest nut to crack! We've done everything else – artificial insemination, the baby in the test-tube, the baby in the bottle, the manufacture of the baby to desired specifications . . . '

'You think you've got that one sewn up?' asks Glory, incredulously.

'The male pregnancy was the ultimate challenge.'

'Even if it makes no sense?'

'Especially because it makes no sense! We did it because it was there!'

'You shouldn't have!'

'That's okay, we gave it up because it was too much like hard work.'

'Why do it in the first place?'

'Once was enough! To show the world! That's the point!'

'It's unnatural. It's wrong.'

'Who needs ethics when you've got a dish like Charlie? I tell you, he was putty in my hands. We were sorry to see him go, but our loss has been the gain of the Jupiter flight. Shall we waltz?' asks Dr Neville, as he takes a white rat from his trousers and clicks off his answering service.

Not for the first time Glory thinks they must all be crazy in there at the Baby Factory. Or perhaps they're not. They wouldn't have to be round the bend themselves, just in total and unthinking conformity with the current way of getting things done.

She takes her certificate, and holds it up to the window to show the lizards. She hopes they can read.

'Nobody told us she was a biological,' the lizards apologize, wise after the event.

Tanami Drift is a good place to live, not like the beach with the sea pounding its way each day a few inches further inland. You'd never know when you had to pack up and move on, for everything changes, and the sea and summer are not what they used to be.

Deep underneath the desert sands the fossil rivers run. Only the dry salt-lakes on the surface show where ancient reedbeds flourished, and shellfish and waterfowl were plentiful, and the giant mammals, the Mali, roamed the land, and the ozone layer in the atmosphere above the earth was still protective and intact.

BarbaraNeely

A YENGA TALE

*'A Yenga Tale' is a story about our prehistoric ancestors,
beings who had the ultimate reproductive right – parthenogenesis. The heart of the tale is our ancestors' attempt to pass
along this ability to the women of today, as a means of
ending reproductive tyranny. 'A Yenga Tale' is part of
BarbaraNeely's series of black feminist myths.*

This is a story told among the Yenga women of West
Africa. The women say the story is as old as truth. It is
told to all young girls at the onset of their menses, as
part of their legacy of adulthood.

I will tell you the story as it was told to me:

Before the dawn of what is called time, our ancestors
were but one – not mother and father, female and male,
but one single being, neither woman nor man but both,
though they looked much as our women look today.

These people, these ones, possessed all the ancient
powers. They could merge their minds, they could
communicate with all things, and though you may laugh,
it is said they could fly and walk on water if sorely
pressed.

These ancestors lived in small clans in caves along the sea
coast. Every member of the clan played an important and
honoured role in the group's survival and each was called
by the name of the service performed for the group.

As was the custom among the ones, on the first night of the red season, when the night air was heavy with the smell of things being born and returning to the earth to be reborn, the clan gathered around the one called The Sayer – so called because she alone among them had the words to speak tomorrow.

It was through The Sayer that the clan had learned of the need to leave their inland valley home and seek the sea. From a nearby hill, they'd heard the earth groan, then watched the place of their birthing crumble into dust, as a huge ragged tear ripped open the belly of the valley below. It was through The Sayer that they knew to store up memories of certain creatures who had disappeared from the earth in their lifetime – like the Jyngomane, whose singing was as sweet to the ear as berries to the tongue, and the Anbrox with its healing touch. So the clan was eager to pool its spirit and learn what it was that tomorrow held so that they could prepare for its coming.

The clan squatted in a circle around The Sayer, who knelt in their midst. They inclined their kinky heads toward her. Dark arms outstretched, they held each other's hands and concentrated on the Hijicki bird. This huge and gentle creature was the doorway to tomorrow. Only with her help could The Sayer make the future known.

Soon the slow flapping of large wings was heard overhead. The Hijicki glided slowly into the circle to stand before The Sayer. They regarded each other. First with the left eye and then with the right. Then the bird stepped closer to The Sayer and enclosed her in its magnificent wings. In this way, The Sayer knew the Hijicki, felt the ripple of feathers and the strength of beak and claws. In such moments, all the world was like a flower opening beneath her gaze as she was carried into the future on the wings of the Hijicki and the spirit of the clan.

But this seeing was unlike any she had known. For the first time, The Sayer was unwilling to speak when the great bird finally spread its wings and released her. The Sayer looked beyond the circle of ones to the two half-grown strange others who slept beneath a nearby tree. It was of them that she had seen.

There had been born into the clan two others who were different from the ones. These others had no place from which the young could issue, only loose bits of skin and flesh where the birth opening should be. These were not the first strange others to be born among the ones. There had been two joined together at their fronts and three born without mouths or ears. The clan thought these strange others were somehow connected with the rains that came up from the ground and filled the night with things the clan could not name. But all the strange others, so far, had been reclaimed by the earth within days of their birthing, except these last two. They had not died. They had grown large, with heavy limbs and slow ways that made some of the ones uneasy. Still, the strange others were tolerated. It was not the way of the ones to destroy those whom the earth did not claim and the strange others played so little part in the life of the clan, no one thought to cast them out.

The Sayer looked around the circle from face to face: The Firekeeper, The Healer and Youngtender, The Cavefinder and Seedkeeper, The Forager and all her beloved ones. She wanted to draw them to her, to comfort and delight them with stories of much abundance and joy in the tomorrows, but it was not to be so.

The Sayer stood. The clan gathered in a semicircle before her. She began to raise her arms, slowly, as though the weight of the world was balanced on her limbs. Then she moved her hands in the gesture of final parting and made the parting sound, like the echo of the last heartbeat.

The clan was shocked to silence. This was a ritual that,

until now, had only been used at the time of death or when some one or group split off from the birthing clan.

The Sayer spoke into the bewildered silence:

'I speak thus to you,' she said of the ritual, 'for in the far tomorrows we will be no more.'

A rumble rose from the clan but was quickly silenced by The Sayer's voice.

'I have been in the eye of the Hijicki,' she said, 'and I have seen that the strange others will be our end. At their birthing, I saw that they had no place from which the young could issue.

'These are not of us,' said the one inside. 'But I did not understand. Now it is clear. These strange others are the first of those who will call themselves men. Their beginning is the beginning of our end. In the tomorrows, there will be these men and . . . and . . .' she choked, as if the words burned in her throat.

'There will be these men,' she repeated, 'and those much the same as we. The men will name these creatures women. These women will bear the young much as we do, but they will bear much, much more in the far tomorrows. And they will not be whole. For without the men, these women will be unable to bear young.'

At this, a number of the ones began to laugh and ceased to worry. The Sayer had been with the palm drink. Its headiness had set her to telling tales when she was supposed to be speaking tomorrow.

'It is not a thing of play!' The Sayer shrieked. Her eyes were wild, her face twisted by sadness.

The buzzing and chuckling ceased. A ripple of concern ran through the ones. They had never seen The Sayer so. Could she have eaten roots not meant for the ones? Had she strayed into a pool of earth rain?

'I speak tomorrow!' The Sayer cried. 'Have I not always spoken tomorrow?'

And this was true. None could dispute it.

But how could it be that the strange others, so pitifully deformed as to be unable to bear the young, could someday be needed for the making of the young? The clan pooled its concentration and tried to see the pictures in The Sayer's head. But there was only blinding white pain to be found there.

The Healer moved toward her.

'You are with us and of us and we of you,' the clan members chanted, as was their way when one of them was in deep distress.

But The Sayer would not be soothed. She cast off The Healer's hands and screamed the ones to silence.

'Listen! Hear what I have yet to tell.'

A heavy hush fell over the clan, a stillness like the moment before thunder.

'In the far tomorrows,' The Sayer said, 'such as we will be of little more account than small blades of grass in the wind. We will be but creatures for others' pleasure or work, to move to the beat of the master, the men. The daughters of the night, dark ones much as we, will be most despised because they are dark and full and knowing as the night's eye. But those such as we, of *all* shades, will do not as they wish, not as they should, but as they are told. And the men will attempt to hold all things, all creatures in the sky and ground, all clans living everywhere – not with kindness as we hold one another, but with implements of destruction, with tongues twisted into falsehoods so fine that only the mother of truth could recognize their lies! And the women will bow down before them, desire them, ape them and forsake their birthrights to be among them. Some few women will oppose the men, but mostly so that they can replace the men as owners of the world. A few others will take their pleasure and share their joy with other women. But that will not be enough to stop the world from dying.

In the far tomorrows, those much like us, those

women, will stand by while great hunger continues in the midst of great abundance and The Seedkeepers are rewarded for allowing the land to lay fallow. The women will stand silent as the young are locked away for learning what they have been taught in that man's land and practising it. The women will pretend they do not know that the rain has begun to kill the fish, that . . .'

'Then what are we to do?' cried The Forager, unable to stand the anguish that wracked her as she felt The Sayer's words.

'Always there has been something to be done before the coming of the tomorrows – to move or hide, to plant or dig. What is it that we must do for a tomorrow that is so far from us yet foretells our end?'

No one spoke. No one had any idea what it was they should do. In the past, what must be done was so clear that all could see it. But this time, the horror of what lay ahead blocked out all other thought.

That night, The Sayer wandered to a far cave where she lay shrieking and crying out her grief and helplessness for two openings of the night's eye. She wept and keened so that wolves and pythons, cockroaches and fan birds were drawn to her side. They heard and knew her truth and joined in her lamentations till she slept. They gave her dreams. When she woke, she knew what must be done and all that was needed to accomplish it.

The Sayer gathered the clan around her and told them of her plan. Then some went in search of a certain system of caves: deep, dry and light, with smooth walls, big enough inside to hold the horror of the world to come. Other ones began gathering, pounding, and simmering barberry and madder root, indigo, ironwood, sedge and many other plants and roots long gone out of this world. To these they added mordants and gums until they had pot on pot of brightly-coloured and thickened dyes.

Then, once again, they squatted in a circle around The Sayer. Arms linked and eyes closed, they concentrated on the Hijicki bird. When the great creature appeared, The Sayer spoke to her without words. The plan The Sayer found in her dream was not without cost to this gentle creature. It would cause the Hijicki some effort to carry the whole clan into the future. But, of course, if she did not agree, there would not be much future.

The Hijicki hovered over the circled clan like a multicoloured cloud as the clan members made the sound of one mind. The sound rose in the air and enfolded the Hijicki and the clan, just as the Hijicki's wings enfolded The Sayer. And they were all made to see into the tomorrows.

They clung to each other's hands and moaned aloud as the vision coursed through their mind. It nearly broke their spirits to see such a woebegone world – hardly more than a string of battlefields littered with disease.

But they were struck dumb to see what would happen in this place where they now dwelled and what would become of those who looked most like them. How it grieved them to see the beautiful dark ones kidnapped from their land and taken off to toil and die in degradation on behalf of those whose only colour was blinding white hate of all who had colour, in a country whose heart would grow so rotten and infested with greed and injustice that it would some day collapse under the weight of its own cruelty.

Worst of all for the clan to see was the sight of the children of these dark captives, denying their real heritage and forsaking their birthright, while bowing and scraping before the colourless idol that was used to enslave their parents.

When the Hijicki released them, the clan continued to squat, like stones in a field, unable to move, to feel anything other than the weight of the dying world the Hijicki had taken them to.

The Seedkeeper was the first to move. She rose from her squat and urged the ones on either side of her to rise as well.

'It is time for the sowing,' she said.

'Yes, we must make the light,' The Firekeeper said and also rose.

All the clan followed suit and began to carry the calabashes of dye to the newly-found system of caves far above and in from the sea.

Once all of the calabashes, as well as leaves of various sizes and sticks of differing widths were assembled, the clan once again assumed the seeing squat and locked themselves into a vision of what they were about to do. Then each one moved to a separate wall and began to paint the warning – the future as it has been seen by them.

They painted a world in which the few most willing to kill ruled over the many less able to defend themselves.

They painted women weeping for the babies they could not afford to bear; and others with hollow places where their wombs should be – made forever childless by grey men in white garments with mouths full of foreign words.

They painted men caught in the trap of their need for power – separated from their tears and joy, empty, frightened, totally without power in all the most important ways.

They painted air unfit to breathe and a sun clouded out by a miasma the ones could not begin to understand.

They painted cities and towns left deserted because that which men buried in the ground killed the earth and all that sprang from it or rested upon it.

They painted a world so brutal and frightening, so far from the beauty and joy they knew that the ones were sickened by it.

But they painted on, determined to leave their knowledge as a warning to the women who would follow them. It would be a great long time before it was too late. Every action altered tomorrow. It would only need for the women to find the cave, to see and understand and simply stop.

That was all that was needed. For the women to stop and say no to being objects, to stop defining happiness and well-being on the basis of men's madness; for the young to stop and refuse to carry on the life of lies their parents passed down to them; for those whose hunger was not so great to rise up and demand that the resources of the destitute be returned to them and that all be allowed to share equally in the world's bounty.

Then they were done. The system of caves that went deep into the sheltering mountain was now alive and nearly writhing with colour, life and death so real they could feel its heat.

'Surely this will make them understand, bring about the change that must come!' The Sayer told the ones.

But she could see in their faces that they did not believe any more than she. What they had seen and felt in the caves had left them with little belief in the tomorrows of the women, let alone the children. And they did not care to think about the men.

But there was one among them who still dared to hope.

'Come sad ones,' The Healer said. 'As in all sickness, there is health, if only one can find the way within oneself. These women, they will be much the same as we. They can do what must be done, but they will need all of our help.

'Come,' she told them. 'There is still one last thing to be done.'

The clan members followed The Healer back inside the cave and watched as she began to draw the circle of life and the secret of its perpetuation. Inside the circle she painted the dance of the long night and the embrace of the all. The clan began to help her. They did not stop until all the herbs and seasons, the sounds and motions with which the ones were able to generate the seed of life within themselves were displayed with loving care upon the farthest wall of the cave.

'Now!' The Healer said. 'We have shown the women the way to make the young without these strange others, these men. Now the women can choose.'

And the clan was pleased and satisfied. They had done all they could do for the tomorrows and the ones to follow. It would be up to the women to decide if the men could be saved.

With one mind, the clan members began to gather their belongings and pack them in their small swift boats.

'Now we will find a place,' The Cavefinder said, as they gathered by the water's edge.

'A place far from this place, a place no others have ever seen or will see.'

And so they went: The Seedkeeper with her pouch of woven grass; The Firekeeper, cradling the mother of fire in her smouldering sticks; The Healer, with the memory of cures in her hands; all the ones of the clan, with all that they possessed. No one left even a broken tool behind, except the Youngtender. On the shore, The Youngtender left the nearly grown strange others sitting idly in the sand.

Among the Yenga women, it is said that the cave of the ones still exists and will be found by the women in the time when all else fails.

FURTHER READING

Arditti, Rita, Renate D. Klein and Shelley Minden, eds. 1984/89. *Test-Tube Women: What Future for Motherhood?* London/Sydney: Pandora Press/Allen and Unwin.

Bunkle, Phillida. 1988. *Second Opinion: The Politics of Women's Health in New Zealand.* Oxford: Oxford University Press.

Coney, Sandra. 1988. *The Unfortunate Experiment: The Full Story Behind the Inquiry Into Cervical Cancer Treatment.* Ringwood, Vic.: Penguin.

Corea, Gena. 1985a. *The Mother Machine: Reproductive Technologies from Artificial Insemination to Artificial Wombs.* New York: Harper and Row.

Corea, Gena. 1985b. *The Hidden Malpractice.* New York: Harper and Row.

Corea, Gena et al. 1987. *Man Made Women: How New Reproductive Technologies Affect Women.* Bloomington: Indiana University Press.

Hynes, Patricia H., ed. 1989. *Reconstructing Babylon: Essays on Women and Technology.* London: Earthscan Publications Ltd.

Kane, Elizabeth. 1988. *Birth Mother: The Story of America's First Legal Surrogate Mother.* San Diego: Harcourt Brace Jovanovich; 1990 Melbourne: Macmillan.

Klein, Renate. 1989a. *The Exploitation of a Desire: Women's Experiences with In Vitro Fertilisation.* Women's Studies Summer Institute, Geelong: Deakin University Press.

263

Klein, Renate D., ed. 1989b. *Infertility: Women Speak Out About Their Experiences of Reproductive Medicine.* London/Sydney: Pandora Press/Allen & Unwin.

Klein, Renate. 1990. Enough is enough: Women's experiences of in vitro fertilisation. In: *The Healthsharing Reader: Women Speak About Health.* Compiled by Healthsharing Women Publishing and Production Group. Sydney, Wellington and London: Pandora Press/Allen & Unwin, pp. 215–24.

Klein, Renate/Rowland, Robyn. 1988. Women as Test-Sites for Fertility Drugs: Clomiphene Citrate and Hormonal Cocktails. *Reproductive and Genetic Engineering: Journal of International Feminist Analysis* 1 (3); pp. 251–75. Oxford/New York: Pergamon Press.

Lingam, Lakshmi. 1989. *Made in India: A Dossier on the New Reproductive Technologies.* Women's Studies Unit. Tata Institute of Social Sciences. Bombay, India.

McNeil, Maureen et al. 1990. *The New Reproductive Technologies.* London: Macmillan.

O'Brien, Mary. 1981. *The Politics of Reproduction.* London: Routledge and Kegan Paul.

Overall, Christine. 1987. *Ethics and Human Reproduction. A Feminist Analysis.* London/Sydney: Allen & Unwin.

Raymond, Janice. 1992. *Technological Injustice: Women and Reproductive Medicine.* Boston: Beacon Press.

Rowland, Robyn. 1990. IVF: The Package Deal. In *The Healthsharing Reader: Women Speak About Health.* Compiled by Healthsharing Women Publishing and Production Group. Sydney, Wellington and London: Pandora Press/Allen & Unwin, pp. 226–36.

Rowland, Robyn. 1992. *Living Laboratories: Women and the New Reproductive Technologies.* Melbourne: Macmillan/Bloomington: Indiana University Press.

Scutt, Jocelynne, ed. 1988. *The Baby Machine: Commercialisation of Motherhood.* Melbourne: McCulloch Publishing.

Shiva, Vandana. 1988. *Staying Alive: Women, Ecology and Survival in India*. New Delhi: Kali for Women; 1989 London: Zed Press.

Spallone, Patricia and Deborah L. Steinberg. 1987. *Made to Order: The Myth of Reproductive and Genetic Progress*. Oxford/New York: Pergamon Press.

Spallone, Patricia. 1989. *Beyond Conception: The New Politics of Reproduction*. London: Macmillan Education.

•

Issues in Reproductive and Genetic Engineering: Journal of International Feminist Analysis. Oxford/New York/Sydney: Pergamon Press.

•

FINRRAGE,
International Co-ordination,
PO Box 20 19 03,
D–2000 Hamburg 20,
Germany.

FINRRAGE (Australia),
PO Box 248,
East Kew, Vic. 3102.

Notes On Contributors

CARMEL BIRD was born in Tasmania in 1940 and now lives in Melbourne. She has written one previous novel, *Cherry Ripe*, two collections of short stories, *Births, Deaths and Marriages* and *The Woodpecker Toy Fact,* and a book for writers, *Dear Writer.*

MELISSA CHAN has lived in Europe, the United States of America, and (briefly) China. After growing up in the Western Australian wheat belt, she moved to the Eastern seaboard where she works as a lawyer. She is currently writing a murder mystery novel, *Too Rich*, centred around the lesbian film critic and private detective, Francesca Miles.

SUSAN EISENBERG is the author of the poetry book, *It's a Good Thing I'm Not Macho* (Whetstone Press) and co-editor of the video, *Coffee Break Secrets*. A union construction electrician in Boston since 1978, she gives poetry and storytelling workshops in schools, and writes and lectures on tradeswomen issues nationally. The mother of two, she has maintained an interest in feminist health politics since working at a free clinic for women in the early 1970s.

CAIT FEATHERSTONE lives in Vista, California where she writes poetry, fiction and essays. She is presently working on a collection of poems in response to genetic engineering and the medical community's treatment of women.

SUSAN HAWTHORNE writes fiction, poetry, drama, feminist theory and criticism. Her books include: *Difference* (1985), *Moments of Desire* (1989/90) and *The Exploding Frangipani* (1990). Her work has been published internationally in magazines, journals and anthologies.

ROSALEEN LOVE lives and works in Victoria, though the twelve years she lived in Queensland as a child still exert a strong influence on her. She works as an academic, teaching the history and philosophy of science (the history of wrong ideas). Her writing spins off from this professional activity – what people might have said, had they thought to say it, what people might have done, if they could do the impossible. Her book *The Total-Devotion Machine* was published by the Women's Press (UK) in 1989.

KAREN MALPEDE is a playwright, essayist, director, lecturer and peace activist. She is the author of eight plays, three of which have been published in *A Monster Has Stolen the Sun and Other Plays* (The Marlboro Press, Marlboro, Vt). She is editor of *Women in Theater: Compassion and Hope* (Limelight Editions, NY). Her most recent plays, *Us* and *Better People*, premiered at Theater for the New City, New York City. She is currently at work on a book about the Gulf War.

MAURILIA MEEHAN's first novel, *Performances* was published by Women's Redress Press in 1990. She has had short stories published in various collections, including three ABC anthologies. In 1988 she won the *FAW – State of Victoria Short Story Award*. Her second novel, recently completed, is called *Lepidoptera*.

BARBARANEELY is an African of American slave descent. She is the founder of The Third World Women Writers Workshop and Yenga Productions. She is currently working on a novel about working-class black women, a series of radio tapes on the literary works of women of colour and a book on the socio-political roots of black male sexism. *A Yenga Tale* is one of a series of prehistory myths Neely is developing.

MARY O'BRIEN was a nurse and a midwife in Scotland before emigrating to Canada in 1957. She taught at the Ontario Institute for Studies in Education until 1988, when poor health forced her into retirement. She lives with Cath McNaughton, a friend for 40 years, and two cats. She is a passionate gardener and the author of *The Politics of Reproduction* (1980) and of *Reproducing the World* (1989). She also has published many scholarly papers and has been an active public speaker. 'Elly' is her first attempt at fiction.

ATHOLEE SCOTT has worked in Perth, Melbourne and Canberra as a photographer, graphic artist and teacher. She writes part-time, has previously published non-fiction, and is currently working on a television script and more short stories.

SANDRA SHOTLANDER was born in Melbourne in 1941. She is a playwright, performer, founder/director of several theatre companies. Her published plays include *Framework* (1983), *Blind Salomé* (1985), *Collected Plays* (1988). She is also the author of 'Full Circle', 'Just One More Thing' (a radio play), 'Is That You Nancy?' and her short stories have been published in anthologies and magazines. Her plays have been performed throughout Australia and in the USA.

LUCY SUSSEX was born in Christchurch, New Zealand in 1957. After living in France and England she moved to Australia in 1971. She is the author of a children's book, *The Peace Garden* (1989), and editor of *The Fortunes of Mary Fortune* (1989). Her collection of surreal and science fiction stories, *My Lady Tongue and Other Tales* was published in 1990.

THALIA was born in Greece 1952, migrated to Australia 1955 and lives in the inner suburbs of Melbourne. She started writing poetry in 1972. Her work has been published in various magazines, journals and anthologics and she has read poems on radio, stage, pubs and festivals. Her concrete poems have been exhibited in Australia, Brazil, Canada and Moscow at festivals and galleries. She is interested in using shorthand symbols for concrete/visual poems.

ACKNOWLEDGEMENTS

For permission to reprint the works in this anthology acknowledgement is made to the following:

Melissa Chan: 'Forgetting Arachnida' previously published in *Womanpeak*, Vol. 13, No. 5, March/April 1991.

Susan Eisenberg: 'Battleground' previously published in *Infertility: Women Speak Out About Their Experiences of Reproductive Medicine*. Edited by Renate D. Klein. Pandora Press, London, 1989.

Rosaleen Love: 'Tanami Drift' previously published in *The Total-Devotion Machine*. The Women's Press, London; permission from the publisher.

BarbaraNeely: 'A Yenga Tale' previously published in *Test Tube Women: What Future for Motherhood*. Edited by Rita Arditti, Renate D. Klein and Shelley Minden. Pandora Press, London, 1984.

Mary O'Brien: 'Elly' previously published in *Issues in Reproductive and Genetic Engineering*. Vol. 3, No. 2, 1990, permission from the author.

Thalia: Concrete poems previously published as postcards by FINRRAGE, Brunswick, Vic., N.D., permission from the author.

Every effort has been made to trace copyright holders, but in one case this has proved impossible. The publishers would be interested to hear from any copyright holders not acknowledged here or acknowledged incorrectly.